THE BIBLE DOCUMENTS
A PARISH RESOURCE

THE BIBLE DOCUMENTS
A PARISH RESOURCE

LITURGY
TRAINING
PUBLICATIONS

Editor: David A. Lysik
Production editors: Marie McLaughlin and Audrey Novak Riley
Cover designer: Larry Cope
Production artist: Mark Hollopeter
Indexer: Mary Laur

Cover artist: Laura James. The cover art depicts members of a lively study and discussion group, Bibles in hand, gathered with their leader. Laura James, who lives in Brooklyn, paints in the iconographic tradition of Ethiopian Christian art, using bright colors and intricate patterns to express a unique vision.

THE BIBLE DOCUMENTS: A PARISH RESOURCE © 2001 Archdiocese of Chicago: Liturgy Training Publications, 1800 North Hermitage Avenue, Chicago IL 60622-1101; 1-800-933-1800; orders@ltp.org; fax 1-800-933-7094. All rights reserved.

Printed in Toronto, Canada, by Webcom Limited.

See our website: www.ltp.org

05 04 03 02 01   5 4 3 2 1

ISBN 1-56854-249-6
BDOC

CONTENTS

ABBREVIATIONS

AAS   *Acta Apostolicae Sedis* (1909–)

AG   Vatican Council II, decree *Ad gentes divinitus* (on the church's mission activity) (December 7, 1965)

CCC   *Catechism of the Catholic Church* (1992)

CDW   Congregation for Divine Worship

CR   Congregation of Rites

CSEL   *Corpus scriptorum ecclesiasticorum latinorum* (Vienna, 1866–)

DAS   Pius XII, encyclical letter *Divino afflante spiritu* (on the most opportune way to promote biblical studies) (September 30, 1943)

DV   Vatican Council II, dogmatic constitution *Dei verbum* (on divine revelation) (November 18, 1965)

EB   *Enchiridion biblicum* (2nd edition, 1954)

EM   CR, instruction *Eucharisticum mysterium* (on the worship of the eucharist (May 25, 1967)

GIRM   CDW, *General Instruction of the Roman Missal* (1975)

GS   Vatican Council II, pastoral constitution *Gaudium et spes* (on the church in the modern world) (December 7, 1965)

IBC   PBC, *The Interpretation of the Bible in the Church* (April 15, 1993)

LG   Vatical Council II, dogmatic constitution *Lumen gentium* (on the church) (November 21, 1964)

LM   *Lectionary for Mass*, second *editio typica* (1981)

LMIn   Lectionary for Mass: Introduction (1981)

n., nn.   number, numbers

NAB   New American Bible

PBC   Pontifical Biblical Commission

PD   Leo XIII, encyclical letter *Providentissimus Deus* (on the study of holy scripture) (November 18, 1893)

PG   J. P. Migne, *Patrologiae cursus completus: Series Graeca*

PL   J. P. Migne, *Patrologiae cursus completus: Series Latina*

PO   Vatican Council II, decree *Presbyterorum ordinis* (on the life and ministry of priests) (December 7, 1965)

RomM   *The Roman Missal*

SC   Vatican Council II, constitution *Sacrosanctum concilium* (on the sacred liturgy) (December 4, 1963

SME   PBC, instruction *Sancta mater ecclesia* (on the historical truth of the gospels) (April 21, 1964)

SP   Benedict XV, encyclical letter *Spiritus Paraclitus* (on the fifteenth centenary of the death of Saint Jerome) (September 15, 1920)

UR   Vatican Council II, decree *Unitatis redintegratio* (on ecumenism) (November 21, 1964)

GENERAL INTRODUCTION

Eugene LaVerdiere, sss

The twentieth century was a time of church renewal, revolving around the Second Vatican Council (1962–1965). Nine days before the Council opened, the Council Fathers issued a message endorsed by Pope John XXIII on the purpose of Vatican II:

> In this assembly, under the guidance of the Holy Spirit, we wish to inquire how we ought to renew ourselves, so that we may be found increasingly faithful to the gospel of Christ. We shall take pains so to present [to the people] of this age God's truth in its integrity and purity that they may understand it and gladly assent to it.[1]

The purpose of the Second Vatican Council was twofold: to renew the church and to proclaim God's truth effectively. Like the Council, every book in the New Testament, indeed the whole Bible, has the same twofold purpose: to renew the people of God and to proclaim the word of God in deed and in word that the people "may understand it and gladly assent to it."

In the last century, before, during and after the Council, the church reflected on every aspect of its doctrine, of its theology, of its practice, of its teaching and of its liturgy, relating them to the scriptures.[2] We were reflecting on the life and the mission of Jesus, on the role of the Holy Spirit, and on our relationship with God the Father, especially through the scriptures, applying them to this era or to different social contexts and cultures.

At the same time, we were studying the theology of revelation and the theology of the scriptures, especially their nature as a living word and as the written word, their interpretation, their sources and their role in Christian life and liturgy. Taking seriously the purpose of the Council, we were reflecting on scriptures "that we may be found increasingly to be faithful to the gospel of Christ."

At the beginning of a new century, Liturgy Training Publications (LTP) presents in this book as a parish resource the church's most important documents on the scriptures. The collection includes six documents:

1. Pope Pius XII's encyclical *Divino afflante spiritu:* On the Most Opportune Way to Promote Biblical Studies (1943);

2. The Pontifical Biblical Commission's instruction *Sancta mater ecclesia:* On the Historical Truth of the Gospels (1964);

3. The Second Vatican Council's Dogmatic Constitution on Divine Revelation *Dei verbum* (1965);

4. *Lectionary for Mass:* Introduction (1981);

5. The Pontifical Biblical Commission's instruction "The Interpretation of the Bible in the Church" (1993);

6. The *Catechism of the Catholic Church:* excerpts on the transmission of divine revelation (paragraphs 74–100) and sacred scripture (paragraphs 101–141) (1992).

Obviously, the six documents are not on the same level. As a document of an ecumenical council, the Dogmatic Constitution on Divine Revelation demands more respect than a papal encyclical. The documents of the Pontifical Biblical Commission are temporal, prudential decisions on practical problems. As such, they required obedience when issued, but they are less binding than a document of Vatican II or a papal encyclical.[3]

We need to read each document alongside the other documents. We need to study the six documents as a corpus, comparing their teaching, their purpose and their contexts. Just as the encyclical *Divino afflante spiritu* builds on the encyclical *Providentissimus Deus*, issued by Leo XIII in 1893, each document in this book builds on the teaching of the earlier documents. Comparing the document of the Second Vatican Council with the encyclical of Pope Pius XII, we can recognize that the church made a giant step in its theology. Consequently, we need to read and interpret Pius' encyclical in the light of the Dogmatic Constitution on Divine Revelation.

Each of the six documents is introduced by a detailed outline and an excellent overview that describes the contents of the document, its purpose, its context, its theology and its contribution to our understanding the Word of God.

It is very traditional for Christians to reflect personally on the Bible as the sacred scriptures. Even the scriptures reflect on themselves. As we read in the second letter to Timothy (3:14–15):

> But you, remain faithful to what you have learned and believed, because you know from whom you learned it, and that from infancy you have known [the] sacred scriptures, which are capable of giving you wisdom for salvation through faith in Christ Jesus.

The sacred scriptures *are able* to give us wisdom for salvation through our Christian faith. But they do not do so automatically. In the early church, every newly baptized person, old or young, was like a newborn infant (see 1 Peter 2:2), to be nourished by the scriptures and the bread of life. They knew that "all flesh is like grass . . . but the word of the Lord remains forever" (1 Peter 1:24–25). The new Christians were taught by a mature Christian, who had imbibed the scriptures as the living word of God, applying them to his or her life.

From the beginning, the Jewish scriptures had to be interpreted for the Christian communities, as well as for other times and other cultures. "All scripture is inspired by God and is useful for teaching, for refutation, for correction, and for training in righteousness, so that one who belongs to God may be competent, equipped for every good work" (2 Timothy 3:16–17). Everyone in the early church needed to be helped to understand the scriptures. They had to study the scriptures with a competent teacher, inspired by the Holy Spirit.

According to 2 Peter, at the beginning of the second century, there was a tendency to interpret the prophetic passages in the scriptures personally. That is why the letter says "there is no prophecy of scripture that is a matter of personal interpretation, for no prophecy ever came through human will; but rather human beings moved by the Holy Spirit spoke under the influence of God" (2 Peter 1:20–21). The scriptures, inspired by the Holy Spirit, are to be read and interpreted by someone who speaks as a representative of the community and who is likewise inspired by the Holy Spirit.

Many distorted the meaning or misinterpreted the scriptures, which can at times be difficult to understand: "And consider the patience of our Lord as salvation, as our beloved brother Paul, according to the wisdom given to him, also wrote to you, speaking of these things as he does in all his letters. In them there are some things hard to understand that the ignorant and unstable distort to their own destruction, just as they do the other scriptures" (2 Peter 3:15–16). 2 Peter admits that some things in Paul's letters are hard to understand.

Like our ancestors in the faith, we, too, need to be helped to understand the scriptures. Our modern tendency is also to interpret them individually or personally. But if we compare the scriptures to the person of Jesus Christ, we see something else. Jesus is not only *my* Savior and *my* Lord, nor only *our* Savior and *our* Lord. Jesus is the Savior and the Lord of *all*. Likewise, the scriptures are not only addressed to me or to us. As the word of God, the scriptures are addressed to the whole human family. Therefore, we need the Spirit to help us read and interpret the scriptures.

And we need the directives of the church to help us read and interpret the scriptures in every age, every nation, every language and every culture. As the early church did (see 2 Peter 1:12–21; 3:14–16; 2 Timothy 3:14—4:5), the contemporary church has given us many documents to be made available to pastoral ministers, catechists, liturgists, teachers and students, to help us read and interpret the scriptures for our times.

Before the Second Vatican Council the majority of Catholics did not read the Bible. We were afraid to open it. For us, the Bible was like a forbidden book that could be dangerous to our faith and our morals. Now, in the wake of Vatican II, we are very interested in the Bible. For us, the Bible is the word of God written in human words.

Many Catholics, like many other Christians, open the Bible every day to read the scriptures personally, to meditate on them, to study their historical background and their literary dimensions, to relate them to daily life. Many Catholic women and men read the scriptures publicly in the liturgy of the word. After each reading they proclaim, "The word of the Lord," and the assembly responds to the living word, "Thanks be to God."

The Bible has come alive for us, giving life to the church throughout the world. Like the documents of Vatican II, the *Catechism of the Catholic Church* refers to the scriptures almost in every paragraph,[4] inviting us to read the catechism in the context of the scriptures. Many Catholics belong to Bible study groups that read and study the scriptures, applying them to daily life. We pray with the scriptures, individually or communally. Every Christian ministry, including evangelization, catechesis and the liturgical ministries, is based on Jesus' ministry and the ministries of the early church as described in the scriptures.

Just a few years ago, the interpretation of the Bible was a preserve for a few specialists. Now, at the beginning of the 21st century, everyone tries to interpret the scriptures. From the book of Genesis to the book of Revelation, we read the Bible through the lens of our culture and our history, as well as through the lens of our personal faith, our life experience and our limited knowledge. By reading the scriptures publicly, especially in the liturgy, we are interpreting them through our voice, facial expressions, posture and gestures.

There is no escaping the interpretation of the scriptures. Even Jesus interpreted the scriptures, applying Isaiah 61:1–2 to his mission (see Luke 4:18–19, 21). When he was teaching the crowds, he answered a question from the Pharisees on Moses' commandment on marriage and divorce (see Deuteronomy 24:1–4). In his answer, he first placed the commandment in its historical context (Mark 10:5). Then he interpreted Moses' commandment by the law of creation (Mark 10:6–8; see Genesis 1:27; 2:24).

Paul interpreted the early traditions of the Lord's Supper (1 Corinthians 11:23–25) and the baptismal creed (1 Corinthians 15:3–5), challenging the members of the Corinthian community on their behavior in their assembly (1 Corinthians 11:17–22, 26–34) and on their belief in the resurrection (1 Corinthians 15:12–58). He also interpreted the story of Abraham and Sarah for the Roman community when he was reflecting on the mission to the Gentiles (Romans 4:1–25; see Galatians 3:6–29; 4:21–31).

The gospel writers interpreted Jesus' life, mission and ministry according to the scriptures. They applied many verses, particularly from Psalm 22 and Isaiah's fourth Song of the Suffering Servant (Isaiah 52:13—53:12), to Jesus' passion and resurrection. They interpreted Jesus' parables and sayings by setting them within the context of a particular story. For example, in Luke's gospel, Jesus taught the Lord's Prayer in a certain place when he was praying before his disciples (Luke 11:1–4). In Matthew's gospel, Jesus taught the Lord's Prayer on the mountain when he was teaching his disciples in the hearing of a large crowd (Matthew 5:1–2; 6:9–13). In Luke's gospel, the risen Lord appeared to the members of the community in Jerusalem and opened their minds to understand the scriptures, applying them to his suffering and his resurrection and their mission to all the nations (Luke 24:45–48; see 24:27).

There is no escaping the interpretation of the scriptures. Jesus, Paul and the gospel writers inherited their principles of interpretation from the scriptures themselves and also from the synagogue. Reading the scriptures and explaining the early tradition, they could presuppose that their hearers and readers understood the literary forms and symbols in the Bible. The world of the New Testament was very small, including only the Eastern Mediterranean cultures.

In our modern age, the biblical symbols are foreign to many even in the Western church. And now, the gospel has been preached in every country of the world, including China, India and Indonesia. As in every era of the church, we need to reflect on the nature of the scriptures, applying them to contemporary cultures. After two thousand years, we need modern principles to interpret the scriptures for our various ministries.

This collection of the Bible documents responds to our needs to appreciate the scriptures, to read them personally and publicly and to interpret them for our times. We need to renew ourselves according to the scriptures in order to preach and teach the word of God effectively.

NOTES

1. Walter M. Abbott, SJ, general editor, *The Documents of Vatican II* (New York: The America Press, 1966) 3–4.

2. Like the members of the early church, the New Testament writers referred to the Old Testament as "the scriptures" (see 1 Corinthians 15:3–5), not as a "Bible" or as a "text."

3. Raymond E. Brown, SS, and Thomas Aquinas Collins, OP, "Church Pronouncements," in *The New Jerome Biblical Commentary*, edited by Raymond E. Brown, SS, Joseph A. Fitzmyer, SJ, and Roland E. Murphy, OCARM (Englewood Cliffs, New Jersey: Prentice Hall, 1990), 1167.

4. In its index of citations, the English-language edition of the *Catechism of the Catholic Church* has over 31 pages of citations to the scriptures.

ENCYCLICAL LETTER *DIVINO AFFLANTE SPIRITU*

ON THE MOST

OPPORTUNE WAY

TO PROMOTE

BIBLICAL STUDIES

PIUS XII
1943

OVERVIEW OF *DIVINO AFFLANTE SPIRITU*
Murray Watson

It is probably difficult for most contemporary Catholics to imagine a time when the Bible did *not* play a central part in the life and prayer of the Roman Catholic church. All over the world today, millions of Catholics participate in Bible study groups where they read, study, discuss and pray over the scriptures in their own languages, sometimes together with Christians of other churches. The structure of the revised Order of Mass places a clear emphasis on the readings and psalm that comprise the liturgy of the word, on Christ's presence *in* and action *through* the proclaimed scriptures. References to the books of the Bible abound in contemporary church documents, and more than a century's worth of popes have warmly encouraged scripture study on the part of Catholics. These are things that, for the most part, contemporary Catholics take for granted.

But it has not always been so. It is not that long since many Catholic schoolchildren received little or no encouragement in reading the sacred scriptures. Although many families possessed a beautifully-bound family Bible, it was more often a storehouse of family history than a living, accessible message to be read and meditated on. Although passages from the Bible were read at every Mass, they were proclaimed in Latin; those who followed along generally did so with a parallel English translation in their missals. For many Catholics, the Bible was primarily associated with Protestant churches, whose services they were forbidden to attend, and about which they harbored a vague mistrust. The work of Catholic scripture scholars was carefully monitored, and the establishment of graduate-level institutes in scripture study (such as the Dominican *École Biblique* in Jerusalem, founded in 1890) did not always meet with enthusiastic endorsement.

Then, on September 30, 1943, in the midst of World War II, Pope Pius XII issued his now-famous encyclical letter *Divino afflante spiritu* (DAS) (literally, "by the inspiring by the divine Spirit"). In the half-century since, it has become almost trite to refer to Pius' document as the Magna Carta of Catholic biblical study, and yet no one can deny that his encyclical gave a stamp of approval to a new and more positive attitude that has profoundly marked Catholic life ever since.

THE ROAD TO *DIVINO AFFLANTE SPIRITU*

As significant as it was, however, DAS did not appear out of an historical vacuum; it expressed an outlook that had already been slowly evolving in the church for several decades. Indeed, it was the fiftieth anniversary of an *earlier* document, *Providentissimus Deus* (PD) (by Pope Leo XIII) that occasioned Pius' 1943 letter. The fifty years that separated Leo's document (itself a milestone in biblical research) from that of his successor were a time of tremendous upheaval, struggle and growth for the church with regard to the field of Bible study. Indeed, the very different tones adopted by PD and DAS reflect the change in circumstances, as well as the extensive progress that had occurred in those five decades.

In the four centuries following the Reformation, whole-hearted devotion to the Bible had become for many people the distinguishing mark of Protestant Christianity. The Catholic response to Luther's rallying cry, "I stand on the Word of God alone," was a certain distancing from the Bible as an essentially "Protestant" book, and one that held the potential for serious misinterpretation (and schism) in the hands of the laity. It was a no-win situation for *both* sides, but it would take almost 350 years for this biblical "Cold War" to begin to thaw.

But thaw it did, beginning with PD, and the subsequent encyclical letter of Pope Benedict XV, *Spiritus Paraclitus* (SP), written in 1920 to mark the fifteen-hundredth anniversary of the death of Saint Jerome. The need to defend the Bible in the face of rationalistic, reductionistic and anti-clerical theories gave these encyclical letters a definite apologetic flavor. While firmly reasserting the divine inspiration of the Bible and its consequent inerrancy, these papal texts began to use the language of modern science and history, of archaeology and ancient cultures as they broached important questions about the *nature, background* and *methods* of the human authors chosen by God. When interpreters today look beyond the specific historical controversies and false directions the popes were trying to address, it is clear that both PD and SP are characterized by an attitude of openness (albeit limited and conditional) to the value of modern critical scholarship.

THE MODERNIST CRISIS

Both PD and SP were reacting against certain popular currents in scholarship that seemed to deny (or at least seriously question) the divine inspiration and permanent value of the scriptures. Methods developed during the Renaissance for the study of ancient texts, and later honed by German Protestant scholars, were being applied to the books of the Bible in ways that suggested that they were merely human compositions, borrowing heavily from the cultures around them. On the basis of new archeological and textual discoveries in the Middle East, questions were increasingly raised about the historical reliability of large sections of the Old Testament and the gospels. Many postulated that it might be possible to accept minor factual errors in parts of the Bible that were *obiter dicta*—comments merely made in passing—which did not directly impact on faith or morals. In some cases, non-Catholic scholars sought to "free" Christians from the "tyranny of dogma" by a return to an allegedly more pristine (and institution-free) version of the primitive Christian faith, which could be "distilled" from its later canonical form.

The church quickly recognized the threat such investigations posed to a traditional reading of the Bible, and the scandal they represented for the faith of millions of Catholics. A wide range of Catholic intellectuals at the turn of the twentieth century, collectively grouped under the rubric of "Modernists," quickly became a focus of concern and censure on the part of the church's official teachers; many of their writings were officially banned in Catholic universities and seminaries as heretical. Although they embraced a wide range of theses—and a variety of attitudes toward the church—these authors were increasingly condemned as undermining the historicity and inspiration of the scriptures. Teachers suspected of Modernist leanings were reported to the Vatican by local vigilante groups, and a number of prominent scholars were dismissed from teaching positions in Catholic institutes. To further complicate the issue, the Pontifical Biblical Commission (PBC) (established in 1902) issued a series of disciplinary rulings between 1905 and 1915 that officially rejected many of the conclusions proposed by Modernist authors: traditional attributions of biblical authorship were to be upheld, texts were generally to be understood historically, and attempts to isolate sources or to identify composite works were largely rejected as dangerous. In the light of these declarations, Catholic exegetes found their sphere of research and publication severely restricted, and generally considered it safer to adhere to traditional patristic and Scholastic interpretations. The "Modernist crisis" marked a painful and uncertain era for those who worked in the biblical field, and the future direction of Catholic biblical research was far from clear.

With the events of World War I, concern over Modernist heresies gradually faded, and the church was able to re-examine biblical issues in a more serene, less polemical way. In 1927, the Holy Office clarified its own 1897 ruling on certain text-critical questions in the gospel of John, stating that it had simply been meant "to restrain rash speculation," rather than to forbid further discussion or study. Although a 1934 response from the PBC required that biblical texts intended for *liturgical* use be made from the Latin Vulgate, a subsequent letter in August 1943 clarified that this text could be "fleshed out" in preaching by use of the original languages if this helped to make the meaning clearer. The "return to the sources" that characterized liturgical and patristic studies in this period went hand-in-hand with a revival of study of the original languages of the Bible. A wealth of new archeological, manuscript and literary evidence became available, offering valuable new insights into the culture, language and literary forms of the ancient Middle East. Things were clearly changing.

While marking the fiftieth anniversary of Leo's famous encyclical, DAS was also not-so-subtly addressing a series of common criticisms that had been expressed most publicly in an anonymous 48-page Italian booklet circulated to the Pope and cardinals in early 1941, entitled "A Most Serious Danger for the Church and for Souls: The Scientific-Critical System in the Study and Interpretation of Sacred Scripture, Its Disastrous Deviancies and Its Aberrations." Its author argued that the Vulgate alone should be the object of the church's attention. Textual criticism brought about a "massacring" of the Bible, its author contended; the study of ancient languages led to excessive pride and presumption, and much greater spiritual benefit could be derived by simply meditating on the allegorical meaning of the text in its Latin translation and patristic commentaries. The Pope's response—embodied in DAS—would not be at all what the pamphlet's author had hoped for.

THE STRUCTURE OF THE ENCYCLICAL

Pius XII introduces DAS with an overview of the history of the church's teaching on the Bible (#1–9). After reviewing the major statements of the Council of Trent (1545–63) and the First Vatican Council (1869–70), Pius devotes several paragraphs to the teachings of recent popes, with particular emphasis on Pope

Leo XIII and PD, which, he says, "is considered the supreme guide in biblical studies" (#2). He clarifies and reiterates Leo's teaching on the essential inerrancy of the Bible, alluding to some of the erroneous theological positions it was meant to correct, but also providing for a much more nuanced view of what inerrancy means (#3). Among Leo's numerous accomplishments in this field, Pius mentions Leo's approval of the Dominican *École Biblique* in Jerusalem, and his establishment of the PBC. He then refers to the efforts of Popes Pius X and Pius XI in establishing the Pontifical Biblical Institute in Rome and requiring rigorous academic formation of those who would teach scripture in seminary or university settings. Citing Pius X's own support of the Society of Saint Jerome (a lay group dedicated to promoting familiarity with the scriptures), he underscores the value—and even the necessity—of Bible reading and meditation by all members of the church, and demolishes once and for all the claim that the Catholic church was opposed to Bible reading, or vernacular editions of the scriptures. In article 10 of the document, the Pope concludes his introduction with words of praise and encouragement for the work of exegetes and scholars in all fields of scripture study.

In articles 11 to 16, Pius explains some of the reasons that have caused the church to re-evaluate scientific study of the scriptures: new discoveries from archeological excavations in the Middle East, the availability of new and better manuscripts for textual study, an increased knowledge of ancient cultures and literature, and the modern renaissance of study in Greek, Hebrew and other Oriental languages, which had been largely neglected in the Catholic church because of the centrality of the Vulgate.

Articles 17 and 18 of DAS specifically address the need for textual criticism—for a serious, scholarly study of the available manuscripts, to restore and correct the text as accurately as possible, to ensure that future research might be based on the most authentic version attainable. Against those who had railed against this effort, the Pope recalls the words of Saint Augustine: "The correction of the codices should first of all engage the attention of those who wish to know the Divine Scripture, so that the uncorrected may give way to the corrected."

The issue of translations, and specifically the authority of the Latin Vulgate, is taken up in articles 19 to 22. Pius warmly promotes the publication of editions of the scriptures, particularly critical editions of the ancient versions. The Council of Trent's decree authorizing the Vulgate as the "authentic" Latin edition did not in any way detract from, or replace, the value of the original Hebrew and Greek versions; in the midst of a plethora of varying Latin editions, it declared that the Vulgate was certified to be an accurate and reliable translation, due to its long tradition of use in the church. Indeed, the Pope recalled, the Fathers of the Council of Trent had desired that corrected Greek and Hebrew texts be prepared as well, but the state of scholarship at the time precluded this. Today, translations from the original languages are to be promoted, and efforts necessary to permit this should be fostered: "Let all know that this prolonged labor is not only necessary for the right understanding of the divinely-given writings, but also is urgently demanded by that piety by which it behooves us to be grateful to the God of all providence" (#19).

Articles 23 to 34 form one of the key elements of DAS, and one of its most revolutionary: While carefully re-asserting the genuinely divine inspiration of the Bible, Pius insists on the priority of the *literal* meaning as the foundation upon which all other meanings are to be based, and he states that this meaning is to be discerned through a study of the human author's intention and way of speaking. This task, which the Pope calls "the greatest of all those tasks imposed on Catholic exegetes," is absolutely necessary for an accurate understanding of biblical meaning, and "spiritual" or "mystical" interpretation cannot substitute for it.

However, the Pope cautions against a merely "academic" approach; the goal of Catholic exegesis, he says, is to explain the *theological* meaning of the scriptures, to situate them within the life and faith of the church. This demands due respect for the church's official declarations, traditional patristic interpretations and the analogy of faith (the interrelationship existing between all aspects of faith, which allows each of them to cast light on the others).

While the Bible clearly contains a "spiritual sense," an essential rootedness in the *literal* sense will restrain arbitrary, overly imaginative interpretations, and will help to establish if such are indeed clearly intended by God, and not mere human speculation. As the original meaning inspired by God, the literal sense *itself* possesses a richness of meaning to be plumbed and appreciated. In this connection, Pius XII heartily recommends in articles 28–30 the study of patristic commentaries, since "they are distinguished by a certain subtle insight into heavenly things and by a marvelous keenness of intellect, which enables them to penetrate to the very innermost meaning of the divine Word" (#28). Since the Holy Spirit's inspiration respected the uniqueness of each human author, anything that can be learned about the character and background of each sacred writer ultimately contributes to a better understanding of what is being said in the text: "[T]he supreme rule of interpretation is to discover and define what the writer intended to express." (#34)

Articles 35 to 41 deal with the issue of "form criticism," the treatment of which is relatively new in papal documents. Exegetes must attempt to "go back in spirit to those remote centuries," to understand the modes of expression that were in use at the time, along with their specific rules of interpretation. A correct evaluation of the literary form of a work will often clarify, and sometimes resolve, questions of historicity or suggestions of error in the text. Whereas the Modernists had focused excessively on the human contribution to the Bible, and perhaps earlier Vatican officials had insisted a bit too strongly on the divine aspect, Pius XII suggests that a more moderate and fruitful path is suggested by an analogy with the Incarnation: Neither the human nor the divine may be ignored in the Bible, "for as the substantial Word of God became like to men in all things, 'except sin,' so the words of God, expressed in human language, are made like to human speech in every respect, except error" (#37). And "of the modes of expression which . . . human language used to express its thought, none is excluded from the Sacred Books, provided the way of speaking adopted in no wise contradicts the holiness and truth of God" (#37). As a result, Catholic exegetes were called to take into account the contributions of all the relevant fields of human knowledge toward a correct understanding and interpretation of the scriptures: "[L]et him be convinced that this part of his office cannot be neglected without serious detriment to Catholic exegesis." (#38)

Articles 42 to 49 offer a positive overview of the contributions of Catholic exegesis, and a hopeful vision that modern study will assist in resolving some of the long-standing questions of the Bible. While respecting the infinite mystery of God's word, Pius XII calls upon Catholic scholars to "grapple again and again with these difficult problems, hitherto unsolved," to attempt to uncover answers that are in accordance both with faith and with the conclusions of the sciences. In this task, the Pope assures scripture scholars of an appropriate freedom of study:

> [I]n the Sacred Books . . . there are but few texts whose sense has been defined by the authority of the Church, nor are those more numerous about which the teaching of the Holy Fathers is unanimous. There remain, therefore, many things, and of the greatest importance, in the discussion and exposition of which the skill and genius of Catholic commentators may and ought to be freely exercised. (#47)

In praising the work of two millennia of exegetes, Pius XII calls upon all Catholics to demonstrate patience, love and respect regarding the work in which they are involved: "[T]he efforts of these resolute laborers in the vineyard of the Lord should be judged not only with equity and justice, but also with the greatest charity." (#47)

Articles 50 to 58 are devoted to promoting study and love of the Bible on the part of priests and bishops, recalling their primary responsibility to communicate the message of the scriptures accurately and reverently in their preaching and teaching. Bishops should not only support initiatives dedicated to educate Catholics about the word of God, but should promote the distribution of Bibles and scripture reading in the family home. They are to see to it that priests receive a solid formation in biblical matters in the seminary, learning to know and love the Bible and to preach its message of salvation in a spiritually fruitful way. In articles 56 to 58, Pius XII alludes to the sufferings of the modern world, and especially to the war throughout Europe; only in God—encountered in and through the Bible—will people find comfort, hope and the faith to sustain them in times of distress. As Saint Jerome said, "If there is anything in this life which sustains a wise man and induces him to maintain his serenity amidst the tribulations and adversities of the world, it is in the first place, I consider, the meditation and knowledge of the Scriptures." (#57)

The Pope's concluding remarks, contained in articles 59 to 62, are directed primarily to exegetes and biblical scholars who are, he says, the object of his special affection and encouragement: "[F]or what is more sublime than to scrutinize, explain, propose to the faithful and defend from unbelievers the very Word of God, communicated to men under the inspiration of the Holy Spirit?" (#59) It is a call to serious scholarly dedication, but also (and more importantly) to let oneself become steeped in the Bible, to make it one's daily spiritual nourishment. The task of the modern exegete is to help people grasp "all the splendor, stimulating language, and joy contained in the Holy Scriptures," and to model their lives on the example of their saintly predecessors.

The significance of DAS can perhaps best be seen in the tremendous flowering that has occurred in Catholic exegesis and biblical study in the years since 1943. Within a decade of its publication, the uncertainty and fears of the Modernist era gave way to a burst of energy, scholarship and new creative initiatives. Chief among these are the two major new English-language Catholic translations of the Bible that appeared in this era: the *Jerusalem Bible* (original French edition 1948–1954, English translation 1966) and the Confraternity edition (the ancestor of the *New American Bible*), both of which were (to quote the title page of the *New American Bible*) "translated from the original languages with critical use of all the ancient sources." Highly praised for their English style, the accuracy of their translations and the extensive introductions and readers' notes that accompanied them, they have become familiar to readers throughout the world through their use in the liturgy and translation into other languages, and are rightly considered monuments of modern English-language Catholic scholarship.

Similarly, the desire by educated Catholics for accurate and accessible information on the current state of biblical research led to the publication of several major Catholic commentaries, including *A Catholic Commentary on Holy Scripture* (1953, revised 1969), and the monumental one-volume *Jerome Biblical Commentary* (1968, updated and expanded 1990). These volumes bring together under a single cover a collection of concise book-by-book commentaries, as well as excellent topical articles on biblical theology, geography, archeology, church pronouncements, and the lives of Jesus and Saint Paul. Each of these volumes distills the best of modern scholarship; each owes its existence to the revival that received its impetus from DAS.

Taken together with the papal teachings that preceded it and laid its foundations, DAS remains a remarkable and relevant document nearly sixty years after its publication. The wartime Pope Pius XII struck a critical balance between the wisdom of the church's tradition and the insights offered by modern critical study. His openness and positive regard for the efforts of exegetes, and his concern to hold together both divine inspiration and the concrete situation of the human author, continue to mark a healthy direction for Catholics to this day. It will be interesting to see how the next generation of Catholics will respond to Pius XII's appeal to take the necessary next step—from exegesis to its theological significance, from isolated scholarly conclusions to their relevance for everyday Christian living, morality and prayer.

The debate over the proper way to interpret the scriptures remains as lively as ever in the Catholic church, and the historical-critical method continues to grow and evolve, in response to valid criticism. Despite some overstatements and mistakes, hopefully no one would wish to reverse the innumerable gains of that period, or surrender the piercing new insights it has provided. "By the inspiring of the divine Spirit," the church has set out once more to plumb the depths of God's word, and the entire church must work together in pursuit of that goal—exegetes, translators, pastors, preachers, catechists and readers of the Bible. To break open the scriptures with love, faith and learning—this is the marvelous adventure that lies ahead of us in the new millennium. Pope Pius XII would be rightfully proud.

BIBLIOGRAPHY

Brown, SS, Raymond E., and Thomas Aquinas Collins, OP. "Church Pronouncements" in Raymond E. Brown, SS, Joseph A. Fitzmyer, SJ, and Roland E. Murphy, OCARM, eds. *The New Jerome Biblical Commentary*. Englewood Cliffs, New Jersey: Prentice Hall, 1990.

Crehan, SJ, F. J. "The Bible in the Roman Catholic Church from Trent to the Present Day" in S. L. Greenslade, *Cambridge History of the Bible* (Vol. 3). Cambridge: Cambridge University Press, 1963.

Filippi, Alfio and Erminio Lora, eds. *Enchiridion Biblicum: Documenti della Chiesa sulla Sacra Scrittura* (seconda edizione bilingue). Bologna: Edizione Dehoniane, 1994.

Fogarty, SJ, Gerald P. *American Catholic Biblical Scholarship: A History from the Early Republic to Vatican II*. San Francisco: Harper & Row, 1989.

Prior, Joseph G. *The Historical Critical Method in Catholic Exegesis* (doctoral dissertation). Rome: Editrice Pontificia Università Gregoriana, 1999.

Robinson, Robert Bruce. *Roman Catholic Exegesis Since* Divino afflante spiritu: *Hermeneutical Implications*. Atlanta: Scholars Press/Society of Biblical Literature, 1988.

Whealon, J. F. "Divino afflante spiritu" in *New Catholic Encyclopedia* (Vol. 4). Washington: The Catholic University of America Press, 1967.

OUTLINE

ENCYCLICAL LETTER *DIVINO AFFLANTE SPIRITU*

ON THE MOST OPPORTUNE WAY
TO PROMOTE BIBLICAL STUDIES

To Our Venerable Brethren, Patriarchs, Primates, Archbishops, Bishops and other Local Ordinaries Enjoying Peace and Communion with the Apostolic See

INTRODUCTION

1.   Inspired by the Divine Spirit, the Sacred Writers composed those books, which God, in His paternal charity towards the human race, deigned to bestow on them in order "to teach, to reprove, to correct, to instruct in justice: that the man of God may be perfect, furnished to every good work."[1] This heaven-sent treasure Holy Church considers as the most precious source of doctrine on faith and morals. No wonder therefore that, as she received it intact from the hands of the Apostles, so she kept it with all care, defended it from every false and perverse interpretation and used it diligently as an instrument for securing the eternal salvation of souls, as almost countless documents in every age strikingly bear witness. In more recent times, however, since the divine origin and the correct interpretation of the Sacred Writings have been very specially called in question, the Church has with even greater zeal and care undertaken their defense and protection. The sacred Council of Trent ordained by solemn decree that "the entire books with all their parts, as they have been wont to be read in the Catholic Church and are contained in the old vulgate Latin edition, are to be held sacred and canonical."[2] In our own time the Vatican Council, with the object of condemning false doctrines regarding inspiration, declared that these same books were to be regarded by the Church as sacred and canonical "not because, having been composed by human industry, they were afterwards approved by her authority, nor merely because they contain revelation without error, but because, having been written under the inspiration of the Holy Spirit, they have God for their author, and as such were handed down to the Church herself."[3] When, subsequently, some Catholic writers, in spite of this solemn definition of Catholic doctrine, by which such divine authority is claimed for the "entire books with all their parts" as to secure freedom from any error whatsoever, ventured to restrict the truth of Sacred Scripture solely to matters of faith and morals, and to regard other matters, whether in the domain of physical science or history, as "obiter dicta" and—as they contended—in no wise connected with faith, Our Predecessor of immortal memory, Leo XIII in the Encyclical Letter *Providentissimus Deus*, published on November 18th in the year 1893, justly and rightly condemned these errors and safe-guarded the studies of the Divine Books by most wise precepts and rules.

2.   Since then it is fitting that We should commemorate the fiftieth anniversary of the publication of this Encyclical Letter, which is considered the supreme guide in biblical studies, We, moved by that solicitude for sacred studies, which We manifested from the very beginning of Our Pontificate,[4] have considered that this may most opportunely be done by ratifying and inculcating all that was wisely laid down by Our Predecessor and ordained by His Successors for the consolidating and perfecting of the work, and by pointing out what seems necessary in the present day, in order to incite ever more earnestly all those sons of the Church who devote themselves to these studies, to so necessary and so praiseworthy an enterprise.

I. HISTORICAL PART: WORK OF LEO XIII AND OF HIS SUCCESSORS IN FAVOR OF BIBLICAL STUDIES

§1—WORK OF LEO XIII

3.   The first and greatest care of Leo XIII was to set forth the teaching on the truth of the Sacred Books and to defend it from attack. Hence with grave words did he proclaim that there is no error whatsoever if the sacred writer, speaking of things of the physical order "went by what sensibly appeared" as the Angelic Doctor says[5], speaking either "in figurative language, or in terms which were commonly used at the time, and which in many instances are in daily use at this day, even among the most eminent men of science." For "the sacred writers, or to speak more accurately—the words are St. Augustine's[6]—the Holy Ghost, Who spoke by them, did not intend to teach men these things—that is the essential nature of the things of the universe—things in no way profitable to salvation";[7] which principle "will apply to cognate sciences, and especially to history," that is, by refuting, "in a somewhat similar way the fallacies of the adversaries and defending the historical truth of Sacred Scripture from their attacks."[8] Nor is the sacred writer to be taxed with error, if "copyists have made mistakes in the text of the Bible," or, "if the real meaning of a passage remains ambiguous." Finally it is absolutely wrong and forbidden "either to narrow inspiration to certain passages of Holy Scripture, or to admit that the sacred writer has erred," since divine inspiration "not only is essentially incompatible with error but excludes and rejects it as absolutely and necessarily as it is impossible that God Himself, the supreme Truth, can utter that which is not true. This is the ancient and constant faith of the Church."[9]

4.   This teaching, which Our Predecessor Leo XIII set forth with such solemnity, We also proclaim with Our authority and We urge all to adhere to it religiously. No less earnestly do We inculcate obedience at the present day to the counsels and exhortations which he, in his day, so wisely enjoined. For whereas there arose new and serious difficulties and questions, from the wide-spread prejudices of rationalism and more especially from the discovery and investigation of the antiquities of the East, this same Our Predecessor, moved by zeal of the apostolic office, not only that such an excellent source of Catholic revelation

might be more securely and abundantly available to the advantage of the Christian flock, but also that he might not suffer it to be in any way tainted, wished and most earnestly desired "to see an increase in the number of the approved and persevering laborers in the cause of Holy Scripture; and more especially that those whom Divine Grace has called to Holy Orders, should day-by-day, as their state demands, display greater diligence and industry in reading, meditating and explaining it."[10]

IMPULSE GIVEN TO BIBLICAL STUDIES

5.   Wherefore the same Pontiff, as he had already praised and approved the school for biblical studies, founded at St. Stephen's, Jerusalem, by the Master General of the Sacred Order of Preachers—from which, to use his own words, "biblical science itself had received no small advantage, while giving promise of more"[11]—so in the last year of his life he provided yet another way, by which these same studies, so warmly commended in the Encyclical Letter *Providentissimus Deus*, might daily make greater progress and be pursued with the greatest possible security. By the Apostolic Letter *Vigilantiae*, published on October 30 in the year 1902, he founded a Council or Commission, as it is called, of eminent men, "whose duty it would be to procure by every means that the sacred texts may receive everywhere among us that more thorough exposition which the times demand, and be kept safe not only from every breath of error, but also from all inconsiderate opinions."[12] Following the example of Our Predecessors, We also have effectively confirmed and amplified this Council using its good offices, as often before, to remind commentators of the Sacred Books of those safe rules of Catholic exegesis, which have been handed down by the Holy Fathers and Doctors of the Church, as well as by the Sovereign Pontiffs themselves.[13]

§2—WORK OF THE SUCCESSORS OF LEO XIII

6.   It may not be out of place here to recall gratefully the principal and more useful contributions made successively by Our Predecessors toward this same end, which contributions may be considered as the complement or fruit of the movement so happily initiated by Leo XIII. And first of all Pius X, wishing "to provide a sure way for the preparation of a copious supply of teachers, who, commended by the seriousness and the integrity of their doctrine, might explain the Sacred Books in Catholic schools . . ." instituted "the academic degrees of licentiate and doctorate in Sacred Scripture . . .; to be conferred by the Biblical Commission";[14] he later enacted a law "concerning the method of Scripture studies to be followed in Clerical Seminaries" with this end in view viz: that students of the sacred sciences "not only should themselves fully understand the power, purpose and teaching of the Bible, but should also be equipped to engage in the ministry of the Divine Word with elegance and ability and repel attacks against the divinely inspired books";[15] finally "in order that a center of higher biblical studies might be established in Rome, which in the best way possible might promote the study of the Bible and all cognate sciences in accordance with the mind of the Catholic Church" he founded the Pontifical Biblical Institute, entrusted to the care of the illustrious Society of

Jesus, which he wished endowed "with a superior professorial staff and every facility for biblical research"; he prescribed its laws and rules, professing to follow in this the "salutary and fruitful project" of Leo XIII.[16]

7.   All this in fine Our immediate Predecessor of happy memory Pius XI brought to perfection, laying down among other things "that no one should be appointed professor of Sacred Scripture in any Seminary, unless, having completed a special course of biblical studies, he had in due form obtained the academic degrees before the Biblical Commission or the Biblical Institute." He wished that these degrees should have the same rights and the same effects as the degrees duly conferred in Sacred Theology or Canon Law; likewise he decreed that no one should receive "a benefice having attached the canonical obligation of expounding the Sacred Scripture to the people, unless, among other things, he had obtained the licentiate or doctorate in biblical science." And having at the same time urged the Superiors General of the Regular Orders and of the religious Congregations, as well as the Bishops of the Catholic world, to send the more suitable of their students to frequent the schools of the Biblical Institute and obtain there the academical degrees, he confirmed these exhortations by his own example, appointing out of his bounty an annual sum for this very purpose.[17]

8.   Seeing that, in the year 1907, with the benign approval of Pius X of happy memory, "to the Benedictine monks had been committed the task of preparing the investigations and studies on which might be based a new edition of the Latin version of the Scriptures, commonly called the Vulgate[18], the same Pontiff, Pius XI, wishing to consolidate more firmly and securely this "laborious and arduous enterprise," which demands considerable time and great expense, founded in Rome and lavishly endowed with a library and other means of research, the monastery of St. Jerome, to be devoted exclusively to this work.[19]

§3—SOLICITUDE OF SOVEREIGN PONTIFFS

9.   Nor should We fail to mention here how earnestly these same Our Predecessors, when the opportunity occurred, recommended the study or preaching or in fine the pious reading and meditation of the Sacred Scriptures. Pius X most heartily commended the society of St. Jerome, which strives to promote among the faithful—and to facilitate with all its power—the truly praiseworthy custom of reading and meditating on the holy Gospels; he exhorted them to persevere in the enterprise they had begun, proclaiming it "a most useful undertaking, as well as most suited to the times," seeing that it helps in no small way "to dissipate the idea that the Church is opposed to or in any way impedes the reading of the Scriptures in the vernacular."[20] And Benedict XV, on the occasion of the fifteenth centenary of the death of St. Jerome, the greatest Doctor of the Sacred Scriptures, after having most solemnly inculcated the precepts and examples of the same Doctor, as well as the principles and rules laid down by Leo XIII and by himself, and having recommended other things highly

opportune and never to be forgotten in this connection, exhorted "all the children of the Church, especially clerics, to reverence the Holy Scripture, to read it piously and meditate it constantly"; he reminded them "that in these pages is to be sought that food, by which the spiritual life is nourished unto perfection," and "that the chief use of Scripture pertains to the holy and fruitful exercise of the ministry of preaching"; he likewise once again expressed his warm approval of the work of the society called after St. Jerome himself, by means of which the Gospels and Acts of the Apostles are being so widely diffused, "that there is no Christian family any more without them and that all are accustomed to read and meditate them daily."[21]

§4—FRUITS OF MANIFOLD INITIATIVE

10. But it is right and pleasing to confess openly that it is not only by reason of these initiatives, precepts and exhortations of Our Predecessors that the knowledge and use of the Sacred Scriptures have made great progress among Catholics; for this is also due to the works and labors of all those who diligently cooperated with them, both by meditating, investigating and writing, as well as by teaching and preaching and by translating and propagating the Sacred Books. For from the schools in which are fostered higher studies in theological and biblical science, and especially from Our Pontifical Biblical Institute, there have already come forth, and daily continue to come forth, many students of Holy Scripture who, inspired with an intense love for the Sacred Books, imbue the younger clergy with this same ardent zeal and assiduously impart to them the doctrine they themselves have acquired. Many of them also, by the written word, have promoted and do still promote, far and wide, the study of the Bible; as when they edit the sacred text corrected in accordance with the rules of textual criticism or expound, explain, and translate it into the vernacular; or when they propose it to the faithful for their pious reading and meditation; or finally when they cultivate and seek the aid of profane sciences which are useful for the interpretation of the Scriptures. From these therefore and from other initiatives which daily become more wide-spread and vigorous, as, for example, biblical societies, congresses, libraries, associations for meditation on the Gospels, We firmly hope that in the future reverence for, as well as the use and knowledge of, the Sacred Scriptures will everywhere more and more increase for the good of souls, provided the method of biblical studies laid down by Leo XIII, explained more clearly and perfectly by his Successors, and by Us confirmed and amplified— which indeed is the only safe way and proved by experience—be more firmly, eagerly and faithfully accepted by all, regardless of the difficulties which, as in all human affairs, so in this most excellent work will never be wanting.

II. DOCTRINAL PART: BIBLICAL STUDIES
AT THE PRESENT DAY

11. There is no one who cannot easily perceive that the conditions of biblical studies and their subsidiary sciences have greatly changed within the last fifty

years. For, apart from anything else, when Our Predecessor published the Encyclical Letter *Providentissimus Deus,* hardly a single place in Palestine had begun to be explored by means of relevant excavations. Now, however, this kind of investigation is much more frequent and, since more precise methods and technical skill have been developed in the course of actual experience, it gives us information at once more abundant and more accurate. How much light has been derived from these explorations for the more correct and fuller understanding of the Sacred Books all experts know, as well as all those who devote themselves to these studies. The value of these excavations is enhanced by the discovery from time to time of written documents, which help much towards the knowledge of the languages, letters, events, customs, and forms of worship of most ancient times. And of no less importance is the discovery and investigation, so frequent in out times, of papyri which have contributed so much to the knowledge of letters and institutions, both public and private, especially of the time of Our Savior.

12.   Moreover ancient codices of the Sacred Books have been found and edited with discerning thoroughness; the exegesis of the Fathers of the Church has been more widely and thoroughly examined; in fine the manner of speaking, relating and writing in use among the ancients is made clear by innumerable examples. All these advantages which, not without a special design of Divine Providence, our age has acquired, are as it were an invitation and inducement to interpreters of the Sacred Literature to make diligent use of this light, so abundantly given, to penetrate more deeply, explain more clearly and expound more lucidly the Divine Oracles. If, with the greatest satisfaction of mind, We perceive that these same interpreters have resolutely answered and still continue to answer this call, this is certainly not the last or least of the fruits of the Encyclical Letter *Providentissimus Deus,* by which Our Predecessor Leo XIII, foreseeing as it were this new development of biblical studies, summoned Catholic exegetes to labor and wisely defined the direction and the method to be followed in that labor.

13.   We also, by this Encyclical Letter, desire to insure that the work may not only proceed without interruption, but may also daily become more perfect and fruitful; and to that end We are specially intent on pointing out to all what yet remains to be done, with what spirit the Catholic exegete should undertake, at the present day, so great and noble a work, and to give new incentive and fresh courage to the laborers who toil so strenuously in the vineyard of the Lord.

§1—RECOURSE TO ORIGINAL TEXTS

14.   The Fathers of the Church in their time, especially Augustine, warmly recommended to the Catholic scholar, who undertook the investigation and explanation of the Sacred Scriptures, the study of the ancient languages and recourse to the original texts.[22] However, such was the state of letters in those times, that not many,—and these few but imperfectly—knew the Hebrew language. In the middle ages, when Scholastic Theology was at the height of its vigor, the knowledge of even the Greek language had long since become so rare

in the West, that even the greatest Doctors of that time, in their exposition of the Sacred Text, had recourse only to the Latin version, known as the Vulgate.

15.   On the contrary in this our time, not only the Greek language, which since the humanistic renaissance has been, as it were, restored to new life, is familiar to almost all students of antiquity and letters, but the knowledge of Hebrew also and of other oriental languages has spread far and wide among literary men. Moreover there are now such abundant aids to the study of these languages that the biblical scholar, who by neglecting them would deprive himself of access to the original texts, could in no wise escape the stigma of levity and sloth. For it is the duty of the exegete to lay hold, so to speak, with the greatest care and reverence of the very least expressions which, under the inspiration of the Divine Spirit, have flowed from the pen of the sacred writer, so as to arrive at a deeper and fuller knowledge of his meaning.

16.   Wherefore let him diligently apply himself so as to acquire daily a greater facility in biblical as well as in other oriental languages and to support his interpretation by the aids which all branches of philology supply. This indeed St. Jerome strove earnestly to achieve, as far as the science of his time permitted; to this also aspired with untiring zeal and no small fruit not a few of the great exegetes of the sixteenth and seventeenth centuries, although the knowledge of languages then was much less than at the present day. In like manner therefore ought we to explain the original text which, having been written by the inspired author himself, has more authority and greater weight than any even the very best translation, whether ancient or modern; this can be done all the more easily and fruitfully, if to the knowledge of languages be joined a real skill in literary criticism of the same text.

IMPORTANCE OF TEXTUAL CRITICISM

17.   The great importance which should be attached to this kind of criticism was aptly pointed out by Augustine, when, among the precepts to be recommended to the student of the Sacred Books, he put in the first place the care to possess a corrected text. "The correction of the codices"—so says this most distinguished Doctor of the Church—"should first of all engage the attention of those who wish to know the Divine Scripture so that the uncorrected may give place to the corrected."[23] In the present day indeed this art, which is called textual criticism and which is used with great and praiseworthy results in the editions of profane writings, is also quite rightly employed in the case of the Sacred Books, because of that very reverence which is due to the Divine Oracles. For its very purpose is to insure that the sacred text be restored, as perfectly as possible, be purified from the corruption due to the carelessness of the copyists and be freed, as far as may be done, from glosses and omissions, from the interchange and repetition of words and from all other kinds of mistakes, which are wont to make their way gradually into writings handed down through many centuries.

18.   It is scarcely necessary to observe that this criticism, which some fifty years ago not a few made use of quite arbitrarily and often in such wise that one would say they did so to introduce into the sacred text their own preconceived

ideas, today has rules so firmly established and secure, that it has become a most valuable aid to the purer and more accurate editing of the sacred text and that any abuse can easily be discovered. Nor is it necessary here to call to mind—since it is doubtless familiar and evident to all students of Sacred Scripture—to what extent namely the Church has held in honor these studies in textual criticism from the earliest centuries down even to the present day.

19. Today therefore, since this branch of science has attained to such high perfection, it is the honorable, though not always easy, task of students of the Bible to procure by every means that as soon as possible may be duly published by Catholics editions of the Sacred Books and of ancient versions, brought out in accordance with these standards, which, that is to say, unite the greatest reverence for the sacred text with an exact observance of all the rules of criticism. And let all know that this prolonged labor is not only necessary for the right understanding of the divinely-given writings, but also is urgently demanded by that piety by which it behooves us to be grateful to the God of all providence, Who from the throne of His majesty has sent these books as so many paternal letters to His own children.

MEANING OF TRIDENTINE DECREE

20. Nor should anyone think that this use of the original texts, in accordance with the methods of criticism, in any way derogates from those decrees so wisely enacted by the Council of Trent concerning the Latin Vulgate.[24] It is historically certain that the Presidents of the Council received a commission, which they duly carried out, to beg, that is, the Sovereign Pontiff in the name of the Council that he should have corrected, as far as possible, first a Latin, and then a Greek, and Hebrew edition, which eventually would be published for the benefit of the Holy Church of God.[25] If this desire could not then be fully realized owing to the difficulties of the times and other obstacles, at present it can, We earnestly hope, be more perfectly and entirely fulfilled by the united efforts of Catholic scholars.

21. And if the Tridentine Synod wished "that all should use as authentic" the Vulgate Latin version, this, as all know, applies only to the Latin Church and to the public use of the same Scriptures; nor does it, doubtless, in any way diminish the authority and value of the original texts. For there was no question then of these texts, but of the Latin versions, which were in circulation at that time, and of these the same Council rightly declared to be preferable that which "had been approved by its long-continued use for so many centuries in the Church." Hence this special authority or as they say, authenticity of the Vulgate was not affirmed by the Council particularly for critical reasons, but rather because of its legitimate use in the Churches throughout so many centuries; by which use indeed the same is shown, in the sense in which the Church has understood and understands it, to be free from any error whatsoever in matters of faith and morals; so that, as the Church herself testifies and affirms, it may be quoted safely and without fear of error in disputations, in lectures and in preaching; and so its authenticity is not specified primarily as critical, but rather as juridical.

22.   Wherefore this authority of the Vulgate in matters of doctrine by no means prevents—nay rather today it almost demands—either the corroboration and confirmation of this same doctrine by the original texts or the having recourse on any and every occasion to the aid of these same texts, by which the correct meaning of the Sacred Letters is everywhere daily made more clear and evident. Nor is it forbidden by the decree of the Council of Trent to make translations into the vulgar tongue, even directly from the original texts themselves, for the use and benefit of the faithful and for the better understanding of the divine word, as We know to have been already done in a laudable manner in many countries with the approval of the Ecclesiastical authority.

§2—INTERPRETATION OF SACRED BOOKS

23.   Being thoroughly prepared by the knowledge of the ancient languages and by the aids afforded by the art of criticism, let the Catholic exegete undertake the task, of all those imposed on him the greatest, that namely of discovering and expounding the genuine meaning of the Sacred Books. In the performance of this task let the interpreters bear in mind that their foremost and greatest endeavor should be to discern and define clearly that sense of the biblical words which is called literal. Aided by the context and by comparison with similar passages, let them therefore by means of their knowledge of languages search out with all diligence the literal meaning of the words; all these helps indeed are wont to be pressed into service in the explanation also of profane writers, so that the mind of the author may be made abundantly clear.

24.   The commentators of the Sacred Letters, mindful of the fact that here there is question of a divinely inspired text, the care and interpretation of which have been confided to the Church by God Himself, should no less diligently take into account the explanations and declarations of the teaching authority of the Church, as likewise the interpretation given by the Holy Fathers, and even "the analogy of faith" as Leo XIII most wisely observed in the Encyclical Letter *Providentissimus Deus*.[26] With special zeal should they apply themselves, not only to expounding exclusively these matters which belong to the historical, archaeological, philological and other auxiliary sciences—as, to Our regret, is done in certain commentaries,—but, having duly referred to these, in so far as they may aid the exegesis, they should set forth in particular the theological doctrine in faith and morals of the individual books or texts so that their exposition may not only aid the professors of theology in their explanations and proofs of the dogmas of faith, but may also be of assistance to priests in their presentation of Christian doctrine to the people, and in fine may help all the faithful to lead a life that is holy and worthy of a Christian.

RIGHT USE OF SPIRITUAL SENSE

25.   By making such an exposition, which is above all, as We have said, theological, they will efficaciously reduce to silence those who, affirming that they scarcely ever find anything in biblical commentaries to raise their hearts to God,

to nourish their souls or promote their interior life, repeatedly urge that we should have recourse to a certain spiritual and, as they say, mystical interpretation. With what little reason they thus speak is shown by the experience of many, who, assiduously considering and meditating the word of God, advanced in perfection and were moved to an intense love for God; and this same truth is clearly proved by the constant tradition of the Church and the precepts of the greatest Doctors. Doubtless all spiritual sense is not excluded from the Sacred Scripture.

26.   For what was said and done in the Old Testament was ordained and disposed by God with such consummate wisdom, that things past prefigured in a spiritual way those that were to come under the new dispensation of grace. Wherefore the exegete, just as he must search out and expound the literal meaning of the words, intended and expressed by the sacred writer, so also must he do likewise for the spiritual sense, provided it is clearly intended by God. For God alone could have known this spiritual meaning and have revealed it to us. Now Our Divine Savior Himself points out to us and teaches us this same sense in the Holy Gospel; the Apostles also, following the example of the Master, profess it in their spoken and written words; the unchanging tradition of the Church approves it; and finally the most ancient usage of the liturgy proclaims it, wherever may be rightly applied the well-known principle: "The rule of prayer is the rule of faith."

27.   Let Catholic exegetes then disclose and expound this spiritual significance, intended and ordained by God, with that care which the dignity of the divine word demands; but let them scrupulously refrain from proposing as the genuine meaning of Sacred Scripture other figurative senses. It may indeed be useful, especially in preaching, to illustrate, and present the matters of faith and morals by a broader use of the Sacred Text in the figurative sense, provided this be done with moderation and restraint; it should, however, never be forgotten that this use of the Sacred Scripture is, as it were, extrinsic to it and accidental, and that, especially in these days, it is not free from danger, since the faithful, in particular those who are well-informed in the sciences sacred and profane, wish to know what God has told us in the Sacred Letters rather than what an ingenious orator or writer may suggest by a clever use of the words of Scripture. Nor does "the word of God, living and effectual and more piercing than any two-edged sword and reaching unto the division of the soul and the spirit, of the joints also and the marrow, and a discerner of the thoughts and intents of the heart"[27] need artificial devices and human adaptation to move and impress souls; for the Sacred Pages, written under the inspiration of the Spirit of God, are of themselves rich in original meaning; endowed with a divine power, they have their own value; adorned with heavenly beauty, they radiate of themselves light and splendor, provided they are so fully and accurately explained by the interpreter, that all the treasures of wisdom and prudence, therein contained are brought to light.

28.   In the accomplishment of this task the Catholic exegete will find invaluable help in an assiduous study of those works, in which the Holy Fathers, the Doctors of the Church and the renowned interpreters of past ages have explained the Sacred Books. For, although sometimes less instructed in profane learning and in the knowledge of languages than the scripture scholars of our time, nevertheless by reason of the office assigned to them by God in the Church, they are distinguished by a certain subtle insight into heavenly things and by a marvelous keenness of intellect, which enables them to penetrate to the very innermost meaning of the divine word and bring to light all that can help to elucidate the teaching of Christ and to promote holiness of life.

29.   It is indeed regrettable that such precious treasures of Christian antiquity are almost unknown to many writers of the present day, and that students of the history of exegesis have not yet accomplished all that seems necessary for the due investigation and appreciation of so momentous a subject. Would that many, by seeking out the authors of the Catholic interpretation of Scripture and diligently studying their works and drawing thence the almost inexhaustible riches therein stored up, might contribute largely to this end, so that it might be daily more apparent to what extent those authors understood and made known the divine teaching of the Sacred Books, and that the interpreters of today might thence take example and seek suitable arguments.

30.   For thus at long last will be brought about the happy and fruitful union between the doctrine and spiritual sweetness of expression of the ancient authors and the greater erudition and maturer knowledge of the modern, having as its result new progress in the never fully explored and inexhaustible field of the Divine Letters.

§3—SPECIAL TASKS OF INTERPRETERS

31.   Moreover we may rightly and deservedly hope that our times also can contribute something towards the deeper and more accurate interpretation of Sacred Scripture. For not a few things, especially in matters pertaining to history, were scarcely at all or not fully explained by the commentators of past ages, since they lacked almost all the information which was needed for their clearer exposition. How difficult for the Fathers themselves, and indeed well nigh unintelligible, were certain passages is shown, among other things, by the oft-repeated efforts of many of them to explain the first chapters of Genesis; likewise by the reiterated attempts of St. Jerome so to translate the Psalms that the literal sense, that, namely, which is expressed by the words themselves, might be clearly revealed.

32.   There are, in fine, other books or texts, which contain difficulties brought to light only in quite recent times, since a more profound knowledge of antiquity has given rise to new questions, on the basis of which the point at issue may be more appropriately examined. Quite wrongly therefore do some pretend, not rightly understanding the conditions of biblical study, that nothing remains to be added by the Catholic exegete of our time to what Christian antiquity has

produced; since, on the contrary, these our times have brought to light so many things, which call for a fresh investigation, and which stimulate not a little the practical zest of the present-day interpreter.

CHARACTER OF SACRED WRITER

33. As in our age, indeed new questions and new difficulties are multiplied, so, by God's favor, new means and aids to exegesis are also provided. Among these it is worthy of special mention that Catholic theologians, following the teaching of the Holy Fathers and especially of the Angelic and Common Doctor, have examined and explained the nature and effects of biblical inspiration more exactly and more fully than was wont to be done in previous ages. For having begun by expounding minutely the principle that the inspired writer, in composing the sacred book, is the living and reasonable instrument of the Holy Spirit, they rightly observe that, impelled by the divine motion, he so uses his faculties and powers, that from the book composed by him all may easily infer "the special character of each one and, as it were, his personal traits."[28] Let the interpreter then, with all care and without neglecting any light derived from recent research, endeavor to determine the peculiar character and circumstances of the sacred writer, the age in which he lived, the sources written or oral to which he had recourse and the forms of expression he employed.

34. Thus can he the better understand who was the inspired author, and what he wishes to express by his writings. There is no one indeed but knows that the supreme rule of interpretation is to discover and define what the writer intended to express, as St. Athanasius excellently observes: "Here, as indeed is expedient in all other passages of Sacred Scripture, it should be noted, on what occasion the Apostle spoke; we should carefully and faithfully observe to whom and why he wrote, lest, being ignorant of these points, or confounding one with another, we miss the real meaning of the author."[29]

IMPORTANCE OF MODE OF WRITING

35. What is the literal sense of a passage is not always as obvious in the speeches and writings of the ancient authors of the East, as it is in the works of our own time. For what they wished to express is not to be determined by the rules of grammar and philology alone, nor solely by the context; the interpreter must, as it were, go back wholly in spirit to those remote centuries of the East and with the aid of history, archaeology, ethnology, and other sciences, accurately determine what modes of writing, so to speak, the authors of that ancient period would be likely to use, and in fact did use.

36. For the ancient peoples of the East, in order to express their ideas, did not always employ those forms or kinds of speech which we use today; but rather those used by the men of their times and countries. What those exactly were the commentator cannot determine as it were in advance, but only after a careful examination of the ancient literature of the East. The investigation, carried

out, on this point, during the past forty or fifty years with greater care and diligence than ever before, has more clearly shown what forms of expression were used in those far off times, whether in poetic description or in the formulation of laws and rules of life or in recording the facts and events of history. The same inquiry has also shown the special preeminence of the people of Israel among all the other ancient nations of the East in their mode of compiling history, both by reason of its antiquity and by reason of the faithful record of the events; qualities which may well be attributed to the gift of divine inspiration and to the peculiar religious purpose of biblical history.

37.   Nevertheless no one, who has a correct idea of biblical inspiration, will be surprised to find, even in the Sacred Writers, as in other ancient authors, certain fixed ways of expounding and narrating, certain definite idioms, especially of a kind peculiar to the Semitic tongues, so-called approximations, and certain hyperbolical modes of expression, nay, at times, even paradoxical, which help to impress the ideas more deeply on the mind. For of the modes of expression which, among ancient peoples, and especially those of the East, human language used to express its thought, none is excluded from the Sacred Books, provided the way of speaking adopted in no wise contradicts the holiness and truth of God, as, with his customary wisdom, the Angelic Doctor already observed in these words: "In Scripture divine things are presented to us in the manner which is in common use amongst men."[30] For as the substantial Word of God became like to men in all things, "except sin,"[31] so the words of God, expressed in human language, are made like to human speech in every respect, except error. In this consists that "condescension" of the God of providence, which St. John Chrysostom extolled with the highest praise and repeatedly declared to be found in the Sacred Books.[32]

38.   Hence the Catholic commentator, in order to comply with the present needs of biblical studies, in explaining the Sacred Scripture and in demonstrating and proving its immunity from all error, should also make a prudent use of this means, determine, that is, to what extent the manner of expression or the literary mode adopted by the sacred writer may lead to a correct and genuine interpretation; and let him be convinced that this part of his office cannot be neglected without serious detriment to Catholic exegesis. Not infrequently— to mention only one instance—when some persons reproachfully charge the Sacred Writers with some historical error or inaccuracy in the recording of facts, on closer examination it turns out to be nothing else than those customary modes of expression and narration peculiar to the ancients, which used to be employed in the mutual dealings of social life and which in fact were sanctioned by common usage.

39.   When then such modes of expression are met within the sacred text, which, being meant for men, is couched in human language, justice demands that they be no more taxed with error than when they occur in the ordinary intercourse of daily life. By this knowledge and exact appreciation of the modes of speaking and writing in use among the ancients can be solved many difficulties, which are raised against the veracity and historical value of the Divine

Scriptures, and no less efficaciously does this study contribute to a fuller and more luminous understanding of the mind of the Sacred Writer.

STUDIES OF BIBLICAL ANTIQUITIES

40.   Let those who cultivate biblical studies turn their attention with all due diligence towards this point and let them neglect none of those discoveries, whether in the domain of archaeology or in ancient history or literature, which serve to make better known the mentality of the ancient writers, as well as their manner and art of reasoning, narrating and writing. In this connection Catholic laymen should consider that they will not only further profane science, but moreover will render a conspicuous service to the Christian cause if they devote themselves with all due diligence and application to the exploration and investigation of the monuments of antiquity and contribute, according to their abilities, to the solution of questions hitherto obscure.

41.   For all human knowledge, even the non-sacred, has indeed its own proper dignity and excellence, being a finite participation of the infinite knowledge of God, but it acquires a new and higher dignity and, as it were, a consecration, when it is employed to cast a brighter light upon the things of God.

§4—WAY OF TREATING MORE DIFFICULT QUESTIONS

42.   The progressive exploration of the antiquities of the East, mentioned above, the more accurate examination of the original text itself, the more extensive and exact knowledge of languages both biblical and oriental, have with the help of God, happily provided the solution of not a few of those questions, which in the time of Our Predecessor Leo XIII of immortal memory, were raised by critics outside or hostile to the Church against the authenticity, antiquity, integrity and historical value of the Sacred Books. For Catholic exegetes, by a right use of those same scientific arms, not infrequently abused by the adversaries, proposed such interpretations, which are in harmony with Catholic doctrine and the genuine current of tradition, and at the same time are seen to have proved equal to the difficulties, either raised by new explorations and discoveries, or bequeathed by antiquity for solution in our time.

43.   Thus has it come about that confidence in the authority and historical value of the Bible, somewhat shaken in the case of some by so many attacks, today among Catholics is completely restored; moreover there are not wanting even non-Catholic writers, who by serious and calm inquiry have been led to abandon modern opinion and to return, at least in some points, to the more ancient ideas. This change is due in great part to the untiring labor by which Catholic commentators of the Sacred Letters, in no way deterred by difficulties and obstacles of all kinds, strove with all their strength to make suitable use of what learned men of the present day, by their investigations in the domain of archaeology or history or philology, have made available for the solution of new questions.

44.   Nevertheless no one will be surprised, if all difficulties are not yet solved and overcome; but that even today serious problems greatly exercise the minds of Catholic exegetes. We should not lose courage on this account; nor should we forget that in the human sciences the same happens as in the natural world; that is to say, new beginnings grow little by little and fruits are gathered only after many labors. Thus it has happened that certain disputed points, which in the past remained unsolved and in suspense, in our days, with the progress of studies, have found a satisfactory solution. Hence there are grounds for hope that those also will by constant effort be at last made clear, which now seem most complicated and difficult.

45.   And if the wished-for solution be slow in coming or does not satisfy us, since perhaps a successful conclusion may be reserved to posterity, let us not wax impatient thereat, seeing that in us also is rightly verified what the Fathers, and especially Augustine,[33] observed in their time viz: God wished difficulties to be scattered through the Sacred Books inspired by Him, in order that we might be urged to read and scrutinize them more intently, and, experiencing in a salutary manner our own limitations, we might be exercised in due submission of mind. No wonder if of one or other question no solution wholly satisfactory will ever be found, since sometimes we have to do with matters obscure in themselves and too remote from our times and our experience; and since exegesis also, like all other most important sciences, has its secrets, which, impenetrable to our minds, by no efforts whatsoever can be unraveled.

DEFINITE SOLUTIONS SOUGHT

46.   But this state of things is no reason why the Catholic commentator, inspired by an active and ardent love of his subject and sincerely devoted to Holy Mother Church, should in any way be deterred from grappling again and again with these difficult problems, hitherto unsolved, not only that he may refute the objections of the adversaries, but also may attempt to find a satisfactory solution, which will be in full accord with the doctrine of the Church, in particular with the traditional teaching regarding the inerrancy of Sacred Scripture, and which will at the same time satisfy the indubitable conclusions of profane sciences.

47.   Let all the other sons of the Church bear in mind that the efforts of these resolute laborers in the vineyard of the Lord should be judged not only with equity and justice, but also with the greatest charity; all moreover should abhor that intemperate zeal which imagines that whatever is new should for that very reason be opposed or suspected. Let them bear in mind above all that in the rules and laws promulgated by the Church there is question of doctrine regarding faith and morals; and that in the immense matter contained in the Sacred Books—legislative, historical, sapiential and prophetical—there are but few texts whose sense has been defined by the authority of the Church, nor are those more numerous about which the teaching of the Holy Fathers is unanimous. There remain therefore many things, and of the greatest importance, in

the discussion and exposition of which the skill and genius of Catholic commentators may and ought to be freely exercised, so that each may contribute his part to the advantage of all, to the continued progress of the sacred doctrine and to the defense and honor of the Church.

48. This true liberty of the children of God, which adheres faithfully to the teaching of the Church and accepts and uses gratefully the contributions of profane science, this liberty, upheld and sustained in every way by the confidence of all, is the condition and source of all lasting fruit and of all solid progress in Catholic doctrine, as Our Predecessor of happy memory Leo XIII rightly observes, when he says: "Unless harmony of mind be maintained and principle safeguarded, no progress can be expected in this matter from the varied studies of many."[35]

§5—USE OF SCRIPTURE IN INSTRUCTION OF FAITHFUL

49. Whosoever considers the immense labors undertaken by Catholic exegetes during well nigh two thousand years, so that the word of God, imparted to men through the Sacred Letters, might daily be more deeply and fully understood and more intensely loved, will easily be convinced that it is the serious duty of the faithful, and especially of priests, to make free and holy use of this treasure, accumulated throughout so many centuries by the greatest intellects. For the Sacred Books were not given by God to men to satisfy their curiosity or to provide them with material for study and research, but, as the Apostle observes, in order that these Divine Oracles might "instruct us to salvation, by the faith which is in Christ Jesus" and "that the man of God may be perfect, furnished to every good work."[36]

50. Let priests therefore, who are bound by their office to procure the eternal salvation of the faithful, after they have themselves by diligent study perused the sacred pages and made them their own by prayer and meditations, assiduously distribute the heavenly treasures of the divine word by sermons, homilies and exhortations; let them confirm the Christian doctrine by sentences from the Sacred Books and illustrate it by outstanding examples from sacred history and in particular from the Gospel of Christ Our Lord; and—avoiding with the greatest care those purely arbitrary and far-fetched adaptations, which are not a use, but rather an abuse of the divine word—let them set forth all this with such eloquence, lucidity and clearness that the faithful may not only be moved and inflamed to reform their lives, but may also conceive in their hearts the greatest veneration for the Sacred Scripture.

51. The same veneration the Bishops should endeavor daily to increase and perfect among the faithful committed to their care, encouraging all those initiatives by which men, filled with apostolic zeal, laudably strive to excite and foster among Catholics a greater knowledge of and love for the Sacred Books. Let them favor therefore and lend help to those pious associations whose aim it is to spread copies of the Sacred Letters, especially of the Gospels, among the faithful, and to procure by every means that in Christian families the same be

read daily with piety and devotion; let them efficaciously recommend by word and example, whenever the liturgical laws permit, the Sacred Scriptures translated, with the approval of the Ecclesiastical authority, into modern languages; let them themselves give public conferences or dissertations on biblical subjects, or see that they are given by other public orators well versed in the matter.

52.   Let the ministers of the Sanctuary support in every way possible and diffuse in fitting manner among all classes of the faithful the periodicals which so laudably and with such heartening results are published from time to time in various parts of the world, whether to treat and expose in a scientific manner biblical questions, or to adapt the fruits of these investigations to the sacred ministry, or to benefit the faithful. Let the ministers of the Sanctuary be convinced that all this, and whatsoever else an apostolical zeal and a sincere love of the divine word may find suitable to this high purpose, will be an efficacious help to the cure of souls.

CURRICULUM IN SEMINARIES

53.   But it is plain to everyone that priests cannot duly fulfill all this unless in their Seminary days they have imbibed a practical and enduring love for the Sacred Scriptures. Wherefore let the Bishops, on whom devolves the paternal care of their Seminaries, with all diligence see to it that nothing be omitted in this matter which may help towards the desired end. Let the professors of Sacred Scripture in the Seminaries give the whole course of biblical studies in such a way, that they may instruct the young aspirants to the Priesthood and to the ministry of the divine word with that knowledge of the Sacred Letters and imbue them with that love for the same, without which it is vain to hope for copious fruits of the apostolate.

54.   Hence their exegetical explanation should aim especially at the theological doctrine, avoiding useless disputations and omitting all that is calculated rather to gratify curiosity than to promote true learning and solid piety. The literal sense and especially the theological let them propose with such definiteness, explain with such skill and inculcate with such ardor that in their students may be in a sense verified what happened to the disciples on the way to Emmaus, when, having heard the words of the Master, they exclaimed: "Was not our heart burning within us, whilst He opened to us the Scriptures?"[37]

55.   Thus the Divine Letter will become for the future priests of the Church a pure and never failing source for their own spiritual life, as well as food and strength for the sacred office of preaching which they are about to undertake. If the professors of this most important matter in the Seminaries accomplish all this, then let them rest joyfully assured that they have most efficaciously contributed to the salvation of souls, to the progress of the Catholic faith, to the honor and glory of God, and that they have performed a work most closely connected with the apostolic office.

56.   If these things which We have said, Venerable Brethren and beloved sons, are necessary in every age, much more urgently are they needed in our sorrowful times, when almost all peoples and nations are plunged in a sea of calamities, when a cruel war heaps ruins upon ruins and slaughter upon slaughter, when, owing to the most bitter hatred stirred up among the nations, We perceive with greatest sorrow that in not a few has been extinguished the sense not only of Christian moderation and charity, but also of humanity itself. Who can heal these mortal wounds of the human family if not He, to Whom the Prince of the Apostles, full of confidence and love, addresses these words: "Lord, to whom shall we go? Thou hast the words of eternal life."[37]

57.   To this Our most merciful Redeemer we must therefore bring all back by every means in our power; for He is the divine consoler of the afflicted; He it is Who teaches all, whether they be invested with public authority or are bound in duty to obey and submit, true honesty, absolute justice and generous charity; it is He in fine, and He alone, Who can be the firm foundation and support of peace and tranquillity: "For other foundation no man can lay, but that which is laid: which is Christ Jesus."[38] This the author of salvation, Christ, will men more fully know, more ardently love and more faithfully imitate in proportion as they are more assiduously urged to know and meditate the Sacred Letters, especially the New Testament, for, as St. Jerome the Doctor of Stridon says: "To ignore the Scripture is to ignore Christ";[39] and again: "If there is anything in this life which sustains a wise man and induces him to maintain his serenity amidst the tribulations and adversities of the world, it is in the first place, I consider, the meditation and knowledge of the Scriptures."[40]

58.   There those who are wearied and oppressed by adversities and afflictions will find true consolation and divine strength to suffer and bear with patience; there—that is in the Holy Gospels—Christ, the highest and greatest example of justice, charity and mercy, is present to all; and to the lacerated and trembling human race are laid open the fountains of that divine grace without which both peoples and their rulers can never arrive at, never establish, peace in the state and unity of heart; there in fine will all learn Christ, "Who is the head of all principality and power"[41] and "Who of God is made unto us wisdom and justice and sanctification and redemption."[42]

CONCLUSION

EXHORTATION TO ALL THOSE WHO CULTIVATE BIBLICAL STUDIES

59.   Having expounded and recommended those things which are required for the adaptation of Scripture studies to the necessities of the day, it remains, Venerable Brethren and beloved sons, that to biblical scholars who are devoted sons of the Church and follow faithfully her teaching and direction, We address with paternal affection, not only Our congratulations that they have been chosen and called to so sublime an office, but also Our encouragement to continue

with ever renewed vigor with all zeal and care, the work so happily begun. Sublime office, We say; for what is more sublime than to scrutinize, explain, propose to the faithful and defend from unbelievers the very word of God, communicated to men under the inspiration of the Holy Ghost?

60.   With this spiritual food the mind of the interpreter is fed and nourished "to the commemoration of faith, the consolation of hope, the exhortation of charity."[43] "To live amidst these things, to meditate these things, to know nothing else, to seek nothing else, does it not seem to you already here below a foretaste of the heavenly kingdom?"[44] Let also the minds of the faithful be nourished with this same food, that they may draw from thence the knowledge and love of God and the progress in perfection and the happiness of their own individual souls. Let, then, the interpreters of the Divine Oracles devote themselves to this holy practice with all their heart. "Let them pray, that they may understand";[45] let them labor to penetrate ever more deeply into the secrets of the Sacred Pages; let them teach and preach, in order to open to others also the treasures of the word of God.

61.   Let the present-day commentators of the Sacred Scripture emulate, according to their capacity, what those illustrious interpreters of past ages accomplished with such great fruit; so that, as in the past, so also in these days, the Church may have at her disposal learned doctors for the expounding of the Divine Letters; and, through their assiduous labors, the faithful may comprehend all the splendor, stimulating language, and joy contained in the Holy Scriptures. And in this very arduous and important office let them have "for their comfort the Holy Books"[46] and be mindful of the promised reward: since "they that are learned shall shine as the brightness of the firmament, and they that instruct many unto justice, as stars for all eternity."[47]

62.   And now, while ardently desiring for all sons of the Church, and especially for the professors in biblical science, for the young clergy and for preachers, that, continually meditating on the divine word, they may taste how good and sweet is the spirit of the Lord;[48] as a presage of heavenly gifts and a token of Our paternal goodwill, We impart to you one and all, Venerable Brethren and beloved sons, most lovingly in the Lord, the Apostolic Benediction.

63.   Given at Rome, at St. Peter's, on the 30th of September, the feast of St. Jerome, the greatest Doctor in the exposition of the Sacred Scriptures, in the year 1943, the fifth of Our Pontificate.

NOTES

1. 2 Timothy 3:16 ff.

2. Session IV, decr. I; EB, n. 45.

3. Session III, Cap. 2i EB, n. 62.

4. *Address to the Ecclesiastical students in Rome* (June 24, 1939); AAS XXXI (1939), p. 245–251.

5. Cf. I, q. 70, art. I ad 3.

6. *De Gen. ad litt.* 2, 9, 20; PL 34, col. 270 s.; CSEL 28 (Sectio III, pars. 2), p. 46.

7. Leo XIII *Acta* XIII, p. 355; EB, n. 106; supra, p. 22.

8. Cf. Benedict XV, SP, AAS XII (1920), p. 396; EB, n. 471; supra p. 53.

9. Leo XIII *Acta* XLI, p. 357 sq.; EB, n. 109 sq; supra, pp. 23–25.

10. Leo XIII *Acta* XIII, p. 328; EB, n. 67 sq.

11. Apostolic letter *Hierosolymae in coenobio*, Sept. 17, 1892; Leo XIII *Acta* XII, pp. 239–241; v. p. 240.

12. Cf. Leo XIII *Acta* XXII, p. 232 ss.; EB, n. 130–141; v. nn. 130, 132; supra. p. 31.

13. Letter of the Pontifical Biblical Commission to their Excellencies the Archbishops and Bishops of Italy, Aug. 20, 1941; AAS XXXIII (1941), pp. 465–472; infra, pp. 129–138.

14. Apostolic letter *Scripturae Sanctae*, Feb. 23, 1904; Pius X *Acta* 1, pp. 176–179; EB, nn. 142–150; v nn. 143–144.

15. Cf. Apostolic letter *Quoniam in re biblica*, March 27, 1906; Pius X *Acta* III, p. 72–76; EB, nn. 155–173; v. n. 155; supra. pp. 36–39.

16. Apostolic letter *Vinea electa*, May 7, 1909; AAS 1(1909), pp. 447–449; EB, nn. 293–306; v. nn. 296–306; v. nn. 296 et 294.

17. Cf. Motu proprio *Bibliorum scientiam*, April 27, 1924; AAS XVI (1924), pp. 180–182: EB, nn. 518–525.

18. Letter to the Most Rev. Abbot Aidan Gasquet, Dec. 3, 1907; Pius X *Acta* IV, pp. 117–119, EB, n. 285 sq.

19. Apostolic constitution *Inter praecipuas*, June 15, 1933; AAS XXVI (1934), pp. 85–87.

20. Letter to the Most Eminent Cardinal Casetta *Qui piam*, Jan. 21, 1907; Pius X *Acta* IV, pp. 23–25.

21. SP, Sept. 15, 1920; AAS XII (1920), pp. 385–422; EB, nn. 457–508; v. nn. 457, 495, 497, 491; supra, pp. 43–78.

22. Cf. ex. gr. St. Jerome, *Praef. in IV Evang. ad Damasum*; PL 29, col. 526–527; St. Augustine, *De Doctr. christ.* 11, 16; PL 34, col. 42–43.

23. *De doctr. christ.* 11, 21; PL 34, col. 40.

24. *Decr. de editione et usu Sacrorum Librorum*; Conc. Trid. ed. Soc. Goerres, t. V, p. 91 s.

25. *Ib.*, t. X, p. 471; cf. t. V, pp. 29, 59, 65; t. X, p. 446 sq.

26. Leo XIII *Acta* XIII, pp. 345–346; EB, n. 94–96; infra, pp. 15–16.

27. Hebrews 4:12.

28. Cf. SP; AAS XII (1920), p. 390; EB, n. 461; supra, pp. 46–47.

29. *Contra Arianos* I, 54; PG 26, col. 123.

30. *Comment. ad Hebr.* cap. 1, lectio 4.

31. Hebrews 4:15.

32. Cf. v. gr. *In Gen.* 1, 4 (PG 53, col. 34-35); *In Gen.* II, 21 (ib. col. 121); *In Gen.* III, 8 (ib. col. 135); *Hom. 15 in Joan.*, ad. 1, 18 (PG 59, col. 97 sq.).

33. St. Augustine, *Epist. 149 ad Paulinum*, n. 34 (PL 33, col. 644); *De diversis quaestionibus*, q. 53, n. 2 (ib. XL, col. 36); *Enarr. in Ps.* 146, n. 12 (ib. 37, col. 1907).

34. Apostolic letter *Vigilantiae*; Leo XIII *Acta* XIII, p. 237; EB, n. 136; supra, p. 34. 35. Cf. 2 Timothy 3:15, 17.

36. Luke 24:32.

37. John 6:69.

38. 1 Corinthians 3:11.

39. St. Jerome, *In Isaiam, prologus*; PL 24, col. 17.

40. Id., *In Ephesios, prologus*; PL 26, col. 439.

41. Colossians 2:10.

42. 1 Corinthians 1:30.

43. Cf. St. Augustine, *Contra Faustum* XIII, 18; PL 42, col. 294; CSEL XXV, p. 400.

44. St. Jerome, *Ep. 53*, 10; PL 22, col. 549; CSEL 54, p. 463.

45. St. Augustine, *de doctr. christ.* III, 56; PL 34, col. 89.

46. 1 Maccabees 12:9.

47. Daniel 12:3.

48. Cf. Wisdom 12:1.

INSTRUCTION *SANCTA MATER ECCLESIA*

ON THE HISTORICAL TRUTH
OF THE GOSPELS

PONTIFICAL BIBLICAL COMMISSION
1964

OVERVIEW OF *SANCTA MATER ECCLESIA*
Joseph Prior

"There are also many other things that Jesus did; if every one of them were written down, I suppose that the world itself could not contain the books that would
be written" (John 21:25). The Beloved Disciple ends the Fourth Gospel in these
words, recalling the inexhaustible wealth of Jesus' public ministry. The words
allude to the fact that the mystery that is the Word made flesh (John 1:14) cannot
be exhausted through knowledge, memory or experience. The gospel writer concludes his work with the basic understanding that his presentation and interpretation of Jesus' words and deeds will be neither exhaustive nor complete.

The message of Jesus is reflected in the writings of Matthew, Mark, Luke
and John. The four gospels present and interpret the mission of Jesus the Christ
from four different perspectives. Each work is inspired by the Holy Spirit but is
written by a distinct author, or evangelist. These evangelists were influenced
not only by the Holy Spirit but also by the circumstances surrounding their
activity, including the time period in which they wrote, the place in which
they wrote, and the people for whom they were writing. These varying circumstances influence the purpose of each author. Although the evangelists share
the general intention of giving an interpretation to and a witness of the mystery
of Christ, each evangelist has a specific intention forged by the circumstances
mentioned above. Understanding the human author's intention and purpose in
writing a gospel will help one to understand the portraits of Jesus' life, ministry,
passion, death and resurrection given by Matthew, Mark, Luke and John.

HISTORICAL BACKGROUND AND CONTEXT FOR *SANCTA MATER ECCLESIA*

Biblical studies from the days of the early church until the present have sought
to uncover the meaning of the words of scripture. In the years following the
Renaissance, it was Protestant scholarship that developed critical methods for
studying the scriptures (Catholic exceptions being R. Simon [1638–1712] and
J. Astruc [c. 1753]). Catholic use of such methods began later, in the mid-
nineteenth century. Toward the end of that century questions were raised concerning the value of critical scholarship for interpreting the scriptures. Pope
Leo XIII, in his encyclical letter *Providentissimus Deus* (1893), addressed these
questions and allowed the cautious use of critical biblical studies, emphasizing
the importance of textual criticism and the study of the texts in their original
languages. Fifty years later, Pius XII, in his encyclical letter *Divino afflante
spiritu* (1943), encouraged the use of critical methodologies to determine the
literal sense of the sacred compositions. This literal sense was described as the
meaning intended by the human author. Catholic use of critical methodologies
and scholarship greatly increased following this encyclical.

Throughout the history of the church debates have raged over the
approaches to and methods of interpreting the sacred scriptures. In the early
church the dominant question was the relationship between allegorical and literal interpretation; today the prevailing concern involves the relationship

between spiritual and intellectual interpretation. In the years following *Divino afflante spiritu*, as the Catholic use of critical methodologies increased, a new debate began regarding the value of using such methods in biblical studies. This debate coincided with the preparation for the Second Vatican Council (1962–1965). The pre-conciliar preparatory commissions solicited opinions from bishops, major religious superiors and the faculties of Catholic universities. The responses revealed a growing division between those who valued modern methods of biblical research and those who opposed them. When the Council opened in 1962 the debate was brought to the fore in the discussions on divine revelation and the document that would eventually become the Dogmatic Constitution on Divine Revelation—*Dei verbum*.

One aspect of the debate on the scriptures centered on the historicity of the events recounted in the New Testament. Scholarship had raised such questions as: Was the New Testament historically reliable? Were the details historical? Why were there different accounts for the same events? How can the different accounts be reconciled?

No clear and satisfactory answers were presented. As a result, two extreme movements developed. One suggested that nothing in the New Testament was historically reliable; the other suggested that everything in the New Testament was historically accurate. Recognizing the need for serious discussion on the issue, Pope John XXIII intervened by appointing the Pontifical Biblical Commission (PBC) to discuss the historicity of the gospels. He asked that specific attention be given to the interplay between form criticism and historical information. The PBC began its discussions on this topic in 1963 and concluded with the publication on April 21, 1964, of the instruction *Sancta mater ecclesia* (SME) on the historical truth of the gospels.

ORGANIZATION OF THE DOCUMENT

The document is not a treatise on biblical interpretation, but is a compact treatment of specific issues. Framed by a brief introduction and conclusion, the document is divided into five parts: 1. General Guidelines, 2. The Elaboration of the Gospel Message, 3. Seminary Teachers, 4. Preachers and 5. Biblical Associations.

The PBC begins by acknowledging the advances in biblical scholarship made by Catholic scholars. At the same time, it recognizes the current debate and the divisions caused by the different theological positions. The PBC warns: "Care must be taken 'that the heated atmosphere of dispute does not overstep the bounds of mutual charity; that such disputes do not give the impression that divine truths and sacred Traditions are being called into question'" [2].

(Unlike many Roman documents, *Sancta mater ecclesia* did not originally have numbered articles or paragraphs. In the edition that follows, numbers were added for convenience. References in this *Overview* will be to these added numbers.)

PART ONE: GENERAL GUIDELINES

The first part of SME sets forth the general guidelines for the exegete: "In short the exegete will use any and every means which will enable him to acquire a deeper insight into the nature of the gospel testimony, the religious life of the early churches, and the meaning and value of the Apostolic tradition" [5]. Biblical scholars should take into consideration the work of the Fathers and Doctors of the Church, along with using the historical method—including textual criticism, literary criticism, linguistic criticism and the determination of the literary genres used by a particular author. The PBC quotes Pius XII in noting the importance of these studies for biblical exegesis: "Let [the exegete] rest assured that this aspect . . . cannot be neglected without grave detriment to Catholic exegesis" [5]. Yet the PBC does not give a blind endorsement of these methods but suggests that they be employed with care. Special attention should be given to the application of form criticism. Its use is encouraged "if the opportunity presents itself"; however, it should not be "interlaced with inadmissible philosophical and theological principles which frequently vitiate either the method itself or its judgements on literary questions" [6]. In addition to these concerns, the PBC warns exegetes to avoid rationalist presuppositions that have been associated with the development of the method. The rationalist prejudges the impossibility of divine involvement in the creation of the scriptures even to the point of denying revelation itself. As a result, the rationalist will find no historical value in the sacred texts and some will "minimize the authority of the Apostles as witnesses to Christ." The PBC observes that these principles are contrary to Catholic doctrine as well as "devoid of scholarly foundation" [7].

PART TWO: THE ELABORATION OF THE GOSPEL MESSAGE

The second part of the document is its cornerstone as well as its enduring contribution to Catholic biblical studies. In this section the PBC describes the elaboration of the gospel message as developing in three consecutive stages: the teaching of Jesus, the teaching of the apostles, and the writings of the four evangelists. In each stage the teaching is transmitted through words and images that are conditioned by the local setting, the time period and the mentality of the audience. At the same time, the eternal Word reflected in the words and images remains the same and thus the message can be understood and applied to all times and read in all places.

Jesus chose a "select group of disciples" who would be the witnesses of his message to the world, and communicated his teaching to these disciples and others using words, images and expressions understandable to them. He "adapted himself to the mentality of his audience so that his teaching would be firmly impressed on their minds and easily remembered by his disciples" [9]. For example, Jesus used the agricultural and familial images common to his society. He also used forms of speech such as proverbial sayings, parables and stories that were commonly used at the time. And since his audience was overwhelmingly Jewish, he frequently used Old Testament quotations or allusions. In doing this Jesus effectively communicated his teaching to his disciples. Thus, the first stage in the elaboration of the gospel message was that of the teaching of Jesus.

During the public ministry of Jesus, the apostles understood Jesus' words and deeds, but only to a certain point. Numerous times Jesus had rebuked the apostles for not understanding his role in salvation history, namely, that the Son of Man must suffer and die and then be raised on the third day (see, for example, Mark 8:33, 9:32). After the resurrection, the apostles gained new insight into the ministry of Jesus. They came to understand that the miracles and events of Jesus' life were meant to engender faith. The apostles, empowered by the Holy Spirit, then went out and preached the gospel to all the nations. Just as Jesus adapted his teaching to the mentality of the people to whom he spoke, so too the apostles tailored "the format of their preaching to the condition of their audience." The apostles used those means available to them in communicating the gospel and so SME notes that they were "debtors to 'Greeks and to foreigners, to learned and unlearned.'" SME also recognizes the many forms that the apostles used in preaching—"catechetical formulas, narrative reports, eyewitness accounts, hymns, doxologies, prayers, and similar literary genres commonly found in Sacred Scripture and the speech of that period" [12]. And so the second stage in the elaboration of the gospel was the teaching of the apostles.

The movement from oral preaching to the written word occurs in the third stage, the time of the writing of the four evangelists. The evangelists attempt to "'draw up a narrative' of the events connected with the Lord Jesus." As with Jesus and the apostles, the evangelists were affected by the culture and times in which they wrote so that each author gives his own presentation of the teaching and events connected with Christ. SME notes: "Of the many elements at hand [the evangelists] reported some, summarized others, and developed still others in accordance with the needs of the various churches. They used every possible means to ensure that their readers would come to know the validity of the things they had been taught" [14]. The evangelists wrote to particular audiences with particular concerns that needed to be addressed. These needs influenced their decisions on what to include, what to exclude, what to elaborate and what to summarize. The work, always under the influence of the Spirit, was done so that the faith of the community would be strengthened and that Christ's words and deeds might be better understand. Thus, the third stage of the elaboration of the gospel was the writing of the four evangelists.

Understanding the transmission of the gospel as occurring in three stages has consequences for biblical exegesis and interpretation. First, the historical context of the author needs to be identified and understood so that his purpose may be identified.

Second, the exegete must be aware that the truth of the gospel "is not compromised because the Evangelists report the Lord's words and deeds in different order." The Holy Spirit, in inspiring the human authors, provides the guarantee that the truth communicated through the written works is authentic and that the books are thus authoritative. Yet, a certain freedom was allowed to the human author in his composition. The PBC states that the Holy Spirit "undoubtedly guided and directed the sacred writers as they thought about the things which they were going to write down; but He probably allowed each writer to arrange his narrative as he saw fit" [17].

Third, in order to ascertain the intention and purpose of the human author, the exegete needs to consider "all the factors involved in the origin and composition of the Gospels." Scholarly investigations must be undertaken in order to understand these factors. In doing so, the scholar "will be more able to illustrate more clearly the perennial theological value of the Gospels as well as the importance and necessity of the Church's interpretation" [19].

Fourth, the exegete should be "free to exercise his own perspicacity and intelligence," when investigating the Scriptures.

Fifth, the exegete should "always be prepared to obey the magisterium of the Church." Exegetes should also always keep in mind the influence of the Holy Spirit during both the second and third stages of the elaboration of the gospel message.

PART THREE: SEMINARY TEACHERS

The third part of SME addresses teachers in seminaries and "like institutions." Such professors are encouraged to use principles of modern criticism, including those of literary criticism. The methods are to be used to help draw out and elaborate the theological meaning of the scriptures. The PBC warns that teachers "should not stop half-way, content with pointing out literary devices," but rather they should find "that which raises the mind to God, nourishes the spirit, and stimulates the interior life" [23].

PART FOUR: PREACHERS

The fourth part of SME addresses preachers and authors. SME stresses the care that must be taken when presenting theories and proposals concerning the sacred texts. Communicating the truth of salvation needs to be the primary and underlying goal of all preaching and writing. New material should only be presented as a reflection of the truth if it has been thoroughly tested. In other words, the virtue of prudence has to be cultivated in the exegete, the preacher and the scholar. Such individuals "are strictly forbidden to indulge in the pernicious craving for novelty by indiscriminately spreading makeshift solutions to problems, solutions which are not the product of prudent judgement and serious deliberation, and which can, therefore upset the faith of many" [26]. The section concludes with a reference to the magisterium's responsibility and authority regarding publications on the scriptures: The ordinaries are to "keep a very diligent watch over such writings."

PART FIVE: BIBLICAL ASSOCIATIONS

The final and shortest part of SME addresses biblical associations. Such associations are simply reminded to comply with the norms established by the PBC.

CONCLUSION

The effect of SME on biblical scholarship in the Catholic church was immediate and lasting. The immediate effect can be seen in the discussions at the Second Vatican Council on divine revelation. Particularly noteworthy was the Council's treatment of the transmission of the gospel message through the apostles and apostolic authors. The Council's Dogmatic Constitution on Divine Revelation, *Die verbum*, draws from SME and notes the process through which the sacred authors composed the four gospels: They "selected certain of the many elements which had been handed on, either orally or in written form; others they synthesized or explained with an eye to the situation of the churches. They retained the preaching style, but always in such fashion that they have told us the authentic truth about Jesus" (#19).

The lasting effect of SME on biblical scholarship can be seen in the volume of New Testament exegesis produced by Catholic scholars following its publication. Furthermore, to this day in Catholic seminaries and universities many courses on the gospels begin with a presentation of SME as a prerequisite to the study of the gospel texts themselves.

BIBLIOGRAPHY

Kearns, G. A., "The Instruction on the Historical Truth of the Gospels. Some First Impressions," *Angelicum* 41 (1964): 218–34.

Fitzmyer, J. A., "Commentary on the Instruction on the Historical Truth of the Bible," *Theological Studies* 24 (1964): 386–408.

Fogarty, G. P., *American Catholic Biblical Scholarship* (San Franscisco), 1989.

Prior, J. G., *The Historical Critical Method in Catholic Exegesis* (Rome), 1999.

OUTLINE

INSTRUCTION *SANCTA MATER ECCLESIA*

ON THE HISTORICAL TRUTH OF THE GOSPELS

[1]   Holy Mother Church, "the pillar and mainstay of the truth,"[1] has always utilized Sacred Scripture in her task of saving souls, and preserved it from erroneous interpretations. There will never be a lack of problems in explaining God's word and trying to solve vexing difficulties, so the Catholic exegete should not lose heart. Rather he should strive diligently to clarify the true meaning of Scripture, relying on his own forces and, most of all, on God's help and the Church's guiding light.

PROGRESS IN CATHOLIC EXEGESIS

[2]   It is a source of great joy that today many loyal sons of the Church are expert in biblical studies, as the times demand. Complying with the exhortations of the Supreme Pontiffs, they devote themselves unstintingly to this serious and arduous task. "All the children of the Church are reminded to judge the efforts of these industrious workers in the Lord's vineyard with absolute fairness and great charity."[2] For even such illustrious commentators as St. Jerome sometimes had relatively little success in explaining more difficult questions.[3] Care must be taken "that the heated atmosphere of dispute does not overstep the bounds of mutual charity; that such disputes do not give the impression that divine truths and sacred Traditions are being called into question. If the spirit of harmony and full respect for principles does not exist, we cannot expect much progress in this field from the varied studies undertaken by many different people."[4]

EXEGESIS IMPORTANT TODAY

[3]   The work of exegetes is all the more necessary today because many writings in circulation question the truth of the events and sayings reported in the Gospels. Hence the Pontifical Biblical Commission, in order to carry out the task entrusted to it by the Supreme Pontiffs, deems it advisable to set forth and to stress the following points.

I. GENERAL GUIDELINES FOR THE EXEGETE

[4]   The Catholic exegete, under the guidance of the Church, should take advantage of all the contributions made by earlier commentators, by the Fathers and Doctors of the Church in particular, and carry on their work. In order to shed

full light on the perennial truth and authority of the Gospels, he will adhere to the norms of scholarly, Catholic hermeneutics; and he will make appropriate use of the new exegetical techniques, particularly those advocated by the historical method taken as a whole.

THE HISTORICAL METHOD

[5]   This method thoroughly investigates the sources, and analyzes their nature and value, relying on the help of textual criticism, literary criticism, and linguistic knowledge.

The commentator will pay heed to the insistent admonition of Pius XII. "Let him prudently examine what the manner of expression or the literary genre used by the sacred writer contributes to a true and accurate interpretation; and let him rest assured that this aspect of his work cannot be neglected without grave detriment to Catholic exegesis."[5] Pius XII's admonition lays down a general principle of hermeneutics, valid for the interpretation of both the Old and New Testament, because the sacred writers used the patterns of thought and expression native to their contemporaries.

In short the exegete will use any and every means which will enable him to acquire a deeper insight into the nature of the gospel testimony, the religious life of the early churches, and the meaning and value of the apostolic tradition.

FORM CRITICISM

[6]   If the opportunity presents itself, the exegete may look for the sound elements in the method of "form criticism," and use them to acquire a fuller understanding of the Gospels. However he must move with caution in this area, because the method is often interlaced with inadmissible philosophical and theological principles, which frequently vitiate either the method itself or its judgments on literary questions.

ERRONEOUS PREMISES

[7]   Some proponents of this method, motivated by rationalistic prejudices, refuse to recognize the existence of a supernatural order. They deny the intervention of a personal God in the world by means of Revelation in the strict sense, and reject the possibility or actual occurrence of miracles and prophecies. Some start out with an erroneous concept of faith, regarding faith as indifferent to, or even incompatible with, historical truth. Some deny, *a priori* as it were, the historical nature and historical value of the documents of Revelation. And finally, some minimize the authority of the Apostles as witnesses to Christ. Belittling their office and their influence in the primitive community, these people exaggerate the creative power of the community itself.

All these opinions are not only contrary to Catholic doctrine, but also devoid of scholarly foundation and inconsistent with the sound principles of the historical method.

II. THE ELABORATION OF THE GOSPEL MESSAGE

[8]   In order to establish the validity of the things contained in the Gospels, the exegete should carefully note the three stages of the tradition, through which the life and teaching of Jesus have come down to us.

1) OUR LORD'S TEACHING

[9]   Christ the Lord chose a select group of disciples,[6] who followed Him from the very beginning.[7] They saw His works and heard His words. Thus they were in a good position to be witnesses to His life and teaching.[8]

When the Lord set forth His teaching orally, He used the forms of thought and expression prevailing at that time. Thus He adapted Himself to the mentality of his audience so that His teaching would be firmly impressed on their minds and easily remembered by His disciples. The latter realized that the miracles and other events of Christ's life took place so that men might believe in Christ and embrace his message of salvation by faith.

2) THE APOSTLES' TEACHING

[10]   The Apostles rendered testimony to Jesus,[9] announcing first and foremost the Lord's death and resurrection. They faithfully set forth His life and His words,[10] adapting the format of their preaching to the condition of their audience.[11] When Jesus rose from the dead and His divinity became manifest,[12] faith by no means obliterated the memory of the events which had taken place. On the contrary it reinforced these memories, because it rested on the things which Jesus had taught and done.[13] Nor did their worship of Jesus as Lord and Son of God transform Him into a "mythological" figure, or distort His teaching.

[11]   However there is no reason to deny the fact that the apostles, in telling their listeners about our Lord's deeds and words, utilized the fuller understanding which they had acquired from the glorious events of Christ's life[14] and the guidance of the Spirit of truth.[15] After His resurrection Jesus Himself "interpreted to them"[16] His own words and those of the Old Testament.[17] In a similar manner they explained His deeds and words according to the needs of their audience.

[12]   Devoting themselves "to the ministry of the word,"[18] they set about preaching, and utilized the type of presentation appropriate to their purpose and the mentality of their listeners. They were debtors[19] "to Greeks and to foreigners, to learned and unlearned."[20] Indeed we can single out the following categories in the preaching of Christ's heralds: catechetical formulas, narrative reports, eyewitness accounts, hymns, doxologies, prayers, and similar literary genres commonly found in Sacred Scripture and the speech of that period.

3) THE FOUR EVANGELISTS

[12]   This primitive instruction was passed on orally at first, and later written down. Indeed it was not long before many attempted "to draw up a narrative"[21] of the events connected with the Lord Jesus. The sacred authors, each using an

approach suited to his specific purpose, recorded this primitive teaching in the four Gospels for the benefit of the churches.

[14] Of the many elements at hand they reported some, summarized others, and developed still others in accordance with the needs of the various churches. They used every possible means to ensure that their readers would come to know the validity of the things they had been taught.[22]

[15] From the material available to them the Evangelists selected those items most suited to their specific purpose and to the condition of a particular audience. And they narrated these events in the manner most suited to satisfy their purpose and their audience's condition.

Context

[16] Since the meaning of a statement depends, among other things, upon the context in which it is found, the Evangelists reported Christ's deeds and words in varying contexts, choosing whichever one would be of greatest help to the reader in trying to understand a particular utterance. Hence the exegete must try to ascertain what the Evangelist intended by reporting a certain saying or event in a particular manner or a particular context.

Order of treatment

[17] The truth of the Gospel account is not compromised because the Evangelists report the Lord's words and deeds in different order.[23] Nor is it hurt because they report His words, not literally but in a variety of ways, while retaining the same meaning.[24] As St. Augustine says: "It is quite probable that each Evangelist felt duty-bound to narrate his particular account in the order which God suggested to his memory. At least this would seem to hold true for those items in which order of treatment would not affect the authority or truth of the Gospel. After all, the Holy Spirit distributes His gifts to each as He chooses.[25] Since these books were to be so authoritative, He undoubtedly guided and directed the sacred writers as they thought about the things which they were going to write down; but He probably allowed each writer to arrange his narrative as he saw fit. Hence anyone who uses enough diligence, will be able to discover this order with the help of God."[26]

Consequences for the exegete

[18] The exegete will not fulfill his task—finding out what the sacred writers really said and really intended—unless he considers all the factors involved in the origin and composition of the Gospels, and makes proper use of the sound findings of recent investigations.

[19] Recent studies indicate that the life and teaching of Jesus were not simply related so as to be remembered; they were "preached" to provide the basis of faith and morals for the Church. Thus the exegete, by scrutinizing the testimony of the Evangelists over and over again, will be able to illustrate more clearly the

perennial theological value of the Gospels as well as the importance and necessity of the Church's interpretation.

[20] There are many other matters of grave importance to be discussed and explained. In so doing, the Catholic exegete can and should be free to exercise his own perspicacity and intelligence. Only in this way will each person render service to all, contribute to the continuing progress of sacred doctrine, help to form or reinforce the judgment of the Church's Magisterium, and defend and honor the Church.[27]

[21] However, he should always be prepared to obey the Magisterium of the Church. And he should never forget that the apostles were filled with the Holy Spirit when they preached the good news; that the Gospels were written under the inspiration of the Holy Spirit, who preserved their authors from every error. "We have come to know the economy of salvation only through those who have transmitted the Gospel to us. First they preached this Gospel. Then later, following the will of God, they transmitted it to us in the Scriptures so that it would be the pillar and mainstay of our faith. It cannot be said that they preached before they had acquired perfect knowledge. Some dare to make this statement, boasting that they can improve on the apostles. But in reality, after our Lord had risen from the dead and they had received the power of the Spirit from above, they were filled with all gifts and had perfect knowledge. So they set out for the ends of the earth, preaching about God's goodness to us and announcing heavenly peace to men. Each and every one of them possessed God's Gospel."[28]

III. SEMINARY TEACHERS

[22] For those who teach in seminaries and similar institutions "the prime concern should be . . . to teach Sacred Scripture in accordance with the seriousness of the subject and the needs of the day."[29] Teachers should give prime consideration to the presentation of theological doctrine, so that Sacred Scripture "may become the pure and perpetual fountainhead for the spiritual life of every future priest, and the source of nourishment for the preaching office he is about to assume."[30]

USE OF LITERARY CRITICISM

[23] When these teachers utilize the principles of criticism, of literary criticism in particular, they should not present them for their own sake, but as a means to shed clearer light on the meaning intended by God through the sacred writer. They should not stop half-way, content with pointing out literary devices. They should go on to show how these devices help us to understand revealed doctrine more clearly, or if the occasion arises, to refute errors. Teachers who follow these norms, will enable students to find in Sacred Scriptures "that which raises the mind to God, nourishes the spirit, and stimulates the interior life."[31]

IV. PREACHERS

[24] Those who instruct the Christian people by sacred preaching must show the highest degree of prudence. They are to give first place to solid doctrine, keeping in mind the admonition of St. Paul: "Take heed to yourself and to your teaching, be earnest in them. For in so doing you will save both yourself and those who hear you."[32]

[25] They should abstain completely from advancing vain new theories or ones which lack sufficient proof. They may present new opinions which have been solidly proven, if the need arises; but they must do so with caution, taking due account of their audience. When they discuss biblical events, they are not to add fictitious details which hardly fit in with the truth.

WRITERS

[26] The virtue of prudence should be especially cultivated by those whose writings are circulated among the faithful. They should bring out the divine riches contained in God's Word "so that the faithful are aroused and inspired to lead a good life."[33] They should scrupulously avoid departing, at any time or in any way, from the common doctrine and tradition of the Church. They should, however, take advantage of the solid advances made in biblical research and the contributions of modern scholars, while avoiding altogether the rash opinions of innovators.[34] They are strictly forbidden to indulge in the pernicious craving for novelty by indiscriminately spreading makeshift solutions to problems, solutions which are not the product of prudent judgment and serious deliberation, and which can, therefore, upset the faith of many.

BOOKS AND ARTICLES

[27] The Pontifical Biblical Commission has already seen fit to remind people that books and articles in magazines and newspapers, which deal with biblical topics, are also subject to the authority and jurisdiction of Ordinaries.[35] For such works deal with religious subjects and the religious education of the faithful. Ordinaries are asked, therefore, to keep a very diligent watch over such writings.

V. BIBLICAL ASSOCIATIONS

[28] Those who are in charge of Biblical Associations are to comply fully with the norms set up by the Pontifical Biblical Commission.[36]

If all these norms are observed, the study of Sacred Scripture will be of great benefit to the faithful. No one, even in our day, will be able to deny the words of St. Paul: ". . . the sacred writings . . . are able to instruct you unto salvation by the faith which is in Christ Jesus. All Scripture is inspired by God and useful for teaching, for reproving, for correcting, for instructing in justice; that the man of God may be perfect, equipped for every good work."[37]

At an audience graciously granted to the undersigned Secretary on April 21, 1964, His Holiness Pope Paul VI approved this Instruction and ordered its publication.

NOTES

1. 1 Timothy 3:15.

2. DAS; EB 564.

3. Cf. SP; EB 451.

4. Apostolic letter *Vigilantiae*; EB 143.

5. DAS; EB 560.

6. Cf. Mark 3:14; Luke 6:13.

7. Cf. Luke 1:2; Acts 1:21–22.

8. Cf. Luke 24:48; John 14:27; Acts 1:8; 10:39; 13:31.

9. Cf. Luke 24:44–48; Acts 2:32; 3:15; 5:30–32.

10. Cf. Acts 10:36–41.

11. Cf. Acts 13:16–41 together with Acts 17:22–31.

12. Acts 2:36; John 20:28.

13. Acts 2:22; 10:37–39.

14. John 2:22; 12:16; 11:51–52; cf. 14:26; 16:12–13; 7:39.

15. Cf. John 14:26; 16:13.

16. Luke 24:27.

17. Cf. Luke 24:44–45; Acts 1:3.

18. Acts 6:4.

19. 1 Corinthians 9:19–23.

20. Romans 1:14.

21. Cf. Luke 1:1.

22. Cf. Luke 1:4.

23. Cf. St. John Chrysostom, *in Mat., Hom. I*, 3; PG 57, 16–17.

24. Cf. St. Augustine, *De consensu Evang.*, 2, 12, 28; PL 34, 1090–91.

25. 1 Corinthians 12:11.

26. *De consensu Evang.*, 2, 21, 51 ff.; PL 34, 1102.

27. DAS, EB 565.

28. St. Irenaeus, *Adv. Haer.*, III 1, 1; PG 7, 844; Harvey II, 2.

29. Apostolic letter *Quoniam in re biblica*; EB 162.

30. DAS; EB 567.

31. DAS; EB 552.

32. 1 Timothy 4:16.

33. DAS; EB 566.

34. Cf. Apostolic letter *Quoniam in re biblica*; EB 175.

35. Instruction to the Most Reverend Ordinaries of Dioceses, Dec. 15, 1955; EB 626.

36. EB 622–33.

37. 2 Timothy 3:15–17.

DOGMATIC CONSTITUTION *DEI VERBUM*

ON DIVINE REVELATION

VATICAN II
1965

OVERVIEW OF *DEI VERBUM*

Marion Moeser, OSF

While preparing to write this overview I attended a conference of biblical schol-ars where a professor gave a presentation on the use of film to enhance the study of the Bible. She showed us a short clip from the movie *Mr. Holland's Opus* to illustrate her method. That scene also illuminates the notion of revelation taught in the Second Vatican Council's document, *Dei verbum*, the Dogmatic Constitution on Divine Revelation (DV).

In the scene, Glenn Holland, a successful music teacher, and his wife, Iris, are arguing over sign language education for their deaf son, Cole. Glenn is opposed, believing that Cole would have a harder time in the hearing world. During their argument Cole becomes agitated because he is asking for some-thing and Iris cannot understand him. Finally, Iris shouts, "I can't talk to my son! I can't tell him I love him! I can't tell him who I am! I want to talk to my son!" Cole thrives when first Iris and then Glenn communicate with him through signing and music.

The Second Vatican Council (1962–1965) teaches that God tells us: "Who I am," "You are loved," and "You are meant to thrive." According to DV, reve-lation is God's self-communication, out of love, of the divine nature and of our status as God's friends, invited into God's company (see #2). Moreover, our God "moves among us" (#2); God speaks and acts in human history, above all, in the words and deeds of Christ Jesus. It is somehow appropriate, therefore, that the Council's very document on revelation is understood correctly only in the context of its human history. This overview will present a brief history of DV, summarize its contents, describe its major accomplishments and comment on remaining challenges.

HISTORICAL BACKGROUND

A historical context for DV must begin where the Council Fathers began. The Prologue speaks of "following in the steps of the Councils of Trent and Vatican I" (#1). Both of those councils had addressed revelation in light of their own times and problems.

The fourth session of the Council of Trent (1546) presented its teachings within the historical context of the Protestant Reformation. The reformers had reacted against the Roman church and many of its practices for which they did not find a warrant in scripture. This situation gave rise to the question: "Where do we find revelation?" The reformers held that it was to be found in scripture alone, *sola scriptura*. The Council of Trent responded that "the purity of the Gospel" (revelation) comes to us in "written books *and* in unwritten tradition*s*" (emphasis added) and that both of these are received with "an equal attitude of piety and an equal reverence." However, Trent left open the question of the precise interrelationship between scripture and the "unwritten traditions." The council then proceeded to list the books of the Old and the New Testament.

The constitution *Dei Filius* of the First Vatican Council (1869–1870) dealt with divine revelation and faith in the context of the Enlightenment, the "Age of

Reason." Christian faith was being attacked as irrational, and this time the question posed was: "Since we have reason by which we can know or can logically discover what we need to know, why do we need divine revelation?" *Dei Filius* answered that while we can know God naturally, God has given humankind supernatural revelation so that God may be known "rapidly, with firm certainty and without error." This council then cited the teaching of the Council of Trent that revelation is contained in written books and unwritten traditions. Like those of Trent, the fathers of the First Vatican Council did not discuss the relationship between the two. Additionally, *Dei Filius* noted that since scripture is inspired by the Holy Spirit, the books of the Bible have God as their author.

The years from 1870 to 1940 were, at first, colored by cautious acceptance of modern linguistic and scientific study of scripture. However, with the threat of Modernism and its purported misuse of the newer scientific approaches to scripture, Pius X, Benedict XV and the Pontifical Biblical Commission issued a series of conservative statements that generally upheld time-honored responses to questions on the historicity of the contents of the Bible (for example, that Moses was the author of the Pentateuch and Paul of Hebrews). This time period also saw the silencing of prominent Catholic biblical scholars.

Pius XII's 1943 encyclical, *Divino afflante spiritu*, is often referred to as the Magna Carta of modern Roman Catholic biblical scholarship. Pius encouraged scripture scholars to use the modern tools of scientific criticism. They were to work in the original languages of the texts, as opposed to the Latin Vulgate translation, and to prepare translations in modern languages. They should study the literal sense of the texts and, therefore, consider the circumstances of the authors, their sources, their verbal expressions, as well as the literary forms of the texts. Despite this liberating document, Catholic biblical scholars in Rome experienced a backlash and in 1961 the Holy Office issued a statement against all who questioned the historical and objective truth of scripture. This was the situation when the first session of the Second Vatican Council began in 1962.

Before moving to the Council's work, one more document must be mentioned. During the time of the Council, in 1964, the Pontifical Biblical Commission (PBC) published its noteworthy "Instruction on the Historical Truth of the Gospels" *(Sancta mater ecclesia)*. This document endorsed the fruits of scientific scholarship regarding the process of the formation of our canonical gospels. The process involved three stages: 1. the words and deeds of Jesus; 2. the preaching of the apostles after the resurrection, adapted to the experiences and needs of their hearers; and 3. the writing down of the apostolic preaching in the gospels. In this third stage the evangelists "selected some things, reduced others to a synthesis, and still others they explicated, keeping in mind the situation of the churches." In other words, the evangelists interpreted the gospels for their communities. The contents of this PBC statement were incorporated into Chapter 5 of DV (see #19).

DRAFTS

At the time of the Second Vatican Council, the church was not experiencing a threat to its teachings as at the times of the Council of Trent and the First Vatican

Council, and Christians were interested less in doctrinal propositions *per se* than in Christian experience and existential and personal values. The move to speak to these concerns is reflected in the drama surrounding DV.

As we have it, DV is the fifth draft in a series of documents discussed by the bishops of the Second Vatican Council. Prior to the first session (fall, 1962) the bishops received a schema, "On the Sources of Revelation" *(De fontibus revelationis),* produced by the Preparatory Theological Commission. The document was criticized by a number of bishops even before the opening session. They thought the text ignored much recent historical, theological and biblical study and that it sought to canonize in a conciliar document one particular school of theological thought. They believed the document did not fulfill the aim of the Council as proposed by John XXIII. Council debate on the schema was held November 14–20. The discussion was very critical of the text and sharp disagreement arose. A vote was taken on whether to end the discussion of the document, in effect rejecting it. The tally was 1368 yes, 822 no, with 19 nullified votes. While a clear majority of the bishops had rejected the schema, the vote fell 105 short of the two-thirds majority needed to withdraw it. The next day, John XXIII intervened, withdrew the text from the floor and appointed a special commission to rewrite and present a more acceptable document to the Council.

A second schema, entitled "On Divine Revelation," was completed and distributed before the second session of the Council (fall, 1963). This second draft was not debated in that session, but at its close Paul VI indicated that the question of revelation was open business for the next session. Many bishops had submitted remarks on the second schema to the Doctrinal Commission so that a revised third draft was sent out to the bishops prior to the third session.

The third draft was debated at the third session (fall, 1964) and this debate led to another revision, the fourth draft. Voting on that document took place September 20–24, 1965, and Council members were allowed to vote "yes, with a written reservation." These reservations were considered for the fifth and final draft, which was adopted by the Council. The final vote occurred on November 18, 1965, tallying 2081 yes, 27 no, with 7 nullified votes. Paul VI officially promulgated the document that same day. Given the drama involved with this document, one expects that DV is a compromise statement with carefully nuanced wording. As will be seen, it did not settle all theological disputes concerning revelation.

PROLOGUE

This dogmatic constitution begins with a citation of sacred scripture, thus illustrating what it says later in the document that "sacred theology relies on the written word of God" (#24). The text cites 1 John 1:2–3:

> We proclaim to you the eternal life which was with the Father and was made manifest to us—that which we have seen and heard we proclaim also to you, so that you may have fellowship with us; and our fellowship is with the Father and with his Son Jesus Christ. (#1)

By this, the Council intends us to see revelation as a process whereby God manifests to us what we need for our salvation, unity with our Creator and Messiah.

God does this through deeds and words ("that which we have seen and heard"), especially those of Jesus Christ. This revelation is transmitted to us within a community ("so that you may have fellowship with us"). The plan of the document reinforces this intention. One moves through the constitution reading of revelation and its transmission, its manifestation in the written deeds and actions of God, the Old and New Testaments, and the place and purpose of the Bible in our individual and communitarian lives.

CHAPTER I: DIVINE REVELATION ITSELF

Leaving aside the second paragraph of article six, one can see that in the opening chapter the Council Fathers wished to emphasize the understanding of divine revelation as God's gratuitous self-communication for our salvation. The opening three sentences of article two and the first paragraph of article six contain this same understanding; surely the repetition is intentional. Additionally, throughout salvation history, God's self-revelation (see #3) in both deeds and words are meant to shed light on each other (see #2). Moreover, revelation is seen as Christological. Humans have access to God through Christ (see #2) who "completed and perfected revelation and confirmed it with divine guarantees," so that "no new public revelation is to be expected"(#4). The purpose of revelation is our salvation, and our response to God's self-disclosure is an "obedience of faith" involving mind, heart and will (see #3). At the close of this chapter the document adds the teaching of the First Vatican Council that God can be known by human reason, but that revelation gives us certainty of this knowledge.

DV teaches, therefore, that revelation is *essentially* a life—God's self-communication and the human person's lived response—versus a doctrine, a set of propositions, or moral norms, although revelation implies all of these. Moreover, revelation is both historical, taking place in the course of human existence, and personal, inviting hearing and response.

CHAPTER II: THE TRANSMISSION OF DIVINE REVELATION

Here the Council dealt with how revelation reaches us in the present day. The line of transmission runs from Christ to the apostles, and under the guidance of the Holy Spirit to the evangelists and the successors of the apostles (#7). The content of this process—tradition—"comprises everything that serves to make the people of God live their lives in holiness and increase their faith, . . . [the] doctrine, life and worship" of the church (#8). Thus, tradition is more than a set of propositions, and more than traditions: Tradition is the ongoing teaching, life and worship of the church. The apostolic preaching is "expressed in a special way in the inspired books," that is, in scripture. The Council Fathers rejected the theory, an interpretation of Trent and found in the first draft of the document, that there are two separate sources of revelation, scripture and tradition. Nor did they accept the argument that all of revelation is found in scripture. The relevant sentences concerning these points are in articles 9 and 10:

> Sacred tradition and sacred scripture, then, are bound closely together, and communicate one with the other. Flowing from the same divine wellspring, both of them merge, in a sense, and move towards the same goal . . . .

[T]he church does not draw its certainty about all revealed truths from the holy scriptures alone. (#9)

Sacred tradition and scripture make up a single sacred deposit of the word of God, which is entrusted to the church. (#10)

DV does not explicate the precise relationship between scripture and tradition, or their quantitative extents, that is, how much of revelation is contained in each.

This chapter contains two other important teachings. First, there is a growth in our *understanding* of revelation, "a growth in insight into the realities and words that are being passed on" (#8). Second, while the magisterium's task is "an authentic interpretation" of scripture and tradition, "[t]his magisterium is not superior to the word of God, but is rather its servant" (#10). It is interesting to note that while this chapter speaks of both scripture and tradition as containing revelation, the remainder of the document deals only with scripture.

CHAPTER III: SACRED SCRIPTURE: ITS DIVINE INSPIRATION AND ITS INTERPRETATION

This section of DV is set up in the form of an analogy, explicitly stated in article 13 where one reads that the Bible is both divine and human just as Christ, in the incarnation, is both divine and human. The divine element in scripture is treated in article 11, the human in article 12. First, the Council spoke to the controversy over the "historical truth" contained in scripture. Explaining that the Bible is the word of God, under the inspiration of the Holy Spirit, "the books of scripture, firmly, faithfully and without error, *teach that truth which God, for the sake of our salvation,* wished to see confided to the sacred scriptures" (#11; emphasis added). Thus, divine inspiration neither necessitates nor guarantees that every historical detail in scripture is accurate, in our contemporary sense of that word. Second, DV endorsed the modern scientific method of scripture study, declaring that since, in scripture, "God speaks through human beings in human fashion," an interpreter "should carefully search out the meaning which the sacred writers really had in mind" (#12). There follow references to various aspects of the critical study of scripture, many of which are from Pius XII's encyclical letter *Divino afflante spiritu*. Ultimately, however, any interpretation of scripture is "subject to the judgment of the church" (#12).

CHAPTER IV: THE OLD TESTAMENT

Here, DV reinforces the belief that revelation is contained in the Old Testament, which has lasting value (#14).

Nonetheless, the Council Fathers opted for the position that the "primary objective of the plan and lay-out of the Old Testament was that it should prepare for and declare in prophecy the coming of Christ" (#15) and that the Old Testament writings "attain and display their full meaning in the New Testament" (#16). This evaluation of the Old Testament, however, is inadequate in that it fails to recognize the living religious tradition of Judaism and the ongoing place of Judaism in the history of salvation. As Paul writes in Romans 11:29: "the gifts and call of God are irrevocable."

CHAPTER V: THE NEW TESTAMENT

DV gives pride of place for the locus of revelation to the New Testament (see #17), with emphasis placed on the gospels. This emphasis reflects the concern at the time of the Council over some biblical scholars who questioned the historical value of the gospels. Article 19 clearly states that the gospels "faithfully hand on what Jesus, the Son of God, while he lived among men and women, really did and taught for their eternal salvation." Thus, the "truth" in the gospels is that of the whole of scripture already spoken of in Chapter III. Article 19 continues by endorsing the teaching on the three stages of the development of the gospels as taught by the PBC in its Instruction on the Historical Truth of the Gospels *(Sancta mater ecclesia)*. Once again, the Council unambiguously endorsed a crucial result of modern biblical scholarship.

CHAPTER VI: SACRED SCRIPTURE IN THE LIFE OF THE CHURCH

This chapter has had an enormous influence on the life of the church since the Second Vatican Council, and, in many respects, has achieved what the Council desired, namely, "a new impulse of spiritual life" (#26). The role of scripture in the nourishment of the life of the church is presented in the first sentence. The Bread of Life is found at "the *one table* of the word of God and the Body of Christ" (#21; emphasis added). All the preaching of the church "should be nourished and ruled by sacred scripture." For the faithful, the word of God is an "unfailing font of spiritual life." DV then lays out a series of pastoral proposals beginning with a call for wide-open access to scripture for the faithful, as opposed to past directives in which "ordinary faithful" were discouraged from reading the Bible. The church is to provide good vernacular translations of the Bible from the original languages and joint ecumenical endeavors are allowed in this task. Biblical scholars are encouraged in their work (see #23); moreover, theologians are directed to make "the study of the sacred page" the "very soul of sacred theology" (#24). All who are engaged in the ministry of the Word, especially, priests, deacons and catechists should "immerse themselves in the scriptures." Once again, the Council Fathers encourage all the Christian faithful to read and study the sacred texts, and bishops to oversee translations and adequate notes of explanation for this purpose (see #25).

DV ends, as it began, with a reference to scripture. This time the Council reminds us of the constancy of God's revelation by alluding to Isaiah 40:8 (employed in 1 Peter 1:23–25) that "the word of our God . . . 'stands forever'" (#26).

MAJOR ACCOMPLISHMENTS

An often overlooked accomplishment of DV is the process by which the final draft appeared. Its history points out the role of pontiffs in general—and in particular, John XXIII and Paul VI—in an ecumenical council, as well as a process for arriving at consensus. The achievements of DV itself are presented in three areas: theology, biblical scholarship, and the pastoral life of the church.

Theologically, DV moved to a new definition of revelation in terms of God's self-communication. The Council rejected the two-source theory for revelation and opted for "one deposit of revelation." Furthermore, DV answered the questions about the historicity of the Bible by teaching that the "truth" of the Bible is that which is necessary for salvation. While this response is not at all precise, the teaching rejects a fundamentalist concept of the "inerrancy" of the whole of the Bible. Finally, from a theological point of view, DV gave a new emphasis to the role of the human authors of the sacred books. This new emphasis was important for biblical scholarship.

The Council also endorsed the modern critical methods of scripture scholarship. The number of Catholic biblical scholars increased significantly, with appreciable numbers of the laity, particularly women, entering the field. Moreover, Roman Catholic biblical scholars took their place among the leaders in the discipline, both in the academic arena and in the pastoral application of scripture. The field of biblical scholarship became one of great and widespread ecumenical cooperation. Finally, much to the credit of the bishops and the scholars, excellent, fresh translations of the Bible are now available in vernacular languages.

Finally, the spiritual life of the church has been enriched with the flourishing of biblical scholarship, fresh translations and the hunger of the faithful for nourishment from God's word, as evidenced by the growth of Bible study groups and the demand for good homilies at liturgies. The flowering of the place of scripture in Roman Catholic life may be the most lasting of DV's achievements.

REMAINING CHALLENGES

As has already been indicated, in their debates on the sources of revelation the Council Fathers did not adequately define tradition or speak of its quantitative relationship to scripture. There are some who see this as a weakness of the document; however, others view the obscurity as a positive feature, as an opportunity for the church to grow in understanding of this relationship and as an invitation for persons to express differing opinions.

DV does not speak of the presence of divine revelation in non-Christian religions. Other documents of the Second Vatican Council do discuss this (for example, the Declaration on the Relationship of the Church to Non-Christian Religions), but this omission is a major weakness of DV, especially given the topic's importance for Asian and African local churches.

While DV does endorse modern scripture study, it presents a limited understanding of the historical-critical method of exegesis and of the interpretation of scripture. Furthermore, it does not deal sufficiently with the concept of the inculturation of revelation in the time periods of the biblical books and what that might mean for our present situation. Nor does DV offer guidelines on what has come to be termed the "actualization" of a biblical text, that is, having the text come alive for the hearers of today. These topics are covered more fully in the Pontifical Biblical Commission's 1993 text, "The Interpretation of the Bible in the Church."

Despite these weaknesses, DV remains a major work of the Second Vatican Council, a triumph for modern critical biblical scholarship, and a gift to the spiritual life of the church. This constitution reminds us that, like Iris and Glenn Holland who struggled to communicate with their son in a language they all understood, God has spoken to us, has revealed the Divine Self, and has told us that we are loved, in words and actions both human and divine. Cole Holland thrives when his parents communicate with him. The "soul nourishment" on scripture that DV fosters in the church gives concrete evidence that divine communication—revelation—enables men and women to thrive.

OUTLINE

DOGMATIC CONSTITUTION *DEI VERBUM*

ON DIVINE REVELATION

PROLOGUE

1.   Hearing the word of God reverently and proclaiming it confidently, this holy synod makes its own the words of St. John: "We proclaim to you the eternal life which was with the Father and was manifest to us—that which we have seen and heard we proclaim also to you, so that you may have fellowship with us; and our fellowship is with the Father and with his Son Jesus Christ" (1 John 1:2–3). Following, then, in the steps of the councils of Trent and Vatican I, this synod wishes to set forth the authentic teaching on divine revelation and its transmission. For it wants the whole world to hear the summons to salvation, so that through hearing it may believe, through belief it may hope, through hope it may come to love.[1]

CHAPTER I
DIVINE REVELATION ITSELF

2.   It pleased God, in his goodness and wisdom, to reveal himself and to make known the mystery of his will (see Ephesians 1:9), which was that people can draw near to the Father, through Christ, the Word made flesh, in the holy Spirit, and thus became sharers in the divine nature (see Ephesians 2:18, 2 Peter 1:4). By this revelation, then, the invisible God (see Colossians 1:15; 1 Timothy 1:17), from the fullness of his love, addresses men and women as his friends (see Exodus 33:11; John 15; 14–15), and lives among them (see Baruch 3:38), in order to invite and receive them into his own company. The pattern of this revelation unfolds through deeds and words which are intrinsically connected: the works performed by God in the history of salvation show forth and confirm the doctrine and realities signified by the words; the words, for their part, proclaim the works, and bring to light the mystery they contain. The most intimate truth thus revealed about God and human salvation shines forth for us in Christ, who is himself both the mediator and the sum total of revelation.[2]

3.   God, who creates and conserves all things by his Word (see John 1:3), provides constant evidence of himself in created realities (see Romans 1:19–20). Furthermore, wishing to open up the way to heavenly salvation, he manifested himself to our first parents from the very beginning. After the fall, he buoyed them up with the hope of salvation, by promising redemption (see Genesis 3:15); and he has never ceased to take care of the human race, in order to give eternal

life to all those who seek salvation by persevering in doing good (see Romans 2:6–7). In his own time, God called Abraham and made him into a great nation (see Genesis 12:2). After the era of the patriarchs, he taught this nation, through Moses and the prophets, to recognize him as the only living and true God, as a provident Father and just judge. He taught them, too, to look for the promised Savior. And so, throughout the ages, he prepared the way for the Gospel.

4.   After God had spoken many times and in various ways through the prophets, "in these last days he has spoken to us by a Son" (Hebrew 1:1-2). For he sent his Son, the eternal Word who enlightens all humankind, to live among them and to tell them about the inner life of God. Hence, Jesus Christ, sent as "a man being men and women"[3], "speaks the words of God" (John 3:34), and accomplishes the saving work which the Father gave him to do (see John 5:36; 17:4). As a result, he himself—to see whom is to see the Father (see John 14:9)—completed and perfected revelation and confirmed with divine guarantees. Everything to do with his presence and his manifestation of himself was involved in achieving this: his words and works, signs and miracles, but above all his death and glorious resurrection from the dead, and finally his sending of the Spirit of truth. He revealed that God was with us, to deliver us from the darkness of sin and death, and to raise us up to eternal life.

The Christian dispensation, therefore, since it is the new and definitive covenant, will never pass away; and no new public revelation is to be expected before the glorious manifestation of our Lord Jesus Christ (see 1 Timothy 6:14 and Titus 2:13).

5.   "The obedience of faith" (see Romans 16:26; compare Romans 1:5; 2 Corinthians 10:5–6) must be our response to God who reveals. By faith one freely commits oneself entirely to God, making "the full submission of intellect and will to God who reveals"[4], and willingly assenting to the revelation given by God. For this faith to be accorded we need the grace of God, anticipating it and assisting it, as well as the interior helps of the holy Spirit, who moves the heart and converts it to God, and opens the eyes of the mind and "makes it easy for all to accept and believe the truth"[5]. The same holy Spirit constantly perfects faith by his gifts, so that revelation may be more and more deeply understood.

6.   By divine revelation God wished to manifest and communicate both himself and the eternal decrees of his will concerning the salvation of humankind. He wished, in other words, "to share with us divine benefits which entirely surpass the powers of the human mind to understand".[6]

The holy synod professes that "God, the first principle and last end of all things, can be known with certainty from the created world, by the natural light of human reason" (see Romans 1:20). It teaches that it is to his revelation that we must attribute the fact "that those things, which in themselves are not beyond the grasp of human reason, can, in the present condition of the human race, be known by all with ease, with firm certainty, and without the contamination of error".[7]

CHAPTER II
THE TRANSMISSION OF DIVINE REVELATION

7.   God graciously arranged that what he had once revealed for the salvation of all peoples should last forever in its entirety and be transmitted to all generations. Therefore, Christ the Lord, in whom the entire revelation of the most high God is summed up (see 2 Corinthians 1:20; 3:16—4:6), having fulfilled in his own person and promulgated with his own lips the Gospel promised beforehand by the prophets, commanded the apostles to preach it to everyone as the source of all saving truth and moral law, communicating God's gifts to them.[1] This was faithfully done: it was done by the apostles who handed on, by oral preaching, by their example, by their dispositions, what they themselves had received—whether from the lips of Christ, from his way of life and his works, or by coming to know it through the prompting of the holy Spirit; it was done by those apostles and others associated with them who, under the inspiration of the same holy Spirit, committed the message of salvation to writing.[2]

In order that the full and living Gospel might always be preserved in the church the apostles left bishops as their successors. They gave them "their own position of teaching authority."[3] This sacred tradition, then, and the sacred scripture of both Testaments, are like a mirror, in which the church, during its pilgrim journey here on earth, contemplates God, from whom it receives everything, until such time as it is brought to see him face to face as he really is (see John 3:2).

8.   Thus, the apostolic preaching, which is expressed in a special way in the inspired books, was to be preserved in a continuous line of succession until the end of time. Hence the apostles, in handing on what they themselves had received, warn the faithful to maintain the traditions which they had learned either by word of mouth or by letter (see 2 Thessalonians 2:15), and to fight for the faith that had been handed on to them once and for all (see Jude 3).[4] What was handed on by the apostles comprises everything that serves to make the people of God live their lives in holiness and increase their faith. In this way the church, in its doctrine, life and worship, perpetuates and transmits to every generation all that it itself is, all that it believes.

The tradition that comes from the apostles makes progress in the church, with the help of the holy Spirit.[5] There is a growth in insight into the realities and words that are being passed on. This comes about through the contemplation and study of believers who ponder these things in their hearts (see Luke 2:19 and 51). It comes from the intimate sense of spiritual realities which they experience. And it comes from the preaching of those who, on succeeding to the office of bishop, have received the sure charism of truth. Thus, as the centuries go by, the church is always advancing towards the plentitude of divine truth, until eventually the words of God are fulfilled in it.

The sayings of the church Fathers are a witness to the life-giving presence of this tradition, showing how its riches are poured out in the practice and life of the believing and praying church. By means of the same tradition, the full canon of the sacred books is known to the church and the holy scriptures themselves are more thoroughly understood and constantly made effective in the church. Thus God, who spoke in the past, continues to converse with the spouse of his beloved Son. And the holy Spirit, through whom the living voice of the Gospel rings out in the church—and through it in the world—leads believers to the full truth and makes the word of Christ dwell in them in all its richness (see Colossians 3:16).

9.   Sacred tradition and sacred scripture, then, are bound closely together, and communicate one with the other. Flowing from the same divine well-spring, both of them merge, in a sense, and move towards the same goal. Sacred scripture is the utterance of God put down as it is in writing under the inspiration of the holy Spirit. And tradition transmits in its entirety the word of God which has been entrusted to the apostles by Christ the Lord and the holy Spirit; it transmits it to the successors of the apostles so that, enlightened by the Spirit of truth, they may faithfully preserve, expound and disseminate it by their preaching. Thus it is that the church does not draw its certainty about all revealed truths from the holy scriptures alone. Hence, both scripture and tradition must be accepted and honored with equal devotion and reverence.[6]

10.   Tradition and scripture make up a single sacred deposit of the word of God, which is entrusted to the church. By adhering to it the entire holy people, united to its pastors, remains always faithful to the teaching of the apostles, to the communion of life, to the breaking of bread and the prayers (see Acts 2:42 Greek). So, in maintaining, practicing and professing the faith that has been handed on there is a unique interplay between the bishops and the faithful.[7]

But the task of giving an authentic interpretation of the word of God, whether in its written form or in the form of tradition,[8] has been entrusted to the living teaching office of the church alone.[9] Its authority in this matter is exercised in the name of Jesus Christ. This magisterium is not superior to the word of God, but is rather its servant. It teaches only what has been handed on to it. At the divine command and with the help of the holy Spirit, it listens to this devoutly, guards it reverently and expounds it faithfully. All that it proposes for belief as being divinely revealed it draws from this sole deposit of faith.

It is clear, therefore, that, in the supremely wise arrangement of God, sacred tradition, sacred scripture and the magisterium of the church are so connected and associated that one of them cannot stand without the others. Working together, each in its own way under the action of the one holy Spirit, they all contribute effectively to the salvation of souls.

CHAPTER III
SACRED SCRIPTURE: ITS DIVINE INSPIRATION AND ITS INTERPRETATION

11.   Those things revealed by God which are contained and presented in the text of sacred scripture have been written under the inspiration of the holy

Spirit. For holy mother church, relying on the faith of the apostolic age, accepts as sacred and canonical the books of the Old and the New Testaments, whole and entire, with all their parts, on the grounds that, written under the inspiration of the holy Spirit (see John 20:31; 2 Timothy 3:16; 2 Peter 1:19–21; 3:15–16), they have God as their author, and have been handed on as such to the church itself.[1] To compose the sacred books, God chose certain men who, all the while he employed them in this task, made full use of their powers and faculties[2] so that, though he acted in them and by them,[3] it was as true authors that they consigned to writing whatever he wanted written, and no more.[4]

Since, therefore, all that the inspired authors, or sacred writers, affirm should be regarded as affirmed by the holy Spirit, we must acknowledge that the books of scripture, firmly, faithfully and without error, teach that truth which God, for the sake of our salvation, wished to see confided to the sacred scriptures.[5] Thus "all scripture is inspired by God, and is useful for teaching, for reproof, for correction and for training in righteousness, so that everyone who belongs to God may be proficient, equipped for every good work" (2 Timothy 3:16–17, Greek text).

12.   Seeing that, in sacred scripture, God speaks through human beings in human fashion,[6] it follows that the interpreters of sacred scripture, if they are to ascertain what God has wished to communicated to us, should carefully search out the meaning which the sacred writers really had in mind, that meaning which God had thought well to manifest through the medium of their words.

In determining the intention of the sacred writers, attention must be paid, among other things, to literary genres.

The fact is that truth is differently presented and expressed in the various types of historical writing, in prophetical and poetical texts, and in other forms of literary expression. Hence the exegete must look for that meaning which the sacred writers, in given situations and granted the circumstances of their time and culture, intended to express and did in fact express, through the medium of a contemporary literary form.[7] Rightly to understand what the sacred authors wanted to affirm in their work, due attention must be paid both to the customary and characteristic patterns of perception, speech and narrative which prevailed in their time, and to the conventions which people then observed in their dealings with one another.[8]

But since sacred scripture must be read and interpreted with its divine authorship in mind,[9] no less attention must be devoted to the content and unity of the whole scripture, taking into account the tradition of the entire church and the analogy of faith, if we are to derive their true meaning from the sacred texts. It is the task of exegetes to work, according to these rules, towards a better understanding and explanation of the meaning of sacred scripture in order that their research may help the church's judgment to mature. For, of course, all that has been said about the manner of interpreting scripture is ultimately subject to the judgment of the church which exercises the divinely conferred commission and ministry of watching over and interpreting the word of God.[10]

13.   Hence, in sacred scripture, without prejudice to God's truth and holiness, the marvelous "condescension" of eternal wisdom is plain to be seen, "that we may come to know the ineffable loving-kindness of God and see for ourselves the thought and care he has given to accommodating his language to our nature".[11] Indeed the words of God, expressed in human language, are in every way like human speech, just as the Word of the eternal Father, when he took on himself the weak flesh of human beings, became like them.

CHAPTER IV
THE OLD TESTAMENT

14.   In his great love God intended the salvation of the entire human race. In preparation for this, in a special undertaking, he chose for himself a people to whom he would entrust his promises. By his covenant with Abraham (see Genesis 15:18) and, through Moses, with the race of Israel (see Exodus 24:8), he acquired a people for himself, and to them he revealed himself in words and deeds as the one, true, living God. It was his strategy that Israel might learn by experience God's ways with humanity and by listening to the voice of God speaking to them through the prophets might gradually understand his ways more fully and more clearly, and make them more widely known among the nations (see Psalms 21:28–29; 95:1–3; Isaiah 2:14; Jeremiah 3:17). The plan of salvation, foretold, recounted and explained by the sacred authors, appears as the true word of God in the books of the Old Testament, which is why these books, divinely inspired, retain a lasting value: "For whatever was written in former days was written for our instruction, so that by stead-fastness and by the encouragement of the scriptures we might have hope" (Romans 15:4).

15.   The primary objective of the plan and lay-out of the Old Testament was that it should prepare for and declare in prophecy the coming of Christ, universal redeemer, and of the messianic kingdom (see Luke 24:44; John 5:39; 1 Peter 1:10), and should indicate it by means of various foreshadowing signs and symbols (see 1 Corinthians 10:11). For in the context of the human situation before the era of salvation established by Christ, the books of the Old Testament provide an understanding of God and humanity and make clear to all how a just and merciful God deals with humankind. These books, even though they contain matters which are imperfect and provisional, nevertheless contain authentic divine teaching.[1] Christians should accept with reverence these writings, which express a lively sense of God, which are a storehouse of sublime teaching on God and of sound wisdom on human life, as well as a wonderful treasury of prayers; in them, too, the mystery of our salvation is implicitly present.

16.   God, the inspirer and author of the books of both Testaments, in his wisdom has so brought it about that the New should be hidden in the Old and that the Old should be made manifest in the New.[2] For, although Christ founded the New Covenant in his blood (see Luke 22:20; 1 Corinthians 11:25), nevertheless the books of the Old Testament, all of them given a place in the preaching of

the Gospel,[3] attain and display their full meaning in the New Testament (see Matthew 5:17: Luke 24–27; Romans 16:25—26:2; 2 Corinthians 3:14–16) and, in their turn, shed light on it and explain it.

CHAPTER V
THE NEW TESTAMENT

17.   The word of God, which to everyone who has faith contains God's saving power (see Romans 1:16), is set forth and marvelously displays its power in the writings of the New Testament. For when the time has fully come (see Galatians 4:4), the Word became flesh and dwelt among us, full of grace and truth (see John 1:14). Christ established on earth the kingdom of God, revealed his Father and himself by deeds and words and by his death, resurrection and glorious ascension, as well as by sending the holy Spirit, completed his work. Lifted up from the earth he draws all people to himself (see John 10:32, Greek text), for he alone has the words of eternal life (see John 6:68). This mystery was not made known to other generations as it has now been revealed to his holy apostles and prophets by the holy Spirit (see Ephesians 3:4–6, Greek text), that they might preach the Gospel, foster faith in Jesus Christ and the Lord, and bring together the church. The writings of the New Testament stand as a perpetual and divine witness to these realities.

18.   It is common knowledge that among all the inspired writings, including those of the New Testament, the Gospels have a special place, and rightly so, because they are our principal source for the life and teaching of the incarnate Word, our Savior.

The church has always and everywhere maintained, and continues to maintain, the apostolic origin of the four Gospels. The apostles preached, as Christ had charged them to do, and then, under the inspiration of the holy Spirit, they and others of the apostolic age handed on to us in writing the same message they had preached, the foundation of our faith: the fourfold Gospel, according to Matthew, Mark, Luke and John.[1]

19.   Holy mother church has firmly and with absolute constancy maintained and continues to maintain, that these four Gospels, whose historicity it unhesitatingly affirms, faithfully hand on what Jesus, the Son of God, while he lived among men and women, really did and taught for their eternal salvation, until the day when he was taken up (see Acts 1:1–2). For, after the ascension of the Lord, the apostles handed on to their hearers what he had said and done, but with that fuller understanding which they, instructed by the glorious events of Christ and enlightened by the Spirit of truth,[2] now enjoyed.[3] The sacred authors, in writing the four Gospels, selected certain of the many elements which had been handed on, either orally or in written form; others they synthesized or explained with an eye to the situation of the churches. They retained the preaching style, but always in such a fashion that they have told us the authentic truth about Jesus.[4] Whether thy relied on their own memory and recollections or on the

testimony of those who "from the beginning were eyewitnesses and ministers of the word," their purpose in writing was that we might know the "truth" concerning the things of which we have been informed (see Luke 1:2-4).

20. Besides the four Gospels, the New Testament also contains the letters of St Paul and other apostolic writings composed under the inspiration of the holy Spirit. In accordance with God's wise design these writings firmly establish those matters which concern Christ the Lord, formulate more precisely his authentic teaching, preach the saving power of Christ's divine work and foretell its glorious consummation.

For the Lord Jesus was with his apostles as he had promised (see Matthew 28:20) and he had sent to them the Spirit, the Counselor, who would guide them into all the truth (see John 16:13).

CHAPTER VI
SACRED SCRIPTURE IN THE LIFE OF THE CHURCH

21. The church has always venerated the divine scriptures as it has venerated the Body of the Lord, in that it never ceases, above all in the sacred liturgy, to partake of the bread of life and to offer it to the faithful from the one table of the word of God and the Body of Christ. It has always regarded and continues to regard the scriptures, taken together with sacred tradition, as the supreme rule of its faith. For, since they are inspired by God and committed to writing once and for all time, they present God's own word in an unalterable form, and they make the voice of the holy Spirit sound again and again in the words of the prophets and apostles. It follows that all the preaching of church, as indeed the entire Christian religion, should be nourished and ruled by sacred scripture. In the sacred books the Father who is in heave comes lovingly to meet his children, and talks with them. And such is the force and power of the word of God that it is the church's support and strength, imparting robustness to the faith of its daughters and sons and providing food for their souls. It is a pure and unfailing fount of spiritual life. It is eminently true of holy scripture that: "The word of God is living and active" (Hebrew 4:12), and "is able to build you up and to give you the inheritance among all those who are sanctified" (Acts 20:32; see 1 Thessalonians 2:13).

22. Access to sacred scripture ought to be widely available to the christian faithful. For this reason the church, from the very beginning, made its own the ancient translation of the Old Testament called the Septuagint; it honors also the other eastern translations, and the Latin translations, especially those known as the Vulgate. But since the word of God must be readily available at all times, the church, with motherly concern, sees to it that suitable and correct translations are made into various languages, especially from the original texts of the sacred books. If, when the opportunity presents itself and the authorities of the church agree, these translations are made jointly with churches separated from us, they can then be used by all Christians.

23. Taught by the holy Spirit, the spouse of the incarnate Word, which is the church, strives to reach an increasingly more profound understanding of the sacred scriptures, in order to nourish its children with God's words. For this reason also it duly encourages the study of the Fathers, both eastern and western, and of the sacred liturgies. Catholic exegetes and other workers in the field of sacred theology should work diligently together and under the watchful eye of the sacred magisterium. Using appropriate techniques they should together set about examining and explaining the sacred texts in such a way that as many as possible of those who are ministers of God's word may be able to dispense fruitfully the nourishment of the scriptures to the people of God. This nourishment enlightens the mind, strengthens the will and fires the hearts of men and women with the love of God.[1] The holy synod encourages those members of the church who are engaged in biblical studies constantly to renew their efforts, in order to carry on, with complete dedication and in accordance with the mind of the church,[2] the work they have so happily begun.

24. Sacred theology relies on the written word of God, taken together with sacred tradition, as its permanent foundation. By this word it is powerfully strengthened and constantly rejuvenated, as it searches out, under the light of faith, all the truth stored up in the mystery of Christ. The sacred scriptures contain the word of God, and, because they are inspired, they truly are the word of God; therefore, the study of the sacred page should be the very soul of sacred theology.[3] The ministry of the word, too—pastoral preaching, catechetics and all forms of christian instruction, among which the liturgical homily should hold pride of place—gains healthy nourishment and holy vitality from the word of scripture.

25. Therefore, all clerics, particularly priests of Christ and others who, as deacons or catechists, are officially engaged in the ministry of the word, should immerse themselves in the scriptures by constant spiritual reading and diligent study. For it must not happen that any of them become "empty preachers of the word of God to others, not being hearers of the word in their own hearts",[4] when they ought to be sharing the boundless riches of the divine word with the faithful committed to their care, especially in sacred liturgy. Likewise, the holy synod forcefully and specifically exhorts all the christian faithful, especially those who live the religious life, to learn "the surpassing knowledge of Jesus Christ" (Philippians 3:8) by frequent reading of the divine scriptures. "Ignorance of the scriptures is ignorance of Christ".[5] Therefore, let them go gladly to the sacred text itself, whether in the sacred liturgy, which is full of the divine words, or in devout reading, or in such suitable exercises and various other helps which, with the approval and guidance of the pastors of the church, are happily spreading everywhere in our day. Let them remember, however, that prayer should accompany the reading of sacred scripture, so that it becomes a dialogue between God and the human reader. For, "we speak to him when we pray; we listen to him when we read the divine oracles".[6]

It is the duty of bishops, "with whom the apostolic doctrine resides"[7] suitably to instruct the faithful entrusted to them in the correct use of the divine books, especially the New Testament and in particular the Gospels. This is done by translations of the sacred texts which are equipped with necessary and really adequate explanations. Thus, the children of the church can familiarize themselves safely and profitably with the sacred scriptures, and become steeped in their spirit.

Moreover, editions of sacred scripture, provided with suitable notes, should be prepared for the use even of non-Christians, and adapted to their circumstances. These should be prudently circulated, either by pastors of souls, or by Christians of any walk of life.

26.   So may it come that, by the reading and study of the sacred books "the word of God may speed on and triumph" (2 Thessalonians 3:1) and the treasure of revelation entrusted to the church may more and more fill people's hearts. Just as from constant attendance at the eucharistic mystery of the life of the church draws increase, so a new impulse of spiritual life may be expected from increased veneration of the word of God, which "stands forever" (Isaiah 40:8; see 1 Peter 1:23–25).

NOTES

CHAPTER I

a. Prologue and chapters 1, 2, 6 translated by Liam Walsh, OP, chapters 3, 4, 5 by Wilfred Harrington, OP, who have revised their respective chapters for this edition. Further revision was done by Austin Flannery, OP.

1. St. Augustine, *De Catechizandis rudibus*, 4, 8: PL 40, 316.

2. See Matthew 11:27; John 1:14 and 17; 14:6; 17:1–3; 2 Corinthians 3:16 and 4:6; Ephesians 1:3–14.

3. *Letter to Diogentus*, 7, 4: Funk, *Patres Apostolici*, I, p. 403.

4. Vatican Council I, dogmatic constitution on the Catholic faith, *Dei Filius* [=DF], ch. 3: Denz. 1789 (3008).

5. Council of Orange II, canon 7: Denz 180 (377). Vatican Council I, loc. cit.: Denz. 1791 (3010).

6. DF, ch. 2, Denz: 1786 (3005).

7. Ibid.: Denz. 1785 and 1786 (3004 and 3005).

CHAPTER II

1. See Matthew 28:19–20 and Mark 16:15. Council of Trent, decree *On the canonical scriptures* [=OCS]: Denz. 783 (1501).

2. See Council of Trent, loc. cit.; DF, ch. 2: Denz. 1787 (3006).

3. St. Irenaeus, *Adv. Haer.*, III, 3,1: PG 7, 848; Harvey, 2, p. 9.

4. See Council of Nicea II: Denz. 303 (602). Council of Constantinople IV, Session X, can. 1: Denz 336 (650–652).

5. See DF, ch. 4, Denz. 1800 (3020).

6. See OCS: Denz. 783 (1501).

7. See Pius XII, apost. const. *Munificentissimus Deus*, 1 Nov. 1950: AAS 42 (1950), p. 756, taken along with the words of St. Cyprian, *Epist.* 66, 8: CSEL, III, 2, 733: "The church is the people united to its priests, the flock adhering to its shepherd."

8. See DF, ch. 3, Denz. 1972 (3011).

9. See Pius XII, encyclical *Humani Generis*, 12 Aug. 1950: AAS 42 (1950) 568–569: Denz. 2314 (3886).

CHAPTER III

1. See DF, ch. 2: Denz. 1787 (3006). Pontifical Biblical Commission, decree 18 June 1915: Denz. 2180 (3629); EB 420. Holy Office, *Letter*, 22 Dec. 1923: EB 499.

2. See DAS, 30 Sept. 1943: AAS 35 (1943), p. 314; EB 556.

3. In and *through* human beings: see Hebrew 1:1 and 4:7 (in); 2 Kings 23:2; Matthew 1:22 and *passim (through)*; Vatican Council I, Scheme on catholic doctrine, note 9: *Collectio Lacensis*, VII, 522.

4. PD, 18 Nov. 1893: Denz. 1952 (3293); EB 125.

5. See St. Augustine, *De Gen. ad Litt.*, 2, 9, 20: PL 34, 270–271; *Epistola* 82, 3: PL 33, 277; CSEL 34, 2, p. 354. St. Thomas Aquinas, *De Veritate*, q. 12, a 2, C. OCS: Denz. 783 (1501). PD: EB 121, 124, 126–127. DAS: EB 539.

6. St. Augustine, *De Civitate Dei*, XVII, 6, 2: PL 41, 537: CSEL 40, 2, 228.

7. St. Augustine, *De Doctrina Christiana*, III, 18, 26; PL 34, 75–76.

8. DAS: Denz. 2294 (3829-3820); EB 557–562.

9. See SP: EB 469. St. Jerome, *In Gal* 5, 19–21: PL 26, 417 A.

10. See DF, c. 2: Denz. 1788 (3007).

11. St. John Chrysostom, *In Gen* 3, 8 (homily 17, 1): PG 53, 134. *Attemperatio* corresponds to the Greek *synkatabasis*.

CHAPTER IV

1. Pius XI, encyclical *Mit brennender Sorge*, 14 March 1937: AAS 29 (1937), p. 151.

2. St. *Augustine, Quaest. In Hept.* 2, 73: PL 34, 623.

3. St. Irenaeus, *Adv. Haer.*, III, 21, 3: PG 7, 950 (=25, 1) Harvey 2, p. 115. St. Cyril of

Jerusalem, *Catech*, 4, 35: PG 33, 497.
Theodore of Mopsuestia, *In Soph* 1, 4–6:
PG 66, 452D–453A.

CHAPTER V

1. See St. Irenaeus, *Adv. Haer.*, III, 11, 8: PG
   7, 885; ed. Sagnard, p. 194.

2. See John 14:26; 16:13.

3. See John 2:22; 12–16; see 14:26; 16:12–
   13; 7:39.

4. See SME: AAS 56 (1964), p. 715.

CHAPTER VI

1. See DAS: EB 551, 553, 567. Pontifical Biblical Commission, *Instructio de S. Scriptura
   in Clericorum Seminariis et Religiosorum
   Collegiis recte docenda*, 13 May 1950:
   AAS 42 (1950), pp. 495–505.

2. See Pius XII, ibid.: EB 569.

3. See PD: EB 114; SP: EB 483.

4. St. Augustine, *Serm.* 179: PL 38, 966.

5. St. Jerome, *Comm. In Is*, Prol.: PL 24, 17.
   See SP: B 475–480; DAS: EB 544.

6. St. Ambrose, *De Offiis, ministrorum* I,
   20, 88: PL 16, 50.

7. St. Irenaeus, *Adv. Haer.* IV, 32, 1: PG 7,
   1071; (=49, 2) Harvey, 2, p. 255.

LECTIONARY FOR MASS:
INTRODUCTION

1981

OVERVIEW OF THE *LECTIONARY FOR MASS: INTRODUCTION*

Gerard S. Sloyan

Why should anyone read this *Introduction to the Lectionary for Mass* (LMIn), which is as much a defense as an exposition of a liturgical book that has been in use for more than 20 years?

—Many people who were engaged in the church's public worship when it first appeared (1970, revised in 1981) examined it with care and have not returned to it since. There are probably many more—presider-homilists, deacons and regular readers of the Bible in the liturgy—who have not read it for the first time. It provides the rationale underlying an aspect of the practice of the Western church in which they have an intimate part. They should know what it has to say.

—There doubtless are liturgy committees in parishes, monasteries and convents of women and men that have not heard of the document, let alone explored it.

—There are regular complaints against the way the Roman lectionary is constructed, which a careful reading of this *Introduction* might dispel—or confirm.

—And, while there are certain practices regarding the use of the lectionary that this document does not condone, there are many more pastorally beneficial practices that go unemployed because priests and people are unaware of the freedoms it allows.

Two other matters leap out at the reader of this *Introduction*. One is its silence in article 62 on the ecumenical advance represented by the Anglican and Protestant lectionaries that are based on the Roman lectionary and used world-wide. This lends a provincial tone to a piece of writing that bears the proud name of Catholic. The other is the mention of readers who have been "instituted" as such by a liturgical rite (#51 and 52; these are men only, although this is not stated). The reference may surprise readers who have not heard of this under-standably little-used rite.

CATHOLIC LITURGY IS THOROUGHLY BIBLICAL

The best service a background paper can offer to liturgy committees that study LMIn (with priests and deacons sitting in as members) is to highlight things to look for that might be missed. The first is the thoroughly biblical nature of the Catholic liturgy. As LMIn proceeds to specifics, the impression might be derived that Bible readings *in* the eucharistic (or other sacramental) liturgy are the matter at issue. In fact, however, any liturgy is neither more nor less than a celebration of God's word as delivered in the Bible. The prayers of all the rites, including the eucharistic prayer, are either tissues of biblical phrasing or are inspired by the Bible. The Lord's Supper is an act of obedience to a biblical injunction (Luke 22:14c). From the opening sign of the cross (see Matthew 28:19) to the final dismissal (see Psalm 29:11b; Judith 8:35), the participants are invited to live in the world of the Bible as one people with its people. That is why any Catholic should be able to invite a person who is not of this faith but has great veneration for the Bible to attend Sunday Mass saying: "Come to our Bible service." Any Catholic assembly where the Mass is not recognizable as such has not given sufficient attention to what LMIn has to say (see #4–8; 44–48).

Obviously, the eucharistic rite peaks more visibly as biblical in what is called "the liturgy of the word" because there the texts that are read are extracted directly from the Holy Books and are commented on in what ought to be a Bible lesson. If they are not, the hope expressed in the Constitution on the Sacred Liturgy that "the treasures of the Bible are to be opened up more lavishly so that a richer fare may be provided for the faithful at the table of God's word" (#51) will have been thwarted. Any visitor on a single Sunday can tell whether the opening up and sharing of the Bible is lavish or parsimonious, generous or grudging. LMIn tries its best to convince assemblies how to go the better route. "Christ himself is the center and fullness of the whole of Scripture, just as he is of all liturgical celebration. Thus the Scriptures are the living waters from which all who seek life and salvation must drink" (#5).

READERS: AT HOME IN THE SACRED STORIES

Those who hear the scriptures proclaimed in liturgical celebrations should experience themselves as a new people in whom the covenant made in the past is fulfilled (#7). The ordained are *charged* with teaching God's word by virtue of their ordination, but they, or those "who have been entrusted with exercising that ministry" are the ones who must in fact *do* it. Bishops do the entrusting for the whole church. They wisely entrust with the task only those who *can* do it. The clearest impression that comes through from a line-by-line reading of LMIn is that no one should be allowed to read publicly or preach but those who know the Bible.

The word that is heard and the eucharist that is offered and received may be the charge of different or the same ministers, but it is always "one single act of divine worship" (#10). No person who has any ministerial function is absolved from an intimate knowledge of the Bible. That is why these persons have been designated or chosen, not for forensic gifts or personal piety only (although these are assumed), but because they have something of the wisdom that nourishes the church at the table of God's word (#10). That wisdom comes only from an intimate knowledge of the Bible.

This means in practice that the main task of a pastor of a small congregation or of a designated person in a larger one is not the business of recruiting lectors ("getting people to read") but getting the right people and only them to read. It does not matter if a team of four now does what 24 formerly did. The four have proved that they are fit for this task as the others are not. They not only read loudly, clearly and comprehensibly—the great minimum—but are so at home in the sacred stories, commands and exhortations that they never miss the rhetorical intent of the writings or the Anglicized pronunciation of Hebrew and Greek proper nouns. The qualified lector is a person who often reads the Bible privately. His or her intimate knowledge of it and enthusiasm for it is infectious. (See #6.)

Careful study of LMIn regarding the homily (#8, 24) will disclose that all that has been said about those who read the scriptures applies to homilists so much the more. This means, among other things, that not all who have been ordained to the order of deacon should be allowed to preach. All have had the same exposure to a modest theological education but not all have the homilist's gift. Many, in fact, were admitted to this order because they demonstrably had other gifts. Conversely, to reflect on all that is meant by "Christ himself is always present and active in the preaching of his church" and "the homily . . . must always lead the community of the faithful to celebrate the Eucharist actively" (#24) is to realize that some among the nonordained are uniquely qualified to do that. Pastors must therefore ask bishops to authorize others than themselves at times to "explain the text of the Sacred Scriptures proclaimed in the readings," either as an integral part of the liturgy or before or after it (hence, a man or woman) as a "living explanation" of the word of God.

The remaining sticking point is the most important of all. What of men in the presbyteral order who do not seem qualified to expound the scriptures, even though many of these read them tolerably well? Two things must be remembered here: First, such priests were once deemed capable of acquiring the homilist's art and still may, and, second, the whole venture of proclaiming, explaining and being nourished by the scriptures is understood by LMIn to be a corporate venture. (See #8, 9, 19, 20, 24, 48 and especially 40, none of which can be realized without extensive consultation and exchange.) If priests regularly participate in planning sessions on the liturgy as prayerful celebration (not as orchestrated performance), there is everything to be hoped for in their prognosis as effective preachers. If not, then little or nothing.

HOW THE LECTIONARY IS CONSTRUCTED

A word needs to be said about the stress in LMIn on the reading or chanting of the gospel (#13, 17). Everything contained in these two sections must be affirmed strongly. Readings from the gospels always have had pride of place in Christian liturgies because there the Savior speaks directly to his people. In the four gospels, Jesus Christ the Word is embodied in words as nowhere else in the Bible. Hence, the acts of veneration of the book of gospels proposed in LMIn must be taken seriously.

The preeminence of the gospels does not imply, however, that the gospel pericope should always or even usually be the one expounded. The very enlargement of offerings proposed by the three-year lectionary suggests otherwise. Israel's scriptures were not only the Bible of Jesus and the early church, but they are irrevocably the church's scriptures. Paul's letters, too, and perhaps some other New Testament writings were hailed as expressions of the apostolic faith before the first of the gospels was written. "There are certain passages in them hard to understand," as the anonymous author of 2 Peter wrote of Paul's epistles (3:16b). He went on to acknowledge that the ignorant and the unstable were distorting them and the rest of scripture to their own ruin. In the present age, when Catholics everywhere are flooded with doubtful interpretations of the scriptures or confronted by those directly attacking Catholic faith, they must hear clear and accurate expositions of the representative passages contained in the three-year cycle.

The content of articles 58–69, on the way the lectionary is constructed, should be mastered by liturgy committees and *a fortiori* by homilists. It may not give satisfaction but it will at least convey what the lectionary framers tried to achieve. Many people have expressed the wish that the principle of "harmony" among the three readings that marks the major feasts and Advent and Lent might prevail on every Sunday (see #66, 93, 97). They are dismayed by the randomness that they see introduced by the "semicontinuous reading" principle. But if this were done, a false unity then might be imposed on the 72 books of the Catholic canon. The nonarticulation of the second reading with the first and third is a constant reminder of the diversity within this rich collection. If the reading from the First Testament were not in every case chosen because it somehow prefigures a gospel pericope from the Second (the present situation in the Roman and Protestant lectionaries but not always that of the *Common Lectionary* of the Consultation on Common Texts), the diversity would come through more clearly.

Yet the unity of the two testaments is something that never can be submerged. The life of the apostolic church always is seen as a continuation of the life of the people Israel, its ethnic exclusiveness apart. Any reading from either testament can be shown to be related to any other without strain. This is because all convey the relation of the God of Israel whom Jesus called "Father" to the people of God's special love.

Article 64 rather confidently assumes that the selection and arrangement of readings is such that it will satisfy the requirements both of the liturgical seasons and the hermeneutical principles of contemporary biblical research. The Catholic scholars of pastoral bent (including women) who are at ease in the fields of liturgy and biblical interpretation, or who at least can engage in a profitable discussion with those of the other expertise than their own, are painfully few. One does not have to be an expert in gospel scholarship, for example, to see that the lectionary framers think that the incidents in Jesus' life are what must all be presented somehow over three years of Sundays. This is accomplished largely without regard to what Matthew, Mark, Luke and John made of them. People who have been active in adult initiation for several years and have undertaken the necessary study have concluded that the "baptismal and penitential character of this season" (#69) is sometimes in open conflict with itself, with the medieval penitential emphasis usually winning out. The parishes that are taking seriously the "scrutinies" of candidates on the Third, Fourth and Fifth Sundays of Lent have long ago concluded that the readings proposed for Year A should be employed every year (as #97 allows). This is to say that the authors of LMIn take for granted what may not be the case, namely, that the lectionary they have produced is perfectly at ease in face of the requirements of the liturgical seasons and the principles of contemporary biblical research.

TAKING LIBERTIES CAUTIOUSLY

Perhaps the best guidance for liturgy committees, some of whose members are regularly studying the shape of the Roman liturgy, is contained in articles 76–78. There LMIn shares with the prospective ministers of the liturgy its principles on including and omitting "difficult texts," including the ancient custom of lectionaries of not printing every verse in sequence in a given pericope for reasons of length or pastoral unsuitability. An ancient adage says that what is permissible to Jupiter is not necessarily the privilege of the cow *(Quod licet Iovi non licet bovi).* The more applicable adage in this case seems to be "What is sauce for the goose is sauce for the gander." If pastoral judgments were allowable to a team of scholars, some of them not engaged in pastoral work, in a distant city more than two decades ago, these scholars are clearly inviting pastoral teams to make similar wise judgments in their own situations. The options proposed in the choices of certain texts (#78–84) therefore are not to be thought of as confining serious liturgy committees to the ones proposed. Much thought and study must of course go into any departure from the readings prescribed. There have to be good pastoral reasons in every case to justify it.

Some examples of the application of these principles follow. They are prefaced by the observation that omission of one of the three readings is an option that the United States bishops wisely have not entertained. (See #79.)

The gospel pericopes are consistently of sufficient length that the proposal of a shorter form normally does not work against the intended pastoral effect. The same is seldom the case with the first and second readings, many of which, if they were any weaker, would die. They always can be lengthened from a well-marked pulpit Bible. Such treatment might make their selection as lectionary readings understandable to the members of the assembly for the first time. Needless to say, only a skilled hand will know how to lengthen a reading effectively.

In general, the weakness of the lectionary is the constant interruptions within interruptions that it allows. Until a fourth John year is introduced, no liturgical team should be discouraged from plotting either more sequential John readings or fewer. As it is, the lectionary framers give the impression of having ingeniously "worked John in," with the result that they have pitted him against the synoptics when what they wished was to have this gospel complement them.

When the first reading gives every appearance of being brief and inconsequential (because it was chosen for some glancing verbal similarity to the gospel or to have every book of the Bible represented), a powerful reading from that First Testament should be substituted. Article 65 says that the "more significant parts of God's revealed word" have been chosen for the Sundays and solemnities of the Lord to which those chosen for weekdays are complementary; but this can be questioned. Often the nearby weekday first readings are more significant. If parishioners complain because there is departure from the paperback hand missal they take for an inspired book, they must be educated to the freedoms that the official Roman document proposes. The public reading must then be so effective that no one but the very deaf misses a word.

It is impossible for a liturgy committee to pay too much attention to articles 19–22, on the responsorial psalm. The treatment of psalmody in Catholic worship is, after preaching and presiding, the largest liturgical problem the postconciliar church has had to face. In many churches the psalm is recited by the assembly, either antiphonally or in alternation with the lector, but such practices have not yet faced the problem. The problem is musical since the psalms are the lyrics of songs. Only good, simple musical renderings can solve it, in which the people are not exhausted by the feat of memorizing a long or musically difficult antiphon.

Some attention has been paid in this essay to perceived shortcomings in the present Sunday lectionary, but overall these are minor. The task the Consilium set for itself in appointing a subcommittee on the lectionary was major. The product this committee conceived is worthy of almost total admiration. These selections from the Bible, if consistently read well and just as consistently commented on, cannot but have the hoped-for effect. The readings and homilies once again can make Catholics what they were before the invention of printing— a people of the Bible. This means that in the eucharistic liturgy, they will "faithfully [echo] the 'Amen' that Christ, the mediator between God and men and women, uttered once for all as he shed his blood to seal God's new covenant in the Holy Spirit" (#6).

A biblical liturgy is far from an archaic enterprise. It is not one that looks only to an historical past and a heavenly future. It is above all a thing of the present in which "the Holy Spirit makes [our] response effective, so that what is heard in the celebration of the Liturgy may be carried out in a way of life" (#6). To illustrate: unacceptable levels of employment in the labor force, total sexual liberty versus self-discipline, the consumer mentality, the rich nations and the poor—anything that is part of the people's lives is part of the life of the Bible, sometimes in joltingly specific language.

When the liturgy is celebrated well, it proclaims to every worshiper in church or chapel, "Be doers of the word and not hearers only" (James 1:22). Our day-to-day conduct is our chief praise of God. It is to this that the holy liturgy gives tongue.

OUTLINE

SECOND PART: THE STRUCTURE OF THE ORDER
OF THE READINGS FOR MASS

CHAPTER VI: Adaptations, Translations and Format of the Order of Readings

Table I: Seasonal table of principal celebrations of the liturgical year
Table II: Arrangement of the second reading on the Sundays
      of Ordinary Time
Table III: Arrangement of the first reading on the weekdays
      of Ordinary Time

INTRODUCTION

PREAMBLE

CHAPTER I
GENERAL PRINCIPLES FOR THE LITURGICAL CELEBRATION
OF THE WORD OF GOD

1. Certain Preliminaries

A) THE IMPORTANCE OF THE WORD OF GOD IN LITURGICAL CELEBRATION

1.   The Second Vatican Council,[1] the magisterium of the Popes,[2] and various documents promulgated after the Council by the organisms of the Holy See[3] have already had many excellent things to say about the importance of the word of God and about reestablishing the use of Sacred Scripture in every celebration of the Liturgy. The Introduction to the 1969 edition of the Order of Readings for Mass has clearly stated and briefly explained some of the more important principles.[4]

On the occasion of this new edition of the Order of Readings for Mass, requests have come from many quarters for a more detailed exposition of the same principles. Hence, this expanded and more suitable arrangement of the Introduction first gives a general statement on the essential bond between the word of God and the liturgical celebration,[5] then deals in greater detail with the word of God in the celebration of Mass, and, finally explains the precise structure of the Order of Readings for Mass.

B) TERMS USED TO REFER TO THE WORD OF GOD

2.   For the sake of clear and precise language on this topic, a definition of terms might well be expected as a prerequisite. Nevertheless this Introduction will simply use the same terms employed in conciliar and postconciliar documents. Furthermore it will use "Sacred Scripture" and "word of God" interchangeably throughout when referring to the books written under the inspiration of the Holy Spirit, thus avoiding any confusion of language or meaning.[6]

C) THE SIGNIFICANCE OF THE WORD OF GOD IN THE LITURGY

3.   The many riches contained in the one word of God are admirably brought out in the different kinds of liturgical celebration and in the different gatherings of the faithful who take part in those celebrations. This takes place as the unfolding mystery of Christ is recalled during the course of the liturgical year,

as the Church's sacraments and sacramentals are celebrated, or as the faithful respond individually to the Holy Spirit working within them.[7] For then the liturgical celebration, founded primarily on the word of God and sustained by it, becomes a new event and enriches the word itself with new meaning and power. Thus in the Liturgy the Church faithfully adheres to the way Christ himself read and explained the Sacred Scriptures, beginning with the "today" of his coming forward in the synagogue and urging all to search the Scriptures.[8]

2. Liturgical Celebration of the Word of God

A) THE PROPER CHARACTER OF THE WORD OF GOD IN THE LITURGICAL CELEBRATION

4. In the celebration of the Liturgy the word of God is not announced in only one way[9] nor does it always stir the hearts of the hearers with the same efficacy. Always, however, Christ is present in his word,[10] as he carries out the mystery of salvation, he sanctifies humanity and offers the Father perfect worship.[11]

Moreover, the word of God unceasingly calls to mind and extends the economy of salvation, which achieves its fullest expression in the Liturgy. The liturgical celebration becomes therefore the continuing, complete, and effective presentation of God's word.

The word of God constantly proclaimed in the Liturgy is always, then, a living and effective word[12] through the power of the Holy Spirit. It expresses the Father's love that never fails in its effectiveness toward us.

B) THE WORD OF GOD IN THE ECONOMY OF SALVATION

5. When in celebrating the Liturgy the Church proclaims both the Old and New Testament, it is proclaiming one and the same mystery of Christ.

The New Testament lies hidden in the Old; the Old Testament comes fully to light in the New.[13] Christ himself is the center and fullness of the whole of Scripture, just as he is of all liturgical celebration.[14] Thus the Scriptures are the living waters from which all who seek life and salvation must drink.

The more profound our understanding of the celebration of the liturgy, the higher our appreciation of the importance of God's word. Whatever we say of the one, we can in turn say of the other, because each recalls the mystery of Christ and each in its own way causes the mystery to be carried forward.

C) THE WORD OF GOD IN THE LITURGICAL PARTICIPATION OF THE FAITHFUL

6. In celebrating the Liturgy the Church faithfully echoes the "Amen" that Christ, the mediator between God and men and women, uttered once for all as he shed his blood to seal God's new covenant in the Holy Spirit.[15].

When God communicates his word, he expects a response, one that is, of listening and adoring "in Spirit and in truth" (John 4:23). The Holy Spirit makes that response effective, so that what is heard in the celebration of the Liturgy may be carried out in a way of life: "Be doers of the word and not hearers only" (James 1:22).

The liturgical celebration and the participation of the faithful receive outward expression in actions, gestures, and words. These derive their full meaning not simply from their origin in human experience but from the word of God and the economy of salvation, to which they refer. Accordingly, the participation of the faithful in the Liturgy increases to the degree that, as they listen to the word of God proclaimed in the Liturgy, they strive harder to commit themselves to the Word of God incarnate in Christ. Thus, they endeavor to conform their way of life to what they celebrate in the Liturgy, and then in turn to bring to the celebration of the Liturgy all that they do in life.[16]

3. The Word of God in the Life of the People of the Covenant

A) THE WORD OF GOD IN THE LIFE OF THE CHURCH

7.   In the hearing of God's word the Church is built up and grows, and in the signs of the liturgical celebration God's wonderful, past works in the history of salvation are presented anew as mysterious realities. God in turn makes use of the congregation of the faithful that celebrates the Liturgy in order that his word may speed on and be glorified and that his name be exalted among the nations.[17]

Whenever, therefore, the Church, gathered by the Holy Spirit for liturgical celebration,[18] announces and proclaims the word of God, she is aware of being a new people in whom the covenant made in the past is perfected and fulfilled. Baptism and confirmation in the Spirit have made all Christ's faithful into messengers of God's word because of the grace of hearing they have received. They must therefore be the bearers of the same word in the Church and in the world, at least by the witness of their lives.

The word of God proclaimed in the celebration of God's mysteries does not only address present conditions but looks back to past events and forward to what is yet to come. Thus God's word shows us what we should hope for with such a longing that in this changing world our hearts will be set on the place where our true joys lie.[19]

B) THE CHURCH'S EXPLANATION OF THE WORD OF GOD

8.   By Christ's own will there is a marvelous diversity of members in the new people of God and each has different duties and responsibilities with respect to the word of God. Accordingly, the faithful listen to God's word and meditate on it, but only those who have the office of teaching by virtue of sacred ordination or who have been entrusted with exercising that ministry expound the word of God.

This is how in doctrine, life, and worship the Church keeps alive and passes on to every generation all that she is, all that she believes. Thus with the passage of the centuries, the Church is ever to advance toward the fullness of divine truth until God's word is wholly accomplished in her.[20]

C) THE CONNECTION BETWEEN THE WORD OF GOD PROCLAIMED
   ### AND THE WORKING OF THE HOLY SPIRIT

9.   The working of the Holy Spirit is needed if the word of God is to make what we hear outwardly have its effect inwardly. Because of the Holy Spirit's inspiration and support, the word of God becomes the foundation of the liturgical celebration and the rule and support of all our life.

The working of the Holy Spirit precedes, accompanies, and brings to completion the whole celebration of the Liturgy. But the Spirit also brings home[21] to each person individually everything that in the proclamation of the word of God is spoken for the good of the whole gathering of the faithful. In strengthening the unity of all, the Holy Spirit at the same time fosters a diversity of gifts and furthers their multiform operation.

D) THE ESSENTIAL BOND BETWEEN THE WORD OF GOD
   ### AND THE MYSTERY OF THE EUCHARIST

10.   The Church has honored the word of God and the Eucharistic mystery with the same reverence, although not with the same worship, and has always and everywhere insisted upon and sanctioned such honor. Moved by the example of its Founder, the Church has never ceased to celebrate his paschal mystery by coming together to read "what referred to him in all the Scriptures" (Luke 24:27) and to carry out the work of salvation through the celebration of the memorial of the Lord and through the sacraments. "The preaching of the word is necessary for the ministry of the sacraments, for these are sacraments of faith, which is born and nourished from the word."[22]

The Church is nourished spiritually at the twofold table of God's word and of the Eucharist:[23] from the one it grows in wisdom and from the other in holiness. In the word of God the divine covenant is announced; in the Eucharist the new and everlasting covenant is renewed. On the one hand the history of salvation is brought to mind by means of human sounds; on the other it is made manifest in the sacramental signs of the Liturgy.

It can never be forgotten, therefore, that the divine word read and proclaimed by the Church in the Liturgy has as its one purpose the sacrifice of the New Covenant and the banquet of grace, that is, the Eucharist. The celebration of Mass in which the word is heard and the Eucharist is offered and received forms but one single act of divine worship.[24] That act offers the sacrifice of praise to God and makes available to God's creatures the fullness of redemption.

FIRST PART
THE WORD OF GOD IN THE CELEBRATION OF MASS

CHAPTER II
THE CELEBRATION OF THE LITURGY OF THE WORD AT MASS

1. The Elements of the Liturgy of the Word and their Rites

11.   "Readings from Sacred Scripture and the chants between the readings form the main part of the liturgy of the word. The homily, the profession of faith, and the universal prayer or prayer of the faithful carry it forward and conclude it."[25]

A) THE BIBLICAL READINGS

12.   In the celebration of Mass the biblical readings with their accompanying chants from the Sacred Scriptures may not be omitted, shortened, or, worse still, replaced by nonbiblical readings.[26] For it is out of the word of God handed down in writing that even now "God speaks to his people"[27] and it is from the continued use of Sacred Scripture that the people of God, docile to the Holy Spirit under the light of faith, is enabled to bear witness to Christ before the world by its manner of life.

13.   The reading of the Gospel is the high point of the liturgy of the word. For this the other readings, in their established sequence from the Old to the New Testament, prepare the assembly.

14.   A speaking style on the part of the readers that is audible, clear, and intelligent is the first means of transmitting the word of God properly to the congregation. The readings, taken from the approved editions,[28] may be sung in a way suited to different languages. This singing, however, must serve to bring out the sense of the words, not obscure them. On occasions when the readings are in Latin, the manner given in the *Ordo cantus Missae* is to be maintained.[29]

15.   There may be concise introductions before the readings, especially the first. The style proper to such comments must be respected, that is, they must be simple, faithful to the text, brief, well prepared, and properly varied to suit the text they introduce.[30]

16.   In a Mass with the people the readings are always to be proclaimed at the ambo.[31]

17.   Of all the rites connected with the liturgy of the word, the reverence due to the Gospel reading must receive special attention.[32] Where there is an Evangeliary or Book of Gospels that has been carried in by the deacon or reader during the entry procession,[33] it is most fitting that the deacon or a priest, when there is no deacon, take the book from the altar[34] and carry it to the ambo. He is preceded by servers with candles and incense or other symbols of reverence that may be customary. As the faithful stand and acclaim the Lord, they show honor to the Book of Gospels. The deacon who is to read the Gospel, bowing in front

of the one presiding, asks and receives the blessing. When no deacon is present, the priest, bowing before the altar, prays inaudibly, *Almighty God, cleanse my heart.* . . . [35]

At the ambo the one who proclaims the Gospel greets the people, who are standing, and announces the reading as he makes the sign of the cross on forehead, mouth, and breast. If incense is used, he next incenses the book, then reads the Gospel. When finished, he kisses the book, saying the appointed words inaudibly.

Even if the Gospel itself is not sung, it is appropriate for the greeting *The Lord be with you,* and *A reading from the holy Gospel according to* . . . , and at the end *The Gospel of the Lord* to be sung, in order that the congregation may also sing its acclamations. This is a way both of bringing out the importance of the Gospel reading and of stirring up the faith of those who hear it.

18.   At the conclusion of the other readings, *The word of the Lord* may be sung, even by someone other than the reader; all respond with the acclamation. In this way the assembled congregation pays reverence to the word of God it has listened to in faith and gratitude.

B) THE RESPONSORIAL PSALM

19.   The responsorial psalm, also called the gradual, has great liturgical and pastoral significance because it is an "integral part of the liturgy of the word."[36] Accordingly, the faithful must be continually instructed on the way to perceive the word of God speaking in the psalms and to turn these psalms into the prayer of the Church. This, of course, "will be achieved more readily if a deeper understanding of the psalms, according to the meaning with which they are sung in the sacred Liturgy, is more diligently promoted among the clergy and communicated to all the faithful by means of appropriate catechesis."[37]

Brief remarks about the choice of the psalm and response as well as their correspondence to the readings may be helpful.

20.   As a rule the responsorial psalm should be sung. There are two established ways of singing the psalm after the first reading: responsorially and directly. In responsorial singing, which, as far as possible, is to be given preference, the psalmist, or cantor of the psalm, sings the psalm verse and the whole congregation joins in by singing the response. In direct singing of the psalm there is no intervening response by the community; either the psalmist, or cantor of the psalm, sings the psalm alone as the community listens or else all sing it together.

21.   The singing of the psalm, or even of the response alone, is a great help toward understanding and meditating on the psalm's spiritual meaning.

To foster the congregation's singing, every means available in each individual culture is to be employed. In particular, use is to be made of all the relevant options provided in the Order of Readings for Mass[38] regarding responses corresponding to the different liturgical seasons.

22. When not sung, the psalm after the reading is to be recited in a manner conducive to meditation on the word of God.[39]

The responsorial psalm is sung or recited by the psalmist or cantor at the ambo.[40]

C) THE ACCLAMATION BEFORE THE READING OF THE GOSPEL

23. The *Alleluia* or, as the liturgical season requires, the verse before the Gospel, is also a "rite or act standing by itself."[41] It serves as the greeting of welcome of the assembled faithful to the Lord who is about to speak to them and as an expression of their faith through song.

The *Alleluia* or the verse before the Gospel must be sung and during it all stand. It is not to be sung only by the cantor who intones it or by the choir, but by the whole of the people together.[42]

D) THE HOMILY

24. Through the course of the liturgical year the homily sets forth the mysteries of faith and the standards of the Christian life on the basis of the sacred text. Beginning with the Constitution on the Liturgy, the homily as part of the liturgy of the word[43] has been repeatedly and strongly recommended and in some cases it is obligatory. As a rule it is to be given by the one presiding.[44] The purpose of the homily at Mass is that the spoken word of God and the liturgy of the Eucharist may together become "a proclamation of God's wonderful works in the history of salvation, the mystery of Christ."[45] Through the readings and homily Christ's paschal mystery is proclaimed; through the sacrifice of the Mass it becomes present.[46] Moreover Christ himself is always present and active in the preaching of his Church.[47]

Whether the homily explains the text of the Sacred Scriptures proclaimed in the readings or some other text of the Liturgy,[48] it must always lead the community of the faithful to celebrate the Eucharist actively, "so that they may hold fast in their lives to what they have grasped by faith."[49] From this living explanation, the word of God proclaimed in the readings and the Church's celebration of the day's Liturgy will have greater impact. But this demands that the homily be truly the fruit of meditation, carefully prepared, neither too long nor too short, and suited to all those present, even children and the uneducated.[50]

At a concelebration, the celebrant or one of the concelebrants as a rule gives the homily.[51]

25. On the prescribed days, that is, Sundays and holydays of obligation, there must be a homily in all Masses celebrated with a congregation, even Masses on the preceding evening; the homily may not be omitted without a serious reason.[52] There is also to be a homily in Masses with children and with special groups[53]

A homily is strongly recommended on the weekdays of Advent, Lent, and the Easter season for the sake of the faithful who regularly take part in the celebration of Mass; also on other feasts and occasions when a large congregation is present.[54]

26. The priest celebrant gives the homily, standing either at the chair or at the ambo.[55]

27. Any necessary announcements are to be kept completely separate from the homily; they must take place following the prayer after Communion.[56]

E) SILENCE

28. The liturgy of the word must be celebrated in a way that fosters meditation; clearly, any sort of haste that hinders recollection must be avoided. The dialogue between God and his people taking place through the Holy Spirit demands short intervals of silence, suited to the assembled congregation, as an opportunity to take the word of God to heart and to prepare a response to it in prayer.

Proper times for silence during the liturgy of the word are, for example, before this liturgy begins, after the first and the second reading, after the homily.[57]

F) THE PROFESSION OF FAITH

29. The symbol, creed or profession of faith, said when the rubrics require, has as its purpose in the celebration of Mass that the assembled congregation may respond and give assent to the word of God heard in the readings and through the homily, and that before beginning to celebrate in the Eucharist the mystery of faith it may call to mind the rule of faith in a formulary approved by the Church.[58]

G) THE UNIVERSAL PRAYER OR PRAYER OF THE FAITHFUL

30. In the light of God's word and in a sense in response to it, the congregation of the faithful prays in the universal prayer as a rule for the needs of the universal Church and the local community, for the salvation of the world and those oppressed by any burden, and for special categories of people.

The celebrant introduces the prayer; a deacon, another minister, or some of the faithful may propose intentions that are short and phrased with a measure of freedom. In these petitions "the people, exercising its priestly function, makes intercession for all men and women,"[59] with the result that, as the liturgy of the word has its full effects in the faithful, they are better prepared to proceed to the liturgy of the Eucharist.

31. For the prayer of the faithful the celebrant presides at the chair and the intentions are announced at the ambo.[60]

The assembled congregation takes part in the prayer of the faithful while standing and by saying or singing a common response after each intention or by silent prayer.[61]

2. Aids to the Proper Celebration of the Liturgy of the Word

A) THE PLACE FOR THE PROCLAMATION OF THE WORD OF GOD

32. There must be a place in the church that is somewhat elevated, fixed, and of a suitable design and nobility. It should reflect the dignity of God's word and

be a clear reminder to the people that in the Mass the table of God's word and of Christ's body is placed before them.[62] The place for the readings must also truly help the people's listening and attention during the liturgy of the word. Great pains must therefore be taken, in keeping with the design of each church, over the harmonious and close relationship of the ambo with the altar.

33.   Either permanently or at least on occasions of greater solemnity, the ambo should be decorated simply and in keeping with its design.

Since the ambo is the place from which the word of God is proclaimed by the ministers, it must of its nature be reserved for the readings, the responsorial psalm, and the Easter Proclamation (the *Exsultet*). The ambo may rightly be used for the homily and the prayer of the faithful, however, because of their close connection with the entire liturgy of the word. It is better for the commentator, cantor, or director of singing, for example, not to use the ambo.[63]

34.   In order that the ambo may properly serve its liturgical purpose, it is to be rather large, since on occasion several ministers must use it at the same time. Provision must also be made for the readers to have enough light to read the text and, as required, to have modern sound equipment enabling the faithful to hear them without difficulty.

B) THE BOOKS FOR PROCLAMATION OF THE WORD OF GOD IN THE LITURGY

35.   Along with the ministers, the actions, the allocated places, and other elements, the books containing the readings of the word of God remind the hearers of the presence of God speaking to his people. Since in liturgical celebrations the books too serve as signs and symbols of the higher realities, care must be taken to ensure that they truly are worthy, dignified and beautiful.[64]

36.   The proclamation of the Gospel always stands as the high point of the liturgy of the word. Thus the liturgical tradition of both West and East has consistently made a certain distinction between the books for the readings. The Book of Gospels was always fabricated and decorated with the utmost care and shown greater respect than any of the other books of readings. In our times also, then, it is very desirable that cathedrals and at least the larger, more populous parishes and the churches with a larger attendance possess a beautifully designed Book of Gospels, separate from any other book of readings. For good reason it is the Book of Gospels that is presented to a deacon at his ordination and that at an ordination to the episcopate is laid upon the head of the bishop-elect and held there.[65]

37.   Because of the dignity of the word of God, the books of readings used in the celebration are not to be replaced by other pastoral aids, for example, by leaflets printed for the preparation of the readings by the faithful or for their personal meditation.

CHAPTER III
OFFICES AND MINISTRIES IN THE CELEBRATION
OF THE LITURGY OF THE WORD WITHIN MASS

1. The Function of the President at the Liturgy of the Word

38.   The one presiding at the liturgy of the word communicates the spiritual nourishment it contains to those present, especially in the homily. Even if he too is a listener to the word of God proclaimed by others, the duty of proclaiming it has been entrusted above all to him. Personally or through others he sees to it that the word of God is properly proclaimed. He then as a rule reserves to himself the tasks of composing comments to help the people listen more attentively and of preaching a homily that fosters in them a richer understanding of the word of God.

39.   The first requirement for one who is to preside over the celebration is a thorough knowledge of the structure of the Order of Readings, so that he will know how to work a fruitful effect in the hearts of the faithful. Through study and prayer he must also develop a full understanding of the coordination and connection of the various texts in the liturgy of the word, so that the Order of Readings will become the source of a sound understanding of the mystery of Christ and his saving work.

40.   The one presiding is to make ready use of the various options provided in the Lectionary regarding readings, responses, responsorial psalms, and Gospel acclamations;[66] but he is to do so in harmony[67] with all concerned and after listening to the opinions of the faithful in what concerns them.[68]

41.   The one presiding exercises his proper office and the ministry of the word of God also as he preaches the homily.[69] In this way he leads his brothers and sisters to an affective knowledge of Scripture. He opens their minds to thanksgiving for the wonderful works of God. He strengthens the faith of those present in the word that in the celebration becomes sacrament through the Holy Spirit. Finally, he prepares them for a fruitful reception of Communion and invites them to take upon themselves the demands of the Christian life.

42.   The president is responsible for preparing the faithful for the liturgy of the word on occasion by means of introductions before the readings.[70] These comments can help the assembled congregation toward a better hearing of the word of God, because they stir up an attitude of faith and good will. He may also carry out this responsibility through others, a deacon, for example, or a commentator.[71]

43.   As he directs the prayer of the faithful and through their introduction and conclusion connects them, if possible, with the day's readings and the homily, the president leads the faithful toward the liturgy of the Eucharist.[72]

2. The Role of the Faithful in the Liturgy of the Word

44. Christ's word gathers the people of God as one and increases and sustains them. "This applies above all to the liturgy of the word in the celebration of Mass, where there are inseparably united the proclamation of the death of the Lord, the response of the people listening, and the very offering through which Christ has confirmed the New Covenant in his Blood, and in which the people share by their intentions and by reception of the sacrament."[73] For "not only when things are read 'that were written for our instruction' (Romans 15:4), but also when the Church prays or sings or acts, the faith of those taking part is nourished and their minds are raised to God, so that they may offer him rightful worship and receive his grace more abundantly."[74]

45. In the liturgy of the word, the congregation of Christ's faithful even today receives from God the word of his covenant through the faith that comes by hearing, and must respond to that word in faith, so that they may become more and more truly the people of the New Covenant.

   The people of God have a spiritual right to receive abundantly from the treasury of God's word. Its riches are presented to them through use of the Order of Readings, the homily, and pastoral efforts.

   For their part, the faithful at the celebration of Mass are to listen to the word of God with an inward and outward reverence that will bring them continuous growth in the spiritual life and draw them more deeply into the mystery which is celebrated.[75]

46. As a help toward celebrating the memorial of the Lord with eager devotion, the faithful should be keenly aware of the one presence of Christ in both the word of God—it is he himself "who speaks when the Sacred Scriptures are read in the Church"—and "above all under the Eucharistic species."[76]

47. To be received and integrated into the life of Christ's faithful, the word of God demands a living faith.[77] Hearing the word of God unceasingly proclaimed arouses that faith.

   The Sacred Scriptures, above all in their liturgical proclamation, are the source of life and strength. As the Apostle Paul attests, the Gospel is the saving power of God for everyone who believes.[78] Love of the Scriptures is therefore a force reinvigorating and renewing the entire people of God.[79] All the faithful without exception must therefore always be ready to listen gladly to God's word.[80] When this word is proclaimed in the Church and put into living practice, it enlightens the faithful through the working of the Holy Spirit and draws them into the entire mystery of the Lord as a reality to be lived.[81] The word of God reverently received moves the heart and its desires toward conversion and toward a life resplendent with both individual and community faith,[82] since God's word is the food of Christian life and the source of the prayer of the whole Church.[83]

48. The intimate connection between the liturgy of the word and the liturgy of the Eucharist in the Mass should prompt the faithful to be present right from

the beginning of the celebration,[84] to take part attentively, and to prepare themselves in so far as possible to hear the word, especially by learning beforehand more about Sacred Scripture. That same connection should also awaken in them a desire for a liturgical understanding of the texts read and a readiness to respond through singing.[85]

When they hear the word of God and reflect deeply on it, Christ's faithful are enabled to respond to it actively with full faith, hope, and charity through prayer and self-giving, and not only during Mass but in their entire Christian life.

3. Ministries in the Liturgy of the Word

49.   Liturgical tradition assigns responsibility for the biblical readings in the celebration of Mass to ministers: to readers and the deacon. But when there is no deacon or no other priest present, the priest celebrant is to read the Gospel[86] and when there is no reader present, all the readings.[87]

50.   It pertains to the deacon in the liturgy of the word at Mass to proclaim the Gospel, sometimes to give the homily, as occasion suggests, and to propose to the people the intentions of the prayer of the faithful.[88]

51.   "The reader has his own proper function in the Eucharistic celebration and should exercise this even though ministers of a higher rank may be present."[89] The ministry of reader, conferred through a liturgical rite, must be held in respect. When there are instituted readers available, they are to carry out their office at least on Sundays and festive days, especially at the principal Mass of the day. These readers may also be given responsibility for assisting in the arrangement of the liturgy of the word, and, to the extent necessary, of seeing to the preparation of others of the faithful who may be appointed on a given occasion to read at Mass.[90]

52.   The liturgical assembly truly requires readers, even those not instituted. Proper measures must therefore be taken to ensure that there are certain suitable laypeople who have been trained to carry out this ministry.[91] Whenever there is more than one reading, it is better to assign the readings to different readers, if available.

53.   In Masses without a deacon, the function of announcing the intentions for the prayer of the faithful is to be assigned to the cantor, particularly when they are to be sung, to a reader, or to someone else.[92]

54.   During the celebration of Mass with a congregation a second priest, a deacon, and an instituted reader must wear the distinctive vestment of their office when they go up to the ambo to read the word of God. Those who carry out the ministry of reader just for the occasion or even regularly but without institution may go to the ambo in ordinary attire, but this should be in keeping with the customs of the different regions.

55.   "It is necessary that those who exercise the ministry of reader, even if they have not received institution, be truly suited and carefully prepared, so that the

faithful may develop a warm and living love for Sacred Scripture from listening to the sacred readings."[93]

Their preparation must above all be spiritual, but what may be called a technical preparation is also needed. The spiritual preparation presupposes at least a biblical and liturgical formation. The purpose of their biblical formation is to give readers the ability to understand the readings in context and to perceive by the light of faith the central point of the revealed message. The liturgical formation ought to equip the readers to have some grasp of the meaning and structure of the liturgy of the word and of the significance of its connection with the liturgy of the Eucharist. The technical preparation should make the readers more skilled in the art of reading publicly, either with the power of their own voice or with the help of sound equipment.

56. The psalmist, or cantor of the psalm, is responsible for singing, responsorially or directly, the chants between the readings—the psalm or other biblical canticle, the gradual and *Alleluia*, or other chant. The psalmist may, as occasion requires, intone the *Alleluia* and verse.[94]

For carrying out the function of psalmist it is advantageous to have in each ecclesial community laypeople with the ability to sing and read with correct diction. The points made about the formation of readers apply to cantors as well.

57. The commentator also fulfills a genuine liturgical ministry, which consists in presenting to the congregation of the faithful, from a suitable place, relevant explanations and comments that are clear, of marked sobriety, meticulously prepared, and as a rule written out and approved beforehand by the celebrant.[95]

SECOND PART
THE STRUCTURE OF THE ORDER OF READINGS FOR MASS

CHAPTER IV
THE GENERAL ARRANGEMENT OF READINGS FOR MASS

1. The Pastoral Purpose of the Order of Readings for Mass

58. On the basis of the intention of the Second Vatican Council, the Order of Readings provided by the Lectionary of the Roman Missal has been composed above all for a pastoral purpose. To achieve this aim, not only the principles underlying this new Order of Readings but also the lists of texts that it provides have been discussed and revised over and over again, with the cooperation of a great many experts in exegetical, liturgical, catechetical, and pastoral studies from all parts of the world. The Order of Readings is the fruit of this combined effort.

The prolonged use of this Order of Readings to proclaim and explain Sacred Scripture in the Eucharistic celebration will, it is hoped, prove to be an effective step toward achieving the objective stated repeatedly by the Second Vatican Council.[96]

59.   The decision on revising the Lectionary for Mass was to draw up and edit a single, rich, and full Order of Readings that would be in complete accord with the intent and prescriptions of the Second Vatican Council.[97] At the same time, however, the Order was meant to be of a kind that would meet the requirements and usages of particular Churches and celebrating congregations. For this reason, those responsible for the revision took pains to safeguard the liturgical tradition of the Roman Rite, but valued highly the merits of all the systems of selecting, arranging, and using the biblical readings in other liturgical families and in certain particular Churches. The revisers made use of those elements that experience has confirmed, but with an effort to avoid certain shortcomings found in the preceding form of the tradition.

60.   The present Order of Readings for Mass, then, is an arrangement of biblical readings that provides the faithful with a knowledge of the whole of God's word, in a pattern suited to the purpose. Throughout the liturgical year, but above all during the seasons of Easter, Lent, and Advent, the choice and sequence of readings are aimed at giving Christ's faithful an ever-deepening perception of the faith they profess and of the history of salvation.[98] Accordingly, the Order of Readings corresponds to the requirements and interests of the Christian people.

61.   The celebration of the Liturgy is not in itself simply a form of catechesis, but it does contain an element of teaching. The Lectionary of the Roman Missal brings this out[99] and therefore deserves to be regarded as a pedagogical resource aiding catechesis.

This is so because the Order of Readings for Mass aptly presents from Sacred Scripture the principal deeds and words belonging to the history of salvation. As its many phases and events are recalled in the liturgy of the word, it will become clear to the faithful that the history of salvation is continued here and now in the representation of Christ's paschal mystery celebrated through the Eucharist.

62.   The pastoral advantage of having in the Roman Rite a single Order of Readings for the Lectionary is obvious on other grounds. All the faithful, particularly those who for various reasons do not always take part in Mass with the same assembly, will everywhere be able to hear the same readings on any given day or in any liturgical season and to meditate on the application of these readings to their own concrete circumstances. This is the case even in places that have no priest and where a deacon or someone else deputed by the bishop conducts a celebration of the word of God.[100]

63.   Pastors may wish to respond specifically from the word of God to the concerns of their own congregations. Although they must be mindful that they are above all to be heralds of the entire mystery of Christ and of the Gospel, they may rightfully use the options provided in the Order of Readings for Mass. This applies particularly to the celebration of a ritual or votive Mass, a Mass in honor of the Saints, or one of the Masses for various needs and occasions. With due regard for the general norms, special faculties are granted concerning the readings in Masses celebrated for particular groups.[101]

64. To achieve the purpose of the Order of Readings for Mass, the parts have been selected and arranged in such a way as to take into account the sequence of the liturgical seasons and the hermeneutical principles whose understanding and definition have been facilitated by modern biblical research.

It was judged helpful to state here the principles guiding the composition of the Order of Readings for Mass.

A) THE CHOICE OF TEXTS

65. The course of readings in the Proper of Seasons is arranged as follows. Sundays and festive days present the more important biblical passages. In this way the more significant parts of God's revealed word can be read to the assembled faithful within an appropriate period of time. Weekdays present a second series of texts from Sacred Scripture and in a sense these complement the message of salvation explained on festive days. But neither series in these main parts of the Order of Readings—the series for Sundays and festive days and that for weekdays—is dependent on the other. The Order of Readings for Sundays and festive days extends over three years; for weekdays, over two. Thus each runs its course independently of the other.

The sequence of readings in other parts of the Order of Readings is governed by its own rules. This applies to the series of readings for celebrations of the Saints, ritual Masses, Masses for various needs and occasions, votive Masses, or Masses for the dead.

B) THE ARRANGEMENT OF THE READINGS FOR SUNDAYS AND FESTIVE DAYS

66. The following are features proper to the readings for Sundays and festive days:

1. Each Mass has three readings: the first from the Old Testament, the second from an Apostle (that is, either from a Letter or from the Book of Revelation, depending on the season), and the third from the Gospels. This arrangement brings out the unity of the Old and New Testaments and of the history of salvation, in which Christ is the central figure, commemorated in his paschal mystery.

2. A more varied and richer reading of Sacred Scripture on Sundays and festive days results from the three-year cycle provided for these days, in that the same texts are read only every fourth year.[102]

3. The principles governing the Order of Reading for Sundays and festive days are called the principles of "harmony" and of "semicontinuous reading." One or the other applies according to the different seasons of the year and the distinctive character of the particular liturgical season.

67. The best instance of harmony between the Old and New Testament readings occurs when it is one that Scripture itself suggests. This is the case when the doctrine and events recounted in texts of the New Testament bear a more or less explicit relationship to the doctrine and events of the Old Testament. The

present Order of Readings selects Old Testament texts mainly because of their correlation with New Testament texts read in the same Mass, and particularly with the Gospel text.

Harmony of another kind exists between texts of the readings for each Mass during Advent, Lent, and Easter, the seasons that have a distinctive importance or character.

In contrast, the Sundays in Ordinary Time do not have a distinctive character. Thus the text of both the apostolic and Gospel readings are arranged in order of semicontinuous reading, whereas the Old Testament reading is harmonized with the Gospel.

68.   The decision was made not to extend to Sundays the arrangement suited to the liturgical seasons mentioned, that is, not to have an organic harmony of themes devised with a view to facilitating homiletic instruction. Such an arrangement would be in conflict with the genuine conception of liturgical celebration, which is always the celebration of the mystery of Christ and which by its own tradition makes use of the word of God not only at the prompting of logical or extrinsic concerns but spurred by the desire to proclaim the Gospel and to lead those who believe to the fullness of truth.

C) THE ARRANGEMENT OF THE READINGS FOR WEEKDAYS

69.   The weekday readings have been arranged in the following way.

1. Each Mass has two readings: the first is from the Old Testament or from an Apostle (that is, either from a Letter or from the Book of Revelation), and during the Easter season from the Acts of the Apostles; the second, from the Gospels.

2. The yearly cycle for Lent has its own principles of arrangement, which take into account the baptismal and penitential character of this season.

3. The cycle for the weekdays of Advent, the Christmas season, and the Easter season is also yearly and the readings thus remain the same each year.

4. For the thirty-four weeks of Ordinary Time, the weekday Gospel readings are arranged in a single cycle, repeated each year. But the first reading is arranged in a two-year cycle and is thus read every other year. Year I is used during odd-numbered years; Year II, during even-numbered years.

Like the Order for Sundays and festive days, then, the weekday Order of Readings is governed by similar application of the principles of harmony and of semicontinuous reading, especially in the case of seasons with their own distinctive character.

D) THE READINGS FOR CELEBRATIONS OF THE SAINTS

70.   Two series of readings are provided for celebrations of the Saints.

1. The Proper of Saints provides the first series, for solemnities, feasts, or memorials and particularly when there are proper texts for one or other

such celebration. Sometimes in the Proper, however, there is a reference to the most appropriate among the texts in the Commons as the one to be given preference.

2. The Commons of Saints provide the second, more extensive group of readings. There are, first, appropriate texts for the different classes of Saints (martyrs, pastors, virgins, etc.), then numerous texts that deal with holiness in general. These may be freely chosen whenever the Commons are indicated as the source for the choice of readings.

71. As to their sequence, all the texts in this part of the Order of Readings appear in the order in which they are to be read at Mass. Thus the Old Testament texts are first, then the texts from the Apostles, followed by the psalms and verses between the readings, and finally the texts from the Gospels. The rationale of this arrangement is that, unless otherwise noted, the celebrant may choose at will from such texts, in view of the pastoral needs of the congregation taking part in the celebration.

E) READINGS FOR RITUAL MASSES, MASSES FOR VARIOUS NEEDS AND OCCASIONS, VOTIVE MASSES, AND MASSES FOR THE DEAD

72. For ritual Masses, Masses for various needs and occasions, votive Masses, and Masses for the dead, the texts for the readings are arranged as just described, that is, numerous texts are grouped together in the order of their use, as in the Commons of Saints.

F) THE MAIN CRITERIA APPLIED IN CHOOSING AND ARRANGING THE READINGS

73. In addition to the guiding principles already given for the arrangement of readings in the individual parts of the Order of Readings, others of a more general nature follow.

1) The Reservation of Some Books to Particular Liturgical Seasons

74. In this Order of Readings, some biblical books are set aside for particular liturgical seasons on the basis both of the intrinsic importance of subject matter and of liturgical tradition. For example, the Western (Ambrosian and Hispanic) and Eastern tradition of reading the Acts of the Apostles during the Easter season is maintained. This usage results in a clear presentation of how the Church's entire life derives its beginning from the paschal mystery. The tradition of both West and East is also retained, namely the reading of the Gospel of John in the latter weeks of Lent and in the Easter season.

Tradition assigns the reading of Isaiah, especially the first part, to Advent. Some texts of this book, however, are read during the Christmas season, to which the First Letter of John is also assigned.

2) The Length of the Texts

75. A *middle way* is followed in regard to the length of texts. A distinction has been made between narratives, which require reading a fairly long passage

but which usually hold the attention of the faithful, and texts that should not be lengthy because of the profundity of their doctrine.

In the case of certain rather lengthy texts, longer and shorter versions are provided to suit different situations. The editing of the shorter version has been carried out with great caution.

3) Difficult Texts

76. In readings for Sundays and solemnities, texts that present real difficulties are avoided for pastoral reasons. The difficulties may be objective, in that the texts themselves raise profound literary, critical, or exegetical problems; or the difficulties may lie, at least to a certain extent, in the ability of the faithful to understand the texts. But there could be no justification for concealing from the faithful the spiritual riches of certain texts on the grounds of difficulty if the problem arises from the inadequacy either of the religious education that every Christian should have or of the biblical formation that every pastor of souls should have. Often a difficult reading is clarified by its correlation with another in the same Mass.

4) The Omission of Certain Verses

77. The omission of verses in readings from Scripture has at times been the tradition of many liturgies, including the Roman liturgy. Admittedly such omissions may not be made lightly, for fear of distorting the meaning of the text or the intent and style of Scripture. Yet on pastoral grounds it was decided to continue the traditional practice in the present Order of Readings, but at the same time to ensure that the essential meaning of the text remained intact. One reason for the decision is that otherwise some texts would have been unduly long. It would also have been necessary to omit completely certain readings of high spiritual value for the faithful because those readings include some verse that is pastorally less useful or that involves truly difficult questions.

3. Principles to be Followed in the Use of the Order of Readings

A) THE FREEDOM OF CHOICE REGARDING SOME TEXTS

78. The Order of Readings sometimes leaves it to the celebrant to choose between alternative texts or to choose one from the several listed together for the same reading. The option seldom exists on Sundays, solemnities, or feasts, in order not to obscure the character proper to the particular liturgical season or needlessly interrupt the semicontinuous reading of some biblical book. On the other hand, the option is given readily in celebrations of the Saints, in ritual Masses, Masses for various needs and occasions, votive Masses, and Masses for the dead.

These options, together with those indicated in the General Instruction of the Roman Missal and the *Ordo cantus Missae*,[103] have a pastoral purpose. In arranging the liturgy of the word, then, the priest should "consider the general spiritual good of the congregation rather than his personal outlook. He should be mindful that the choice of texts is to be made in harmony with the ministers and others who have any role in the celebration and should listen to the opinions of the faithful in what concerns them more directly."[104]

1) The Two Readings before the Gospel

79.   In Masses to which three readings are assigned, all three are to be used. If, however, for pastoral reasons the Conference of Bishops has given permission for two readings only to be used,[105] the choice between the two first readings is to be made in such a way as to safeguard the Church's intent to instruct the faithful more completely in the mystery of salvation. Thus, unless the contrary is indicated in the text of the Lectionary, the reading to be chosen as the first reading is the one that is more closely in harmony with the Gospel, or, in accord with the intent just mentioned, the one that is more helpful toward a coherent catechesis over an extended period, or that preserves the semicontinuous reading of some biblical book.[106]

2) The Longer and Shorter Forms of Texts

80.   A pastoral criterion must also guide the choice between the longer and shorter forms of the same text. The main consideration must be the capacity of the hearers to listen profitably either to the longer or to the shorter reading; or to listen to a more complete text that will be explained through the homily.

3) When Two Texts Are Provided

81.   When a choice is allowed between alternative texts, whether they are fixed or optional, the first consideration must be the best interest of those taking part. It may be a matter of using the easier texts or the one more relevant to the assembled congregation or, as pastoral advantage may suggest, of repeating or replacing a text that is assigned as proper to one celebration and optional to another.

The issue may arise when it is feared that some text will create difficulties for a particular congregation or when the same text would have to be repeated within a few days, as on a Sunday and on a day during the week following.

4) The Weekday Readings

82.   The arrangement of weekday readings provides texts for every day of the week throughout the year. In most cases, therefore, these readings are to be used on their assigned days, unless a solemnity, a feast, or else a memorial with proper readings occurs.[107]

In using the Order of Readings for weekdays attention must be paid to whether one reading or another from the same biblical book will have to be omitted because of some celebration occurring during the week. With the arrangement of readings for the entire week in mind, the priest in that case arranges to omit the less significant passages or combines in the most appropriate manner them with other readings, if they contribute to an integral view of a particular theme.

5) The Celebrations of the Saints

83.   When they exist, proper readings are given for celebrations of the Saints, that is, biblical passages about the Saint or the mystery that the Mass is celebrating. Even in the case of a memorial these readings must take the place of

the weekday readings for the same day. This Order of Readings makes explicit note of every case of proper readings on a memorial.

In some cases there are accommodated readings, those, namely, that bring out some particular aspect of a Saint's spiritual life or work. Use of such readings does not seem binding, except for compelling pastoral reasons. For the most part references are given to readings in the Commons in order to facilitate choice. But these are merely suggestions: in place of an accommodated reading or the particular reading proposed from a Common, any other reading from the Commons referred to may be selected.

The first concern of a priest celebrating with a congregation is the spiritual benefit of the faithful and he will be careful not to impose his personal preference on them. Above all he will make sure not to omit too often or without sufficient cause the readings assigned for each day in the weekday Lectionary: the Church's desire is that a more lavish table of the word of God be spread before the faithful.[108]

There are also common readings, that is, those placed in the Commons either for some determined class of Saints (martyrs, virgins, pastors) or for the Saints in general. Because in these cases several texts are listed for the same reading, it will be up to the priest to choose the one best suited to those listening.

In all celebrations of Saints the readings may be taken not only from the Commons to which the references are given in each case, but also from the Common of Men and Women Saints, whenever there is special reason for doing so.

84.   For celebrations of the Saints the following should be observed:

1. On solemnities and feasts the readings must be those that are given in the Proper or in the Commons. For solemnities and feasts of the General Roman Calendar proper readings are always assigned.

2. On solemnities inscribed in particular calendars, three readings are to be assigned, unless the Conference of Bishops has decreed that there are to be only two readings.[109] The first reading is from the Old Testament (but during the Easter season, from the Acts of the Apostles or the Book of Revelation); the second, from an Apostle; the third, from the Gospels.

3. On feasts and memorials, which have only two readings, the first reading can be chosen from either the Old Testament or from an Apostle; the second is from the Gospels. Following the Church's traditional practice, however, the first reading during the Easter season is to be taken from an Apostle, the second, as far as possible, from the Gospel of John.

6) Other Parts of the Order of Readings

85.   In the Order of Readings for ritual Masses the references given are to the texts already published for the individual rites. This obviously does not include the texts belonging to celebrations that must not be integrated with Mass.[110]

86.   The Order of Readings for Masses for various needs and occasions, votive Masses, and Masses for the dead provides many texts that can be of assistance in adapting such celebrations to the situation, circumstances, and concerns of the particular groups taking part.[111]

87.   In ritual Masses, Masses for various needs and occasions, votive Masses, and Masses for the dead, since many texts are given for the same reading, the choice of readings follows the criteria already indicated for the choice of readings from the Common of Saints.

88.   On a day when some ritual Mass is not permitted and when the norms in the individual rite allow the choice of one reading from those provided for ritual Masses, the general spiritual welfare of the participants must be considered.[112]

B) THE RESPONSORIAL PSALM AND THE ACCLAMATION BEFORE THE GOSPEL READING

89.   Among the chants between the readings, the psalm which follows the first reading is of great importance. As a rule the psalm to be used is the one assigned to the reading. But in the case of readings for the Common of Saints, ritual Masses, Masses for various needs and occasions, votive Masses, and Masses for the dead the choice is left up to the priest celebrating. He will base his choice on the principle of the pastoral benefit of those present.

But to make it easier for the people to join in the response to the psalm, the Order of Readings lists certain other texts of psalms and responses that have been chosen according to the various seasons or classes of Saints. Whenever the psalm is sung, these texts may replace the text corresponding to the reading.[113]

90.   The chant between the second reading and the Gospel is either specified in each Mass and correlated with the Gospel or else it is left as a choice to be made from those in the series given for a liturgical season or one of the Commons.

91.   During Lent one of the acclamations from those given in the Order of Readings may be used, depending on the occasion.[114] This acclamation precedes and follows the verse before the Gospel.

CHAPTER V
DESCRIPTION OF THE ORDER OF READINGS

92.   It seems useful to provide here a brief description of the Order of Readings, at least for the principal celebrations and the different seasons of the liturgical year. With these in mind, readings were selected on the basis of the rules already stated. This description is meant to assist pastors of souls to understand the structure of the Order of Readings, so that their use of it will become more perceptive and the Order of Readings a source of good for Christ's faithful.

I. Advent

A) THE SUNDAYS

93.   Each Gospel reading has a distinctive theme: the Lord's coming at the end of time (First Sunday of Advent), John the Baptist (Second and Third Sunday), and the events that prepared immediately for the Lord's birth (Fourth Sunday).

The Old Testament readings are prophecies about the Messiah and the Messianic age, especially from the Book of Isaiah.

The readings from an Apostle contain exhortations and proclamations, in keeping with the different themes of Advent.

B) THE WEEKDAYS

94.   There are two series of readings: one to be used from the beginning of Advent until 16 December; the other from 17 to 24 December.

In the first part of Advent there are readings from the Book of Isaiah, distributed in accord with the sequence of the book itself and including the more important texts that are also read on the Sundays. For the choice of the weekday Gospel the first reading has been taken into consideration.

On Thursday of the second week the readings from the Gospel concerning John the Baptist begin. The first reading is either a continuation of Isaiah or a text chosen in view of the Gospel.

In the last week before Christmas the events that immediately prepared for the Lord's birth are presented from the Gospel of Matthew (chapter 1) and Luke (chapter 1). The texts in the first reading, chosen in view of the Gospel reading, are from different Old Testament books and include important Messianic prophecies.

2. The Christmas Season

A) THE SOLEMNITIES, FEASTS, AND SUNDAYS

95.   For the vigil and the three Masses of Christmas both the prophetic readings and the others have been chosen from the Roman tradition.

The Gospel on the Sunday within the Octave of Christmas, Feast of the Holy Family, is about Jesus' childhood and the other readings are about the virtues of family life.

On the Octave Day of Christmas, Solemnity of the Blessed Virgin Mary, the Mother of God, the readings are about the Virgin Mother of God and the giving of the holy Name of Jesus.

On the second Sunday after Christmas, the readings are about the mystery of the Incarnation.

On the Epiphany of the Lord, the Old Testament reading and the Gospel continue the Roman tradition; the text for the reading from the Letters of the Apostles is about the calling of the nations to salvation.

On the Feast of the Baptism of the Lord, the texts chosen are about this mystery.

B) THE WEEKDAYS

96.   From 29 December on, there is a continuous reading of the whole of the First Letter of John, which actually begins earlier, on 27 December, the Feast of St. John the Evangelist, and on 28 December, the Feast of the Holy Innocents. The Gospels relate manifestations of the Lord: events of Jesus' childhood from the Gospel of Luke (29–30 December); passages from the first chapter of the Gospel of John (31 December–5 January); other manifestations of the Lord from the four Gospels (7–12 January).

3. Lent

A) THE SUNDAYS

97.   The Gospel readings are arranged as follows:

The first and second Sundays maintain the accounts of the Temptation and Transfiguration of the Lord, with readings, however, from all three Synoptics.

On the next three Sundays, the Gospels about the Samaritan woman, the man born blind, and the raising of Lazarus have been restored in Year A. Because these Gospels are of major importance in regard to Christian initiation, they may also be read in Year B and Year C, especially in places where there are catechumens.

Other texts, however, are provided for Year B and Year C: for Year B, a text from John about Christ's coming glorification through his Cross and Resurrection and for Year C, a text from Luke about conversion.

On Palm Sunday of the Lord's Passion the texts for the procession are selections from the Synoptic Gospels concerning the Lord's solemn entry into Jerusalem. For the Mass the reading is the account of the Lord's Passion.

The Old Testament readings are about the history of salvation, which is one of the themes proper to the catechesis of Lent. The series of texts for each Year presents the main elements of salvation history from its beginning until the promise of the New Covenant.

The readings from the Letters of the Apostles have been selected to fit the Gospel and the Old Testament readings and, to the extent possible, to provide a connection between them.

B) THE WEEKDAYS

98.   The readings from the Gospels and the Old Testament were selected because they are related to each other. They treat various themes of the Lenten catechesis

that are suited to the spiritual significance of this season. Beginning with Monday of the Fourth week of Lent, there is a semicontinuous reading of the Gospel of John, made up of texts that correspond more closely to the themes proper to Lent.

Because the readings about the Samaritan woman, the man born blind, and the raising of Lazarus are now assigned to Sundays, but only for Year A (in Year B and Year C they are optional), provision has been made for their use on weekdays. Thus at the beginning of the Third, Fourth, and Fifth Weeks of Lent optional Masses with these texts for the Gospel have been inserted and may be used in place of the readings of the day on any weekday of the respective week.

In the first days of Holy Week the readings are about the mystery of Christ's passion. For the Chrism Mass the readings bring out both Christ's Messianic mission and its continuation in the Church by means of the sacraments.

4. The Sacred Triduum and the Easter Season

A) THE SACRED EASTER TRIDUUM

99.   On Holy Thursday at the evening Mass the remembrance of the meal preceding the Exodus casts its own special light because of the Christ's example in washing the feet of his disciples and Paul's account of the institution of the Christian Passover in the Eucharist.

On Good Friday the liturgical service has as its center John's narrative of the Passion of he who was proclaimed in Isaiah as the Servant of the Lord and who became the one High Priest by offering himself to the Father.

At the Vigil on the holy night of Easter there are seven Old Testament readings which recall the wonderful works of God in the history of salvation. There are two New Testament readings, the announcement of the Resurrection according to one of the Synoptic Gospels and a reading from St. Paul on Christian baptism as the sacrament of Christ's Resurrection.

The Gospel reading for the Mass on Easter day is from John on the finding of the empty tomb. There is also, however, the option to use the Gospel texts from the Easter Vigil or, when there is an evening Mass on Easter Sunday, to use the account in Luke of the Lord's appearance to the disciples on the road to Emmaus. The first reading is from the Acts of the Apostles, which throughout the Easter season replaces the Old Testament reading. The reading from the Apostle Paul concerns the living out of the paschal mystery in the Church.

B) THE SUNDAYS

100. The Gospel readings for the first three Sundays recount the appearances of the risen Christ. The readings about the Good Shepherd are assigned to the Fourth Sunday. On the Fifth, Sixth, and Seventh Sundays, there are excerpts from the Lord's discourse and prayer at the end of the Last Supper.

The first reading is from the Acts of the Apostles, in a three-year cycle of parallel and progressive selections: material is presented on the life of the early Church, its witness, and its growth.

For the reading from the Apostles, the First Letter of Peter is in Year A, the First Letter of John in Year B, the Book of Revelation in Year C. These are the texts that seem to fit in especially well with the spirit of joyous faith and sure hope proper to this season.

C) THE WEEKDAYS

101. As on the Sundays, the first reading is a semicontinuous reading from the Acts of the Apostles. The Gospel readings during the Easter octave are accounts of the Lord's appearances. After that there is a semicontinuous reading of the Gospel of John, but with texts that have a paschal character, in order to complete the reading from John during Lent. This paschal reading is made up in large part of the Lord's discourse and prayer at the end of the Last Supper.

D) THE SOLEMNITIES OF THE ASCENSION AND OF PENTECOST

102. For the first reading the Solemnity of the Ascension retains the account of the Ascension according to the Acts of the Apostles. This text is complemented by the second reading from the Apostle on Christ in exaltation at the right hand of the Father. For the Gospel reading, each of the three Years has its own text in accord with the differences in the Synoptic Gospels.

In the evening Mass celebrated on the Vigil of Pentecost four Old Testament texts are provided; any one of them may be used, in order to bring out the many aspects of Pentecost. The reading from the Apostles shows the actual working of the Holy Spirit in the Church. The Gospel reading recalls the promise of the Spirit made by Christ before his own glorification.

For the Mass on Pentecost day itself, in accord with received usage, the account in the Acts of the Apostles of the great occurrence on Pentecost day is taken as the first reading. The texts from the Apostle Paul bring out the effect of the action of the Spirit in the life of the Church. The Gospel reading is a remembrance of Jesus bestowing his Spirit on the disciples on the evening of Easter day; other optional texts describe the action of the Spirit on the disciples and on the Church.

5. Ordinary Time

A) THE ARRANGEMENT AND CHOICE OF TEXTS

103. Ordinary Time begins on the Monday after the Sunday following 6 January; it lasts until the Tuesday before Lent inclusive. It begins again on the Monday after Pentecost Sunday and finishes before evening prayer I of the First Sunday of Advent.

The Order of Readings provides readings for thirty-four Sundays and the weeks following them. In some years, however, there are only thirty-three weeks of Ordinary Time. Further, some Sundays either belong to another season (the Sunday on which the Feast of the Baptism of the Lord falls and Pentecost Sunday) or else are impeded by a solemnity that coincides with that Sunday (e.g. The Most Holy Trinity or Christ the King).

104. For the correct arrangement in the use of the readings for Ordinary Time, the following are to be respected.

1. The Sunday on which the Feast of the Baptism of the Lord falls replaces the First Sunday in Ordinary Time. Therefore the readings of the First Week in Ordinary Time begin on the Monday after the Sunday following 6 January. When the Feast of the Baptism of the Lord is celebrated on Monday because the Epiphany has been celebrated on the Sunday, the readings of the First Week begin on Tuesday.

2. The Sunday following the Feast of the Baptism of the Lord is the Second Sunday of Ordinary Time. The remaining Sundays are numbered consecutively up to the Sunday preceding the beginning of Lent. The readings for the week in which Ash Wednesday falls are interrupted after the Tuesday readings.

3. For the resumption of the readings of Ordinary Time after Pentecost Sunday:

—when there are thirty-four Sundays in Ordinary Time, the week to be used is the one that immediately follows the last week used before Lent;[115]

—when there are thirty-three Sundays in Ordinary Time, the first week that would have been used after Pentecost is omitted, in order to reserve for the end of the year the eschatological texts that are assigned to the last two weeks.[116]

B) THE SUNDAY READINGS

1) The Gospel Readings

105. On the Second Sunday in Ordinary Time the Gospel continues to center on the manifestation of the Lord, which is celebrated on the Solemnity of the Epiphany, through the traditional passage about the wedding feast at Cana and two other passages from the Gospel of John.

Beginning with the Third Sunday, there is a semicontinuous reading of the Synoptic Gospels. This reading is arranged in such a way that as the Lord's life and preaching unfold the doctrine proper to each of these Gospels is presented.

This distribution also provides a certain coordination between the meaning of each Gospel and the progress of the liturgical year. Thus after Epiphany the readings are on the beginning of the Lord's preaching and they fit in well with Christ's baptism and the first events in which he manifests himself. The liturgical year leads quite naturally to a conclusion in the eschatological theme proper to the last Sundays, since the chapters of the Synoptics that precede the account of the Passion treat this eschatological theme rather extensively.

After the Sixteenth Sunday in Year B, five readings are incorporated from John chapter 6 (the discourse on the bread of life). This is the natural place for these readings because the multiplication of the loaves from the Gospel of John takes the place of the same account in Mark. In the semicontinuous reading of Luke for Year C, the introduction of this Gospel has been prefixed to the first text (that is, on the Third Sunday). This passage expresses the author's intention very beautifully and there seemed to be no better place for it.

2) The Old Testament Readings

106. These readings have been chosen to correspond to the Gospel passages in order to avoid an excessive diversity between the readings of different Masses and above all to bring out the unity between the Old and the New Testament. The connection between the readings of the same Mass is shown by a precise choice of the readings prefixed to the individual readings.

To the degree possible, the readings were chosen in such a way that they would be short and easy to grasp. But care has been taken to ensure that many Old Testament texts of major significance would be read on Sundays. Such readings are distributed not according to a logical order but on the basis of what the Gospel reading requires. Still, the treasury of the word of God will be opened up in such a way that nearly all the principal pages of the Old Testament will become familiar to those taking part in the Mass on Sundays.

3) The Readings from the Apostles

107. There is a semicontinuous reading of the Letters of Paul and James (the Letters of Peter and John being read during the Easter and Christmas seasons).

Because it is quite long and deals with such diverse issues, the First Letter to the Corinthians has been spread over the three years of the cycle at the beginning of Ordinary Time. It also was thought best to divide the Letter to the Hebrews into two parts; the first part is read in Year B and the second in Year C.

Only readings that are short and readily grasped by the people have been chosen.

Table II at the end of this Introduction[117] indicates the distribution of Letters of the Apostles over the three-year cycle of the Sundays of Ordinary Time.

C) THE READINGS FOR SOLEMNITIES OF THE LORD DURING ORDINARY TIME

108. On the solemnities of Holy Trinity, Corpus Christi, and the Sacred Heart, the texts chosen correspond to the principal themes of these celebrations.

The readings of the Thirty-Fourth and last Sunday in Ordinary Time celebrate Christ the universal King. He was prefigured by David and proclaimed as king amid the humiliations of his Passion and Cross; he reigns in the Church and will come again at the end of time.

D) THE WEEKDAY READINGS

109. The *Gospels* are so arranged that Mark is read first (First to Ninth Week), then Matthew (Tenth to Twenty- First Week), then Luke (Twenty-Second to

Thirty-Fourth Week). Mark chapters 1–12 are read in their entirety, with the exception only of the two passages of Mark chapter 6 that are read on weekdays in other seasons. From Matthew and Luke the readings comprise all the material not contained in Mark. All the passages that either are distinctively presented in each Gospel or are needed for a proper understanding of its progression are read two or three times. Jesus' eschatological discourse as contained in its entirety in Luke is read at the end of the liturgical year.

110. The *First reading* is taken in periods of several weeks at a time first from one then from the other Testament; the number of weeks depends on the length of the biblical books read.

Rather large sections are read from the New Testament books in order to give the substance, as it were, of each of the Letters.

From the Old Testament there is room only for select passages that, as far as possible, bring out the character of the individual books. The historical texts have been chosen in such a way as to provide an overall view of the history of salvation before the Incarnation of the Lord. But lengthy narratives could hardly be presented; sometimes verses have been selected that make for a reading of moderate length. In addition, the religious significance of the historical events is sometimes brought out by means of certain texts from the wisdom books that are placed as prologues or conclusions to a series of historical readings.

Nearly all the Old Testament books have found a place in the Order of Readings for weekdays in the Proper of Seasons. The only omissions are the shortest of the prophetic books (Obadiah and Zephaniah) and a poetic book (the Song of Songs). Of those narratives of edification requiring a lengthy reading if they are to be understood, Tobit and Ruth are included, but the others (Esther and Judith) are omitted. Texts from these latter two books are assigned, however, to Sundays and weekdays at other times of the year.)

Table III at the end of this Introduction[118] lists the way the books of the Old and the New Testament are distributed over the weekdays in Ordinary Time in the course of two years.

At the end of the liturgical year the readings are from the books that correspond to the eschatological character of this period, Daniel and the Book of Revelation.

CHAPTER VI
ADAPTATIONS, TRANSLATIONS AND FORMAT
OF THE ORDER OF READINGS

1. Adaptations and Translations

111. In the liturgical assembly the word of God must always be read either from the Latin texts prepared by the Holy See or from vernacular translations approved for liturgical use by the Conferences of Bishops, according to existing norms.[119]

112. The Lectionary for Mass must be translated integrally in all its parts, including the Introduction. If the Conference of Bishops has judged it necessary and useful to add certain adaptations, these are to be incorporated after their confirmation by the Holy See.[120]

113. The size of the Lectionary will necessitate editions in more than one volume; no particular division of the volumes is prescribed. But each volume is to contain the explanatory texts on the structure and purpose of the section it contains.

The ancient custom is recommended of having separate books, one for the Gospels and the other for the other readings for the Old and New Testament.

It may also be useful to publish separately a Sunday lectionary (which could also contain selected excerpts from the sanctoral cycle), and a weekday lectionary. A practical basis for dividing the Sunday lectionary is the three-year cycle, so that all the readings for each year are presented in sequence.

But there is freedom to adopt other arrangements that may be devised and seem to have pastoral advantages.

114. The texts for the chants are always to be adjoined to the readings, but separate books containing the chants alone are permitted. It is recommended that the texts be printed with divisions into stanzas.

115. Whenever a text consists of different parts, the typography must make this structure of the text clear. It is likewise recommended that even non-poetic texts be printed with division into sense lines to assist the proclamation of the readings.

116. Where there are longer and shorter forms of a text, they are to be printed separately, so that each can be read with ease. But if such a separation does not seem feasible, a way is to be found to ensure that each text can be proclaimed without mistakes.

117. In vernacular editions the texts are not to be printed without headings prefixed. If it seems advisable, an introductory note on the general meaning of the passage may be added to the heading. This note is to carry some distinctive symbol or is to be set in different type to show clearly that it is an optional text.[121]

118. It would be useful for every volume to have an index of the passages of the Bible, modeled on the biblical index of the present volume.[122] This will provide ready access to texts of the lectionaries for Mass that may be needed or helpful for specific occasions.

2. The Format of Individual Readings

For each reading the present volume carries the textual reference, the headings, and the *incipit*.

119. The text reference (that is, to chapter and verses) is always given according to the Neo-Vulgate edition for the psalms.[123] But a second reference according to the original text (Hebrew, Aramaic, or Greek) has been added wherever there is a discrepancy. Depending on the decrees of the competent Authorities for the individual languages, vernacular versions may retain the enumeration corresponding to the version of the Bible approved for liturgical use by the same Authorities. Exact references to chapter and verses, however, must always appear and may be given in the text or in the margin.

120. These references provide liturgical books with the basis of the "announcement" of the text that must be read in the celebration, but which is not printed in this volume. This "announcement" of the text will observe the following norms, but they may be altered by decree of the competent authorities on the basis of what is customary and useful for different places and languages.

121. The formula to be used is always: "A *reading* from the Book of . . . ," "A *reading* from the Letter of . . . ," or "A *reading* from the holy Gospel according to . . . ," and not: "The *beginning* of . . . ," (unless this seems advisable in particular instances) nor: "The *continuation* of. . . ."

122. The traditionally accepted titles for books are to be retained with the following exceptions.

1. Where there are two books with the same name, the title is to be: The first Book, The second Book (for example, of Kings, of Maccabees) or The first Letter, The second Letter.

2. The title more common in current usage is to be accepted for the following books:

—I and II Samuel instead of I and II Kings;

—I and II Kings instead of III and IV Kings;

—I and II Chronicles instead of I and II Paralipomenon;

—The Books of Ezra and Nehemiah instead of I and II Ezra.

3. The distinguishing titles for the wisdom books are: The Book of Job, Book of Proverbs, Book of Ecclesiastes, the Song of Songs, the Book of Wisdom, and the Book of Sirach.

4. For all the books that are included among the prophets in the Neo-Vulgate, the formula is to be: "A reading from the Book of the prophet Isaiah, or of the prophet Jeremiah or of the prophet Baruch" and: "A reading from the Book of the prophet Ezekiel, of the prophet Daniel, of the prophet Hosea, of the prophet Malachi," even in the case of books not regarded by some as being in actual fact prophetic.

5. The title is to be book of Lamentations and letter to the Hebrews, with no mention of Jeremiah or Paul.

B) THE HEADING

123. There is a *heading* prefixed to each text, chosen carefully (usually from the words of the text itself) in order to point out the main theme of the reading and, when necessary, to make the connection between the readings of the same Mass clear.

C) THE "INCIPIT"

124. In this Order of Readings the first element of the *incipit* is the customary introductory phrase: "At that time," "In those days," "Brothers and Sisters," "Beloved," "Dearly Beloved," "Dearest Brothers and Sisters," or "Thus says the Lord", "Thus says the Lord God." These words are not given when the text itself provides sufficient indication of the time or the persons involved or where such phrases would not fit in with the very nature of the text. For the individual languages, such phrases may be changed or omitted by decree of the competent Authorities.

After the first words of the *incipit* the Order of Readings gives the proper beginning of the reading, with some words deleted or supplied for intelligibility, inasmuch as the text is separated from its context. When the text for a reading is made up of non-consecutive verses and this has required changes in wording, these are appropriately indicated.

D) THE FINAL ACCLAMATION

125. In order to facilitate the congregation's acclamation, the words for the reader *The word of the Lord*, or similar words suited to local custom, are to be printed at the end of the reading for use by the reader.

TABLES

TABLE 1

Principal Celebrations of the Liturgical Year

YEAR	SUNDAY CYCLE	WEEKDAY CYCLE	ASH WEDNESDAY	EASTER	ASCENSION THURSDAY	PENTECOST
2000	B	II	8 March	23 April	1 June	11 June
2001	C	I	28 Feb.	15 April	24 May	3 June
2002	A	II	13 Feb.	31 March	9 May	19 May
2003	B	I	5 March	20 April	29 May	8 June
2004	C	II	25 Feb.	11 April	20 May	30 May
2005	A	I	9 Feb.	27 March	5 May	15 May
2006	B	II	1 March	16 April	25 May	4 June
2007	C	I	21 Feb.	8 April	17 May	27 May
2008	A	II	6 Feb.	23 March	1 May	11 May
2009	B	I	25 Feb.	12 April	21 May	31 May
2010	C	II	17 Feb.	4 April	13 May	23 May
2011	A	I	9 March	24 April	2 June	12 June
2012	B	II	22 Feb.	8 April	17 May	27 May
2013	C	I	13 Feb.	31 March	9 May	19 May
2014	A	II	5 March	20 April	29 May	8 June

WEEKS IN ORDINARY TIME				
BEFORE LENT		AFTER EASTER SEASON		
ENDING	IN WEEK NO.	BEGINNING	IN WEEK NO.	1ST SUNDAY OF ADVENT
7 March	9	12 June	10	3 Dec.
27 Feb.	7	1 June	9	2 Dec.
12 Feb.	5	20 May	7	1 Dec.
4 March	8	9 June	10	30 Nov.
24 Feb.	7	31 May	9	28 Dec.
8 Feb.	5	16 May	7	27 Nov.
28 Feb.	8	5 June	9	3 Dec.
20 Feb.	7	28 May	8	2 Dec.
5 Feb.	4	12 May	6	30 Nov.
24 Feb.	7	1 June	9	29 Nov.
16 Feb.	6	24 May	8	28 Nov.
8 March	9	13 June	11	27 Nov.
21 Feb.	7	28 May	8	2 Dec.
12 Feb.	5	20 May	7	1 Dec.
4 March	8	9 June	10	30 Nov.

TABLE II

Order of the Second Reading on the Sundays of Ordinary Time

SUNDAY	YEAR A	YEAR B	YEAR C
2	1 Corinthians 1–4	1 Corinthians 6–11	1 Corinthians 12–15
3	"	"	"
4	"	"	"
5	"	"	"
6	"	"	"
7	"	2 Corinthians	"
8	"	"	"
9	Romans	"	Galatians
10	"	"	"
11	"	"	"
12	"	"	"
13	"	"	"
14	"	"	"
15	"	Ephesians	Colossians
16	"	"	"
17	"	"	"
18	"	"	"
19	"	"	Hebrews 11–12
20	"	"	"
21	"	"	"
22	"	James	"
23	"	"	Philemon
24	"	"	1 Timothy
25	Philippians	"	"
26	"	"	"
27	"	Hebrews 2–10	2 Timothy
28	"	"	"
29	1 Thessalonians	"	"
30	"	"	"
31	"	"	2 Thessalonians
32	"	"	"
33	"	"	"

TABLE III

Order of the First Reading on the Weekdays of Ordinary Time

WEEK	YEAR I	YEAR II
1	Hebrews	1 Samuel
2	"	"
3	"	2 Samuel
4	"	2 Samuel; 1 Kings 1–16
5	Genesis 1–11	1 Kings 1–16
6	"	James
7	Sirach (Ecclesiasticus)	"
8	"	1 Peter; Jude
9	Tobit	2 Peter; 2 Timothy
10	2 Corinthians	1 Kings 17–22
11	"	1 Kings 17–22; 2 Kings
12	Genesis 12–50	2 Kings; Lamentations
13	"	Amos
14	"	Hosea; Isaiah
15	Exodus	Isaiah; Micah
16	"	Micah; Jeremiah
17	Exodus; Leviticus	Jeremiah
18	Numbers; Deuteronomy	Jeremiah; Nahum; Habakkuk
19	Deuteronomy; Joshua	Ezekiel
20	Judges; Ruth	"
21	1 Thessalonians	2 Thessalonians; 1 Corinthians
22	1 Thessalonians; Colossians	1 Corinthians
23	Colossians; 1 Timothy	"
24	1 Timothy	"
25	Ezra; Haggai; Zechariah	Proverbs, Qoheleth (Ecclesiastes)
26	Zechariah; Nehemiah; Baruch	Job
27	Jonah; Malachi; Joel	Galatians
28	Romans	Galatians; Ephesians
29	"	Ephesians
30	"	"
31	"	Ephesians; Philippians
32	Wisdom	Titus; Philemon; 2 and 3 John
33	1 and 2 Maccabees	Revelation
34	Daniel	"

NOTES

1. See SC, 7, 24, 33, 35, 48, 51, 52, 56; DV, 21, 25, 26; AG, 6; PO, 18.

2. See Paul VI, *motu proprio Ministeria quaedam*, V; apostolic exhortation *Evangelii nuntiandi* (EN), 28, 43, 47; apostolic exhortation *Marialis cultus* (MC), 12; John Paul II, apostolic constitution *Scripturarum thesaurus*, p. v–viii; apostolic exhortation *Catechesi tradendae* (CT), 23, 27, 48; letter *Dominicae cenae* (DC), 10.

3. See EM, 10; CDW, instruction *Liturgicae instaurationes* (LI) 2; GCD, 10–12, 25; GIRM, 9, 11, 24, 33, 60, 62, 316, 320; SDW, instruction *Inaestimabile donum*, (ID), 1, 2, 3.

4. See LMIn (1969), nos. 1–7; decree of promulgation: AAS 61 (1969) 548–549.

5. See SC, 35, 56; EN, 28, 47; DC, 10, 11, 12.

6. CDW, instruction *Liturgicae instaurationes* (LI) 2, for example, the terms, *word of God, sacred Scripture, Old* and *New Testament, reading(s) of the word of God, reading(s) from sacred scripture, celebration(s) of the word of God*, etc.

7. Thus the same text may be read or used for various reasons on various occasions and celebrations of the church's liturgical year. This is to be recalled in the homily, in pastoral exegesis, and in catechesis.

8. See Luke 4:16–21; 24:25–35 and 44–49.

9. Thus, for example, in the celebration of the Mass there is proclamation, reading, etc. (see GIRM, 21, 23, 95, 131, 146, 234, 235). There are also other celebrations of the word of God in the Roman Pontifical, Ritual and Liturgy of the Hours as restored by decree of the Second Vatican Council.

10. See SC, 7, 33; Mark 16:19–20; Matthew 28:20.

11. See SC, 7.

12. See Hebrews 4:12.

13. See Augustine, *Quaestionum in Heptateuchum*, book 2; DV, 16.

14. See Jerome, "If, as St. Paul says (1 Cor 1:24), Christ is the power of God and the wisdom of God, anyone who does not know the Scriptures does not know the power of God or his wisdom. For not to know the Scriptures is not to know Christ" (*Commentarii in Isaiam prophetam*, prologue); DV, 25.

15. See 2 Corinthians 1:20–22.

16. See SC, 10.

17. See 2 Thessalonians 3:1.

18. See RomM, opening prayers A, B and C in Mass for the Universal Church.

19. See RomM, opening prayer for the Twenty-first Sunday in Ordinary Time.

20. See DV, 8.

21. See John 14:15–17, 25–26; 15:26—16:15.

22. See PO, 4.

23. See SC, 51; PO, 18; DV, 21; AG, 6; GIRM, 8.

24. SC, 56.

25. GIRM, 33.

26. See LI, 2; DC, 10; ID, 1.

27. SC, 33.

28. See LMIn, 111.

29. See RomM, *Ordo cantus Missae* (ed. typ., 1972), Praenotanda, 4, 6, 10.

30. See GIRM, 11 .

31. See GIRM, 272; LMIn, 32–34.

32. See GIRM, 35, 95.

33. See GIRM, 82–84.

34. See GIRM, 94, 131.

35. See RomM, Order of Mass, "Liturgy of the Word: The Gospel."

36. See GIRM, 36.

37. Paul VI, apostolic constitution *Laudis canticum*, in *The Liturgy of the Hours*; see also SC, 24, 90; CR, instruction *Musicam Sacram* (MS) 39.

38. See LMIn, 89–90.

39. See GIRM, 18, 39.

40. See GIRM, 272; LMIn, 32ff.

41. See GIRM, 39 .

42. See GIRM, 37—39; RomM, *Ordo cantus Missae*, Praenotanda, 7–9; *Graduale Romanum* (1974), Praenotanda, 7, *Graduale Simple* (2d ed. typ., 1975); Praenotanda, 16.

43. See SC, 52; CR, instruction *Inter oecumenici* (IOe) 54.

44. See GIRM, 42.

45. See SC, 35, 2.

46. See SC, 6, 47.

47. See Paul VI, encyclical, *Mysterium fidei*, 3 Sept 1965; AG, 9; EN, 43.

48. See SC, 35, 2; GIRM, 41.

49. SC, 10.

50. See CT, 48.

51. See GIRM, 165.

52. See GIRM, 42; EM, 28.

53. See AP, 6g; DMC, 48.

54. See GIRM, 42, 338; *Rite of Marriage* (1969), 22, 42, 57 and *Rite of Funerals* (1969), 41, 64.

55. See GIRM, 97.

56. See GIRM, 139.

57. See GIRM, 23.

58. See GIRM, 43.

59. See GIRM, 45.

60. See GIRM, 99.

61. See GIRM, 47.

62. See LMIn, note 23.

63. See GIRM, 272.

64. See SC, 122.

65. See Roman Pontifical, *Ordination of Deacons, Priests and Bishops* (1968): of deacons, 24; of deacons and priests, 21; of a deacon, 24; of a bishop, 25; of bishops, 25.

66. See LMIn, 78–91.

67. See GIRM, 318–320; 324–325.

68. See GIRM, 313.

69. See GIRM, 42; ID, 3.

70. See GIRM, 11.

71. See GIRM, 68.

72. See GIRM, 33, 47.

73. PO, 4.

74. SC, 33.

75. See GIRM, 9.

76. See SC, 7.

77. See SC, 9.

78. See Romans 1:16.

79. See DV, 21.

80. Ibid.

81. See John 14:15–26; 15:26—16:4, 5–15.

82. See AG, 6, 15; DV, 26.

83. See SC, 24; GCD, 25.

84. See SC, 56; ID, 1.

85. See SC, 24, 35.

86. See GIRM, 34.

87. See GIRM, 96.

88. See GIRM, 47, 61, 132; ID 3.

89. GIRM, 66.

90. See MQ, no. V.

91. See ID, 2, 18; DMC, 22, 24, 27.

92. See GIRM, 47, 66, 151.

93. GIRM, 66.

94. See GIRM, 37a, 67.

95. See GIRM, 68.

96. See Paul VI, apostolic constitution, *Missale Romanum*.

97. See SC, 35, 51.

98. See Paul VI, apostolic constitution, *Missale Romanum*: "This is meant to provide a fuller exposition of the continuing process of the mystery of salvation as shown in the words of divine revelation."

99. See SC, 9, 33; IOe, 7; CT, 23.

100. See SC, 35,4; IOe, 37–38.

101. See AP, 6; DMC, 41–47; MC, 12.

102. Each of the years is designated by the letter A, B or C. The following is the procedure to determine which year is A, B, or C. The letter C designates a year whose number is divisible into three equal parts, as though the cycle had taken its beginning from the first year of the Christian era. Thus the year 1 would have been Year A; year 2, Year B; year 3, Year C (as would years 6, 9 and 12). [Thus, year 1998 was Year C; 1999, Year A; 2000, Year B; and 2001, Year C again.] And so forth. Obviously, each cycle runs in accord with the plan of the liturgical year, that is, it begins with the first

week of Advent, which falls in the preceding year of the civil calendar.

The years in each cycle [are] marked in a sense by the principal charadcteristic of the synoptic gospel (Matthew, Mark or Luke) used for the semicontinuous reading of Ordinary Time. Thus the first Year of the cycle is the Year for the reading of the Gospel of Matthew and is so named; the second and third Years are the Year of Mark and the Year of Luke.

103. See GIRM, 36–40.

104. GIRM, 313.

105. See GIRM, 318; ID, 1.

106. For example: in Lent the continuity of the Old Testament readings corresponds to the unfolding of the history of salvation; the Sundays in Ordinary Time provide the semicontinuous reading of one of the letters of the apostles. In these cases it is right that the pastor of souls choose one or other of the readings in a systematic way over a series of Sundays, so that he may establish a coherent plan for catechesis. It is not right to read indiscriminately on one day from the Old Testament, on another from the letter of an apostle, without any orderly plan for the texts that follow.

107. See GIRM, 319.

108. See GIRM, 316c; SC, 51.

109. See GIRM, 318.

110. See *Rite of Penance* (1974), introduction, no. 13.

111. See GIRM, 320.

112. See GIRM, 313.

113. See Lectionary for Mass, nos. 173–174.

114. See Lectionary for Mass, no. 223.

115. So, for example, when there are six weeks before Lent, the seventh week begins on the Monday after Pentecost. The solemnity of the Most Holy Trinity replaces the Sunday of Ordinary Time.

116. When there are, for example, five weeks before Lent, the Monday after Pentecost begins with the Seventh Week of Ordinary Time and the Sixth Week is omitted.

117. See LMIn, Table II.

118. See LMIn, Table III.

119. See Consilium, instruction *De Popularibus interpretationibus conficiendis*, 25 Jan 1969: Notitiae 5 (1969) 3–12; CDW, *Epistola ad Praesides Conferentiarum Episcoporum de linguis vulgaribus in S. Liturgiam inducendis:* Notitiae 12 (1976) 300–302.

120. See LI, 11; GIRM, 325.

121. See GIRM, 11, 29, 68a, 139.

122. See Lectionary for Mass, index of readings.

123. The references for the psalms follow the order of the *Liber Psalmorum*, Pontifical Commission for the Neo-Vulgate.

THE INTERPRETATION
OF THE BIBLE
IN THE CHURCH

PONTIFICAL BIBLICAL COMMISSION
1993

OVERVIEW OF *THE INTERPRETATION OF THE BIBLE IN THE CHURCH*

Ronald D. Witherup, SS

The Pontifical Biblical Commission's (PBC) document, *The Interpretation of the Bible in the Church* (IBC), was issued on April 15, 1993. It commemorated the centenary of Pope Leo XIII's encyclical letter *Providentissimus Deus* (November 18, 1893), and the fiftieth anniversary of Pope Pius XII's groundbreaking encyclical letter *Divino afflante spiritu* (September 30, 1943). Pope John Paul II officially promulgated the document on April 23, 1993, when he delivered an address to the PBC commending the Commission's work on biblical interpretation. The official text was issued in French and was published later that year in other major languages.

CONTENT

IBC contains four major sections, bracketed by a short introduction and conclusion:

Introduction

I. Methods and Approaches for Interpretation

II. Hermeneutical Questions

III. Characteristics of Catholic Interpretation

IV. Interpretation of the Bible in the Life of the Church

Conclusion

(Unlike many Roman documents, IBC did not originally have numbered articles or paragraphs for ease of reference. In the edition that follows, numbers were added for convenience. References in this *Overview* will be to these added numbers as well as to the document's outline-style section identifiers.)

CONTEXT AND PURPOSE

The introduction sets the context for the document and describes its purpose. The context is the use of scientific approaches to biblical study among Catholic exegetes—called the historical-critical method—and the complaints of "many members of the faithful" that this method "is deficient from the point of view of faith." The PBC sees itself responding to a perceived erosion of faith among Catholics allegedly brought about for two reasons: 1. the results of these traditional scientific methods, which concentrate on the history and sources of the scriptures, have made lay people uneasy about the historical foundations of the Bible, and 2. the new methods of contemporary biblical study, which explore such things as literary, sociological and anthropological aspects of the scriptures, are bewildering to lay people.

Consequently, the stated purpose of IBC is "to indicate the paths most appropriate for arriving at an interpretation of the Bible as faithful as possible to its character both human and divine" ([9]; Intro. B).

The lion's share of IBC explains the multiple methods of biblical study that are employed by exegetes, and evaluates them as to their strengths and weaknesses. Part I begins with a brief history of how the historical-critical method—the dominant method of biblical exegesis in the twentieth century—came into being. It also explains its principles and describes its application. The PBC commends the method for making the Bible more accessible in a fresh and invigorating way and for producing many biblical commentaries of great value. It also criticizes the tendency to limit interpretation to determining questions of historicity.

New methods of biblical study are considered next, utilizing the same format of description and evaluation. The PBC examines rhetorical, narrative and semiotic analyses, which are formal methods of biblical study, and also explains a variety of diverse approaches that have been developed in recent years. It subdivides these approaches according to three main categories:

1. approaches based on tradition (canonical criticism, Jewish interpretation, the history of a text's influence);

2. approaches that use human sciences (sociology, cultural anthropology, psychology);

3. contextual approaches (exegesis from the perspective of liberation theology and feminist criticism).

The PBC also analyzes the fundamentalist approach to the Bible, and its sharp criticisms indicate that this approach is incompatible with a Catholic perspective. One should note that the English title for this section ("Fundamentalist Interpretation") does not accurately render the French original ("*Lecture fondamentaliste*"), which refers to fundamentalist "reading" of scripture. Fundamentalism is less a method than it is a perspective on how to interpret the Bible.

This first major section of IBC is significant for three reasons, not the least of which is because it strongly commends the use of the historical-critical method of biblical interpretation. Those who complain that historical-critical study of the Bible endangers the faith or promotes skepticism will likely be disappointed in this PBC statement.

Another significant point is that the document attempts to be as complete and inclusive as possible. Virtually every major form of scientific biblical methodology is examined according to its positive and negative aspects.

A third significant observation is that, although the historical priority of the traditional scientific methods is acknowledged, the PBC emphasizes the need for multiple methods of biblical study:

No scientific method for the study of the Bible is fully adequate to comprehend the biblical texts in all their richness. For all its overall validity, the historical-critical method cannot claim to be totally sufficient in this respect. It necessarily has to leave aside many aspects of the writings which it studies. It is not surprising, then, that at the present time other methods and approaches are proposed which serve to explore more profoundly other aspects worthy of attention. ([33]; I.B)

Part II sets forth some hermeneutical questions essential for any serious study of the Bible. Since philosophers, in particular, have dealt with serious questions of interpretation, the document explains the complexities of hermeneutical theories, concentrating on the philosophical hermeneutical theories of Rudolf Bultmann, Hans Georg Gadamer and Paul Ricoeur. (A footnote acknowledges the different contribution of the theological hermeneutical approach of Gerhard Ebeling and Ernst Fuchs.) Perhaps the most difficult hermeneutical question is how to explain the Bible as "inspired Scripture." This issue is central to current controversies in biblical studies, largely due to the influence of biblical fundamentalists who have a very mechanical and restricted view of inspiration. This section of IBC examines the thorny issue of inspiration, but the introduction had earlier indicated that it would not adopt a particular theory of inspiration. Rather, IBC affirms the existence of different levels of meaning in the biblical texts, all of which are essential:

—the literal meaning (not a "literalist" meaning typical of fundamentalist interpretation);

—the spiritual meaning;

—the "fuller sense" (in Latin, *sensus plenior,* "deeper meaning," often associated with spiritual meanings).

The PBC reiterates the traditional teaching of the church *that* the Bible is inspired, without adopting any specific explanation of *how* inspiration operates. Any naive mechanical view of inspiration is rejected. God, by the power of the Holy Spirit, is the principal author of the Bible, but the Spirit works entirely through the human authors in order to express the fullness of divine truths.

CATHOLIC INTERPRETATION

Part III of IBC discusses the principles of Catholic exegesis. It begins with the statement:

> Catholic exegesis does not claim any particular scientific method as its own. . . . What characterizes Catholic exegesis is that it deliberately places itself within the living tradition of the church, whose first concern is fidelity to the revelation attested by the Bible. ([143–144]; III)

Then the PBC issues a warning to Catholic exegetes not to let a "pre-understanding" (acknowledged biases) of the biblical texts impose upon them a meaning that they do not have. This section also examines biblical interpretation in the tradition of the church under three categories:

1. re-readings of texts (that is, when the Bible itself quotes or alludes to other biblical texts);

2. the complex interrelationship between the Old and New Testaments;

3. the time-honored place of patristic exegesis in the history of Catholic biblical interpretation.

Of particular importance is the statement that biblical exegesis is not merely the domain of scholars. Rather, "all the members of the church have a role in the interpretation of Scripture," including bishops, priests, and individual Christians ([174]; III.B.3). The encouragement given by IBC to personal study of the Bible reinforces the teaching of the Second Vatican Council that Catholics should become familiar with the Bible.

This section concludes with a series of recommendations for Catholic exegetes to pay careful attention to the following:

—the historical character of biblical revelation

—the interpretation of the Bible as God's word

—the christological significance of biblical texts

—the canonical significance of individual parts of the Bible (that is, the meaning each part of the Bible takes on by virtue of it being part of a greater whole)

—the ecclesial significance (that is, the relationship between the Bible and communities of faith)

—the ecumenical significance

—the relationship of biblical interpretation to other branches of theology.

INTERPRETATION IN THE LIFE OF THE CHURCH

The final section of IBC contains some cautions with regard to the limits of biblical interpretation. It also promotes biblical exegesis sensitive to the varieties of cultures in which the Bible is read, and describes the importance of using the Bible in liturgy, personal devotion (traditionally called *lectio divina*), pastoral ministry, and ecumenical discussion. The brief conclusion encourages Bible study as an "indispensable task" for the life of the church, and the continued use of the traditional and newer scientific methods as essential aids to understanding the Bible as God's revelatory word.

EVALUATION OF IBC

The document's length and technical treatment of the subject mater, unfortunately, have made it less accessible to average Catholics than is desirable. It is an important official document that promotes Catholic Bible study of the highest order. I note sixteen features that show the importance of IBC and that clarify the principles of Catholic biblical interpretation.

1. Most noticeable in IBC is the *absence of a polemical tone.* In the past, Catholic teaching on the Bible was frequently defensive. While the PBC is properly concerned about contemporary dangers in biblical interpretation, the style of presentation suggests that its primary goal is to allay fears and not to attack positions.

2. There is also a *balanced approach toward evaluating methods of interpretation.* Equal attention is given to traditional scientific, historical-critical methods and to newer literary, rhetorical, and sociological methods of biblical study. Furthermore, the PBC enunciates strengths and weaknesses of each method or approach in a manner that is fair and objective.

3. IBC is *particularly critical of fundamentalism.* Given the current wide-spread appeal of fundamentalism even among Catholics, such a critique is noteworthy. The PBC clearly rejects fundamentalist biblical interpretation as "dangerous, for it is attractive to people who look to the Bible for ready answers to the problems of life" ([116]; I.F). It criticizes fundamentalist tendencies as being overly literalist and as historicizing biblical stories that were never meant to be understood as historical accounts.

4. IBC *emphasizes the incarnational aspects of the Bible.* From beginning to end, IBC repeats the basic truth that the Bible is God's word in human words. The human dimension of sacred scripture is precisely what requires the careful development and use of methods of interpretation that allow the divine dimension to be found in its human forms.

5. IBC *acknowledges the cultural dimensions of biblical interpretation.* This is a new feature in Catholic treatment of biblical interpretation and it appears in IBC in two ways. First, the PBC explicitly states that the Bible itself reflects inculturation in the way it was formed and in the way it was translated from one language to another. Second, contemporary concern for inculturation is understood to demand a careful translation of the Bible into concepts that make sense in diverse modern cultures.

6. IBC points out that *biblical interpretation is bi-directional.* Interpretation goes in two directions simultaneously, bringing the text in touch with our lives and vice versa. Interpretation requires both a careful reading of the text and an application that speaks to the contemporary world. One specific application of this principle is pointed out in the section on inculturation. There the PBC speaks of a "mutual enrichment" that occurs when diverse cultures allow the word of God to bear "new fruit" because of the new but faithful application of God's word ([220]; IV.B).

7. The PBC *commends the increase of women exegetes* ([99 ff; 179]; I.E.2; III.B.3), although it must also be emphasized that the last paragraph of I.E.2 [106] did not receive unanimous support among the members of the PBC. (Four out of nineteen objected to the section; another four abstained.) Feminist biblical interpretation is evaluated negatively and positively as is each of the other methods of interpretation treated in IBC, but the PBC applauds the benefits of feminist exegesis. "Feminine sensitivity helps to unmask and correct certain commonly accepted interpretations which were tendentious and sought to justify the male domination of women" ([103]; I.E.2).

8. Another striking position is the *insistence on pluralism in interpretation.* "No single interpretation can exhaust the meaning of the whole, which is a symphony of many voices" ([157]; III.A.3). Many people wrongly conceive of biblical texts as having only one meaning. They think that the job of biblical scholars is to ascertain *the* meaning of a text. IBC clearly counters that naive view by recognizing the multiplicity of meanings of texts.

9. The PBC commends the *variety of exegetical methods* that scholars must use to interpret the Bible. Virtually every method has something to contribute to biblical interpretation, though some methods are clearly better than others. Yet, for the PBC to encourage the use a wide variety of means for interpretation, and not to single out one method, gives wide-ranging freedom to Catholic interpreters.

10. Another concern in IBC is *the Bible's role in ecumenical discussion.* The PBC urges all Christians to acquire knowledge of the Bible and encourages ecumenical translations that promote dialogue in biblical interpretation. The PBC acknowledges: "Most of the issues which ecumenical dialogue has to confront are related in some way to the interpretation of biblical texts" ([236]; IV.C.4).

11. IBC's stance on *inspiration* is important. While no particular theory of inspiration is adopted, the PBC clarifies that the inspired status of the Bible in no way interferes with the human dimensions of the text. Thus, the Holy Spirit works through "human psychology and language" to express divine meanings ([132]; II.B.1).

12. IBC's *attention to the literal sense* and its relationship to other senses of scripture is significant. The PBC points out, "It is not sufficient to translate a text word for word in order to obtain its literal sense. One must understand the text according to the literary conventions of the time" ([130]; II.B.1). The literal sense cannot be reduced to a "literalist sense," yet meanings of the text cannot go contrary to the literal sense.

13. IBC emphasizes that *biblical interpretation has an ecclesial dimension.* It is not a "wholly subjective" enterprise. Two basic principles keep improper interpretations in check. One is that the interpreter must understand individual passages within the context of the entire canon of sacred scripture. The second principle is that the Bible was born within ecclesial communities (see [161–180]; III.B). The church itself has declared the Bible "canonical" and maintains authoritative oversight of its interpretation. Individual interpretations must always be placed in this context.

14. IBC highlights two interrelated features, *"re-readings"* (in French, *relectures;* see [149]; III.A.1) and *"actualization"* (see [204–215]; IV.A), which *emphasize the nature of scripture as "living" text.* Just as in ancient times scriptures were sometimes read and re-read in ways that went beyond the original meaning of the texts, so the modern task of interpretation requires application to the contemporary world. In this fashion, the richness of the biblical text is never exhausted but gains new life generation after generation.

15. IBC promotes *dialogue within the church* between the various theological disciplines, especially emphasizing systematic theology and moral theology (see [195–202]; III.D). Biblical exegesis, in other words, is not an end in itself. There are often ramifications to the interpretations of many biblical texts, and biblical exegetes are called upon to foster dialogue with theologians so that the Bible can properly exercise its role in shaping contemporary theology.

16. Finally, the contribution of *patristic exegesis* is acknowledged in several places (for example, see [166–172]; III.B.2) as an important element of Catholic exegesis that respects the multiple layers of meaning in the biblical text. Yet the PBC also notes that one must always be wary of the danger that can accompany Catholic exegesis, namely, the risk "of attributing to biblical texts a meaning which they do not contain but which is the product of a later development within the tradition" ([146]; III). This observation serves as a warning that all interpreters bring a certain "pre-understanding" to biblical texts, but we should not fall into the trap of eisegesis, that is, a reading into the text something that is not there.

IBC is not the last word on how Catholics can and should approach biblical studies, but it advances considerably the Catholic approach to the Bible. It is a very rich document. Catholic appreciation for and use of the Bible has grown enormously since the time of Leo XIII and Pius XII. The Second Vatican Council's Constitution on Divine Revelation *(Dei verbum)*, which is frequently referenced in IBC, was yet another step forward. Some who are fearful of the effect of scientific study on biblical interpretation might wish to "put the genie back in the bottle," but this PBC document precludes such a move. Scientific biblical study is here to stay. One should also note that at the time IBC was promulgated, it contained a preface by Cardinal Joseph Ratzinger, the prefect of the Congregation for the Doctrine of the Faith, who not only commends it but also expresses the desire that it will receive "wide circulation so that it becomes a genuine contribution to the search for deeper assimilation of the word of God in Holy Scripture." As the PBC continues its work, I would hope that future documents would continue in this vein.

One could ask whether IBC goes too far in its openness to the wide variety of methods currently being applied in biblical research. Is this detrimental to the church's desire to interpret the word of God faithfully? I think not. IBC clearly indicates that every method or approach to biblical interpretation has limitations, strengths and weaknesses. Thus, the church must remain vigilant, carefully evaluating each and every method or approach, accepting what is useful and rejecting what is false. If, as the Dogmatic Constitution on Divine Revelation asserts, the study of sacred scripture is "as it were the very soul of theology" (#24), then biblical studies will continue to be central to the church's mission of proclaiming the gospel of Jesus Christ. Biblical interpretation in the life of the church is a never-ending task. The church can be grateful for the careful guidance offered by the PBC and its highly professional and dedicated members.

OUTLINE

THE INTERPRETATION OF
THE BIBLE IN THE CHURCH

PREFACE

The study of the Bible is, as it were, the soul of theology, as the Second Vatican Council says, borrowing a phrase from Pope Leo XIII (*Dei Verbum*, 24). This study is never finished; each age must in its own way newly seek to understand the sacred books.

In the history of interpretation the rise of the historical-critical method opened a new era. With it, new possibilities for understanding the biblical word in its originality opened up. Just as with all human endeavor, though, so also this method contained hidden dangers along with its positive possibilities: The search for the original can lead to putting the word back into the past completely so that it is no longer taken in its actuality. It can result that only the human dimension of the word appears as real, while the genuine author, God, is removed from the reach of a method which was established for understanding human reality.

The application of a "profane" method to the Bible necessarily led to discussion. Everything that helps us better to understand the truth and to appropriate its representations is helpful and worthwhile for theology. It is in this sense that we must seek how to use this method in theological research. Everything that shrinks our horizon and hinders us from seeing and hearing beyond that which is merely human must be opened up. Thus the emergence of the historical-critical method set in motion at the same time a struggle over its scope and its proper configuration which is by no means finished as yet.

In this struggle the teaching office of the Catholic Church has taken up positions several times. First, Pope Leo XIII, in his encyclical *Providentissimus Deus* of Nov. 18, 1893, plotted out some markers on the exegetical map. At a time when liberalism was extremely sure of itself and much too intrusively dogmatic, Leo XIII was forced to express himself in a rather critical way, even though he did not exclude that which was positive from the new possibilities. Fifty years later, however, because of the fertile work of great Catholic exegetes, Pope Pius XII, in his encyclical *Divino Afflante Spiritu* of Sept. 30, 1943, was able to provide largely positive encouragement toward making the modern methods of understanding the Bible fruitful. The Constitution on Divine Revelation of the Second Vatican Council, *Dei Verbum*, of Nov. 18, 1965, adopted all of this. It provided us with a synthesis, which substantially remains, between the lasting insights of patristic theology and the new methodological understanding of the moderns.

In the meantime, this methodological spectrum of exegetical work has broadened in a way which could not have been envisioned 30 years ago. New methods and new approaches have appeared, from structuralism to materialistic, psychoanalytic and liberation exegesis. On the other hand, there are also new attempts to recover patristic exegesis and to include renewed forms of a spiritual interpretation of Scripture. Thus the Pontifical Biblical Commission took as its task an attempt to take the bearings of Catholic exegesis in the present situation 100 years after *Providentissimus Deus* and 50 years after *Divino Afflante Spiritu*.

The Pontifical Biblical Commission, in its new form after the Second Vatican Council, is not an organ of the teaching office, but rather a commission of scholars who, in their scientific and ecclesial responsibility as believing exegetes, take positions on important problems of Scriptural interpretation and know that for this task they enjoy the confidence of the teaching office. Thus the present document was established. It contains a well-grounded overview of the panorama of present-day methods and in this way offers to the inquirer an orientation to the possibilities and limits of these approaches.

Accordingly, the text of the document inquires into how the meaning of Scripture might become known—this meaning in which the human word and God's word work together in the singularity of historical events and the eternity of the everlasting Word, which is contemporary in every age. The biblical word comes from a real past. It comes not only from the past, however, but at the same time from the eternity of God and it leads us into God's eternity, but again along the way through time, to which the past, the present and the future belong.

I believe that this document is very helpful for the important questions about the right way of understanding Holy Scripture and that it also helps us to go further. It takes up the paths of the encyclicals of 1893 and 1943 and advances them in a fruitful way. I would like to thank the members of the biblical commission for the patient and frequently laborious struggle in which this text grew little by little. I hope that the document will have a wide circulation so that it becomes a genuine contribution to the search for a deeper assimilation of the word of God in holy Scripture.

Rome, on the feast of St. Matthew the evangelist 1993.

Cardinal Joseph Ratzinger

INTRODUCTION

[1]   The interpretation of biblical texts continues in our own day to be a matter of lively interest and significant debate. In recent years the discussions involved have taken on some new dimensions. Granted the fundamental importance of the Bible for Christian faith, for the life of the church and for relations between Christians and the faithful of other religions, the Pontifical Biblical Commission has been asked to make a statement on this subject.

A. THE STATE OF THE QUESTION TODAY

[2]   The problem of the interpretation of the Bible is hardly a modern phenomenon, even if at times that is what some would have us believe. The Bible itself bears witness that its interpretation can be a difficult matter. Alongside texts that are perfectly clear, it contains passages of some obscurity. When reading certain prophecies of Jeremiah, Daniel pondered at length over their meaning (Daniel 9:2). According to the Acts of the Apostles, an Ethiopian of the first century found himself in the same situation with respect to a passage from the Book of Isaiah (Isaiah 53:7–8) and recognized that he had need of an interpreter (Acts 8:30–35). The Second Letter of Peter insists that "no prophecy of Scripture is a matter of private interpretation" (2 Peter 1:20), and it also observes that the letters of the apostle Paul contain "some difficult passages, the meaning of which the ignorant and untrained distort, as they do also in the case of the other Scriptures, to their own ruin" (2 Peter 3:16).

[3]   The problem is therefore quite old. But it has been accentuated with the passage of time. Readers today, in order to appropriate the words and deeds of which the Bible speaks, have to project themselves back almost 20 or 30 centuries—a process which always creates difficulty. Furthermore, because of the progress made in the human sciences, questions of interpretation have become more complex in modern times. Scientific methods have been adopted for the study of the texts of the ancient world. To what extent can these methods be considered appropriate for the interpretation of holy Scripture? For a long period the church in her pastoral prudence showed herself very reticent in responding to this question, for often the methods, despite their positive elements, have shown themselves to be wedded to positions hostile to the Christian faith. But a more positive attitude has also evolved, signaled by a whole series of pontifical documents, ranging from the encyclical *Providentissimus Deus* of Leo XIII (Nov. 18, 1893) to the encyclical *Divino Afflante Spiritu* of Pius XII (Sept. 30, 1943), and this has been confirmed by the declaration *Sancta Mater Ecclesia* of the Pontifical Biblical Commission (April 21, 1964) and above all by the dogmatic constitution *Dei Verbum* of the Second Vatican Council (Nov. 18, 1965).

[4]   That this more constructive attitude has borne fruit cannot be denied. Biblical studies have made great progress in the Catholic Church, and the academic value of these studies has been acknowledged more and more in the scholarly world and among the faithful. This has greatly smoothed the path of ecumenical dialogue. The deepening of the Bible's influence upon theology has contributed to theological renewal. Interest in the Bible has grown among Catholics, with resultant progress in the Christian life. All those who have acquired a solid formation in this area consider it quite impossible to return to a precritical level of interpretation, a level which they now rightly judge to be quite inadequate.

[5]   But the fact is that at the very time when the most prevalent scientific method—the "historical-critical method"—is freely practiced in exegesis, including Catholic exegesis, it is itself brought into question. To some extent,

this has come about in the scholarly world itself through the rise of alternative methods and approaches. But it has also arisen through the criticisms of many members of the faithful, who judge the method deficient from the point of view of faith. The historical-critical method, as its name suggests, is particularly attentive to the historical development of texts or traditions across the passage of time—that is, to all that is summed up in the term *diachronic*. But at the present time in certain quarters it finds itself in competition with methods which insist upon a *synchronic* understanding of texts—that is, one which has to do with their language, composition, narrative structure and capacity for persuasion. Moreover, for many interpreters the diachronic concern to reconstruct the past has given way to a tendency to ask questions of texts by viewing them within a number of contemporary perspectives—philosophical, psycho-analytic, sociological, political, etc. Some value this plurality of methods and approaches as an indication of richness, but to others it gives the impression of much confusion.

[6]   Whether real or apparent, this confusion has brought fresh fuel to the arguments of those opposed to scientific exegesis. The diversity of interpretations only serves to show, they say, that nothing is gained by submitting biblical texts to the demands of scientific method; on the contrary, they allege, much is lost thereby. They insist that the result of scientific exegesis is only to provoke perplexity and doubt upon numerous points which hitherto had been accepted without difficulty. They add that it impels some exegetes to adopt positions contrary to the faith of the church on matters of great importance such as the virginal conception of Jesus and his miracles, and even his resurrection and divinity.

[7]   Even when it does not end up in such negative positions, scientific exegesis, they claim, is notable for its sterility in what concerns progress in the Christian life. Instead of making for easier and more secure access to the living sources of God's word, it makes of the Bible a closed book. Interpretation may always have been something of a problem, but now it requires such technical refinements as to render it a domain reserved for a few specialists alone. To the latter some apply the phrase of the Gospel: You have taken away the key of knowledge; you have not entered in yourselves and you have hindered those who sought to enter" (Luke 11:52; cf. Matthew 23:13).

[8]   As a result, in place of the patient toil of scientific exegesis, they think it necessary to substitute simpler approaches such as one or other of the various forms of synchronic reading which may be considered appropriate. Some even, turning their backs upon all study, advocate a so-called "spiritual" reading of the Bible, by which they understand a reading guided solely by personal inspiration—one that is subjective—and intended only to nourish such inspiration. Some seek above all to find in the Bible the Christ of their own personal vision and, along with it, the satisfaction of their own spontaneous religious feelings. Others claim to find there immediate answers to all kinds of questions touching both their own lives and that of the community. There are, moreover, numerous sects which propose as the only way of interpretation one that has been revealed to them alone.

B. PURPOSE OF THIS DOCUMENT

[9]   It is, then, appropriate to give serious consideration to the various aspects of the present situation as regards the interpretation of the Bible—to attend to the criticisms and the complaints as also to the hopes and aspirations which are being expressed in this matter, to assess the possibilities opened up by the new methods and approaches and, finally, to try to determine more precisely the direction which best corresponds to the mission of exegesis in the Catholic Church.

Such is the purpose of this document. The Pontifical Biblical Commission desires to indicate the paths most appropriate for arriving at an interpretation of the Bible as faithful as possible to its character both human and divine. The commission does not aim to adopt a position on all the questions which arise with respect to the Bible such as, for example, the theology of inspiration. What it has in mind is to examine all the methods likely to contribute effectively to the task of making more available the riches contained in the biblical texts. The aim is that the word of God may become more and more the spiritual nourishment of the members of the people of God, the source for them of a life of faith, of hope and of love—and indeed a light for all humanity (cf. *Dei Verbum*, 21).

[10]   To accomplish this goal, the present document:

—1. Will give a brief description of the various methods and approaches,[1] indicating the possibilities they offer and their limitations.

—2. Will examine certain questions of a hermeneutical nature.

—3. Will reflect upon the aspects which may be considered characteristic of a Catholic interpretation of the Bible and upon its relationship with other theological disciplines.

—4. Will consider, finally, the place interpretation of the Bible has in the life of the church.

I. METHODS AND APPROACHES FOR INTERPRETATION

A. HISTORICAL-CRITICAL METHOD

[11]   The historical-critical method is the indispensable method for the scientific study of the meaning of ancient texts. Holy Scripture, inasmuch as it is the "word of God in human language," has been composed by human authors in all its various parts and in all the sources that lie behind them. Because of this, its proper understanding not only admits the use of this method but actually requires it.

1. HISTORY OF THE METHOD

[12]   For a correct understanding of this method as currently employed, a glance over its history will be of assistance. Certain elements of this method of interpretation are very ancient. They were used in antiquity by Greek commentators of classical literature and, much later, in the course of the patristic period

by authors such as Origen, Jerome and Augustine. The method at that time was much less developed. Its modern forms are the result of refinements brought about especially since the time of the Renaissance humanists and their *recursus ad fontes* (return to the sources).

[13]   The textual criticism of the New Testament was able to be developed as a scientific discipline only from about 1800 onward, after its link with the *textus receptus* was severed. But the beginnings of literary criticism go back to the 17th century, to the work of Richard Simon, who drew attention to the doublets, discrepancies in content and differences of style observable in the Pentateuch—discoveries not easy to reconcile with the attribution of the entire text to Moses as single author. In the 18th century, Jean Astruc was still satisfied that the matter could be explained on the basis that Moses had made use of various sources (especially two principal ones) to compose the Book of Genesis. But as time passed biblical critics contested the Mosaic authorship of the Pentateuch with ever growing confidence.

[14]   Literary criticism for a long time came to be identified with the attempt to distinguish in texts different sources. Thus it was that there developed in the 19th century the "documentary hypothesis," which sought to give an explanation of the editing of the Pentateuch. According to this hypothesis, four documents, to some extent parallel with each other, had been woven together: that of the Yahwist (J), that of the Elohist (E), that of the Deuteronomist (D) and that of the priestly author (P); the final editor made use of this latter (priestly) document to provide a structure for the whole.

[15]   In similar fashion, to explain both the agreements and disagreements between the three synoptic Gospels, scholars had recourse to the "two source" hypothesis. According to this, the Gospels of Matthew and Luke were composed out of two principal sources: on the one hand, the Gospel of Mark and, on the other, a collection of the sayings of Jesus (called Q, from the German word *quelle*, meaning "source"). In their essential features, these two hypotheses retain their prominence in scientific exegesis today—though they are also under challenge.

[16]   In the desire to establish the chronology of the biblical texts, this kind of literary criticism restricted itself to the task of dissecting and dismantling the text in order to identify the various sources. It did not pay sufficient attention to the final form of the biblical text and to the message which it conveyed in the state in which it actually exists (the contribution of editors was not held in high regard). This meant that historical-critical exegesis could often seem to be something which simply dissolved and destroyed the text. This was all the more the case when, under the influence of the comparative history of religions, such as it then was, or on the basis of certain philosophical ideas, some exegetes expressed highly negative judgments against the Bible.

[17]   It was Hermann Gunkel who brought the method out of the ghetto of literary criticism understood in this way. Although he continued to regard the books of the Pentateuch as compilations, he attended to the particular texture

of the different elements of the text. He sought to define the genre of each piece (e.g., whether "legend" or "hymn") and its original setting in the life of the community or *sitz im leben* (e.g., a legal setting or a liturgical one, etc.).

To this kind of research into literary genres was joined the "critical study of forms" *(formgeschichte)*, which Martin Dibelius and Rudolf Bultmann introduced into the exegesis of the synoptic Gospels. Bultmann combined form-critical studies with a biblical hermeneutic inspired by the existentialist philosophy of Martin Heidegger. As a result, *formgeschichte* often stirred up serious reservations.

But one of the results of this method has been to demonstrate more clearly that the tradition recorded in the New Testament had its origin and found its basic shape within Christian community or early church, passing from the preaching of Jesus himself to that which proclaimed that Jesus is the Christ. Eventually, form criticism was supplemented by *redaktionsgeschichte* (redaction criticism), the "critical study of the process of editing." This sought to shed light upon the personal contribution of each evangelist and to uncover the theological tendencies which shaped his editorial work.

[18] When this last method was brought into play, the whole series of different stages characteristic of the historical-critical method became complete: From textual criticism one progresses to literary criticism, with its work of dissection in the quest for sources; then one moves to a critical study of forms and, finally, to an analysis of the editorial process, which aims to be particularly attentive to the text as it has been put together. All this has made it possible to understand far more accurately the intention of the authors and editors of the Bible as well as the message which they addressed to their first readers. The achievement of these results has lent the historical-critical method an importance of the highest order.

2. PRINCIPLES

[19] The fundamental principles of the historical-critical method in its classic form are the following:

It is a historical method, not only because it is applied to ancient texts—in this case, those of the Bible—and studies their significance from a historical point of view, but also and above all because it seeks to shed light upon the historical processes which gave rise to biblical texts, diachronic processes that were often complex and involved a long period of time. At the different stages of their production, the texts of the Bible were addressed to various categories of hearers or readers living in different places and different times.

[20] It is a critical method, because in each of its steps (from textual criticism to redaction criticism) it operates with the help of scientific criteria that seek to be as objective as possible. In this way it aims to make accessible to the modern reader the meaning of biblical texts, often very difficult to comprehend.

[21] As an analytical method, it studies the biblical text in the same fashion as it would study any other ancient text and comments upon it as an expression of human discourse. However, above all in the area of redaction criticism, it does allow the exegete to gain a better grasp of the content of divine revelation.

3. DESCRIPTION

[22] At the present stage of its development, the historical-critical method moves through the following steps:

Textual criticism, as practiced for a very long time, begins the series of scholarly operations. Basing itself on the testimony of the oldest and best manuscripts, as well as of papyri, certain ancient versions and patristic texts, textual-criticism seeks to establish, according to fixed rules, a biblical text as close as possible to the original.

[23] The text is then submitted to a linguistic (morphology and syntax) and semantic analysis, using the knowledge derived from historical philology. It is the role of literary criticism to determine the beginning and end of textual units, large and small, and to establish the internal coherence of the text. The existence of doublets, of irreconcilable differences and of other indicators is a clue to the composite character of certain texts. These can then be divided into small units, the next step being to see whether these in turn can be assigned to different sources.

[24] Genre criticism seeks to identify literary genres, the social milieu that gave rise to them, their particular features and the history of their development. Tradition criticism situates texts in the stream of tradition and attempts to describe the development of this tradition over the course of time. Finally, redaction criticism studies the modifications that these texts have undergone before being fixed in their final state, it also analyzes this final stage, trying as far as possible to identify the tendencies particularly characteristic of this concluding process.

[25] While the preceding steps have sought to explain the text by tracing its origin and development within a diachronic perspective, this last step concludes with a study that is synchronic: At this point the text is explained as it stands, on the basis of the mutual relationships between its diverse elements, and with an eye to its character as a message communicated by the author to his contemporaries. At this point one is in a position to consider the demands of the text from the point of view of action and life *(fonction pragmatique)*.

[26] When the texts studied belong to a historical literary genre or are related to events of history, historical criticism completes literary criticism so as to determine the historical significance of the text in the modern sense of this expression.

It is in this way that one accounts for the various stages that lie behind the biblical revelation in its concrete historical development.

4. EVALUATION

[27] What value should we accord to the historical-critical method, especially at this present stage of its development?

It is a method which, when used in an objective manner, implies of itself no a priori. If its use is accompanied by a priori principles, that is not something pertaining to the method itself, but to certain hermeneutical choices which govern the interpretation and can be tendentious.

Oriented in its origins toward source criticism and the history of religions, the method has managed to provide fresh access to the Bible. It has shown the Bible to be a collection of writings, which most often, especially in the case of the Old Testament, are not the creation of a single author, but which have had a long prehistory inextricably tied either to the history of Israel or to that of the early church. Previously, the Jewish or Christian interpretation of the Bible had no clear awareness of the concrete and diverse historical conditions in which the word of God took root among the people; of all this it had only a general and remote awareness.

[28] The early confrontation between traditional exegesis and the scientific approach, which initially consciously separated itself from faith and at times even opposed it, was assuredly painful; later however it proved to be salutary: Once the method was freed from external prejudices, it led to a more precise understanding of the truth of sacred Scripture (cf. *Dei Verbum*, 12). According to *Divino Afflante Spiritu*, the search for the literal sense of Scripture is an essential task of exegesis and, in order to fulfill this task, it is necessary to determine the literary genre of texts (cf. *Enchiridion Biblicum*, 560), something which the historical-critical method helps to achieve.

[29] To be sure, the classic use of the historical-critical method reveals its limitations. It restricts itself to a search for the meaning of the biblical text within the historical circumstances that gave rise to it and is not concerned with other possibilities of meaning which have been revealed at later stages of the biblical revelation and history of the church. Nonetheless, this method has contributed to the production of works of exegesis and of biblical theology which are of great value.

[30] For a long time now scholars have ceased combining the method with a philosophical system. More recently, there has been a tendency among exegetes to move the method in the direction of a greater insistence upon the form of a text, with less attention paid to its content. But this tendency has been corrected through the application of a more diversified semantics (the semantics of words, phrases, text) and through the study of the demands of the text from the point of view of action and life *(aspect pragmatique)*.

[31] With respect to the inclusion in the method of a synchronic analysis of texts, we must recognize that we are dealing here with a legitimate operation, for it is the text in its final stage, rather than in its earlier editions, which is the expression of the word of God. But diachronic study remains indispensable for making known the historical dynamism which animates sacred Scripture and for

shedding light upon its rich complexity: For example, the covenant code (Exodus 21–23) reflects a political, social and religious situation of Israelite society different from that reflected in the other law codes preserved in Deuteronomy (Chapters 12–26) and in Leviticus (the holiness code, Chapters 17–26). We must take care not to replace the historicizing tendency, for which the older historical-critical exegesis is open to criticism, with the opposite excess, that of neglecting history in favor of an exegesis which would be exclusively synchronic.

[32] To sum up, the goal of the historical-critical method is to determine, particularly in a diachronic manner, the meaning expressed by the biblical authors and editors. Along with other methods and approaches, the historical-critical method opens up to the modern reader a path to the meaning of the biblical text such as we have it today.

B. NEW METHODS OF LITERARY ANALYSIS

[33] No scientific method for the study of the Bible is fully adequate to comprehend the biblical texts in all their richness. For all its overall validity, the historical-critical method cannot claim to be totally sufficient in this respect. It necessarily has to leave aside many aspects of the writings which it studies. It is not surprising, then, that at the present time other methods and approaches are proposed which serve to explore more profoundly other aspects worthy of attention.

[34] In this Section B, we will present certain methods of literary analysis which have been developed recently. In the following sections (C, D, E), we will examine briefly different approaches, some of which relate to the study of the tradition, others to the "human sciences," others still to particular situations of the present time. Finally (F), we will consider the fundamentalist reading of the Bible, a reading which does not accept any systematic approach to interpretation.

Taking advantage of the progress made in our day by linguistic and literary studies, biblical exegesis makes use more and more of new methods of literary analysis, in particular rhetorical analysis narrative analysis and semiotic analysis.

1. RHETORICAL NALYSIS

[35] Rhetorical analysis in itself is not, in fact, a new method. What is new is the use of it in a systematic way for the interpretation of the Bible and also the start and development of a "new rhetoric."

[36] Rhetoric is the art of composing discourse aimed at persuasion. The fact that all biblical texts are in some measure persuasive in character means that some knowledge of rhetoric should be part of the normal scholarly equipment of all exegetes. Rhetorical analysis must be carried out in a critical way, since scientific exegesis is an undertaking which necessarily submits itself to the demands of the critical mind.

[37] A considerable number of recent studies in the biblical area have devoted considerable attention to the presence of rhetorical features in Scripture. Three different approaches can be distinguished. The first is based upon classical Greco-Roman rhetoric; the second devotes itself to Semitic procedures of composition; the third takes its inspiration from more recent studies—namely, from what is called the "new rhetoric."

[38] Every situation of discourse involves the presence of three elements: the speaker (or author), the discourse (or text) and the audience (or the addressees). Classical rhetoric distinguished accordingly three factors which contribute to the quality of a discourse as an instrument of persuasion: the authority of the speaker, the force of the argument and the feelings aroused in the audience. The diversity of situation and of audience largely determines the way of speaking adopted. Classical rhetoric since Aristotle distinguishes three modes of public speaking: the judicial mode (adopted in a court of law); the deliberative mode (for the political assembly) and the demonstrative mode (for celebratory occasions).

[39] Recognizing the immense influence of rhetoric in Hellenistic culture, a growing number of exegetes make use of treatises on classical rhetoric as an aid toward analyzing certain aspects of biblical texts, especially those of the New Testament.

Other exegetes concentrate upon the characteristic features of the biblical literary tradition. Rooted in Semitic culture, this displays a distinct preference for symmetrical compositions, through which one can detect relationships between different elements in the text. The study of the multiple forms of parallelism and other procedures characteristic of the Semitic mode of composition allows for a better discernment of the literary structure of texts, which can only lead to a more adequate understanding of their message.

[40] The new rhetoric adopts a more general point of view. It aims to be something more than a simple catalogue of stylistic figures, oratorical stratagems and various kinds of discourse. It investigates what makes a particular use of language effective and successful in the communication of conviction. It seeks to be "realistic" in the sense of not wanting to limit itself to an analysis that is purely formal. It takes due account of the actual situation of debate or discussion. It studies style and composition as means of acting upon an audience. To this end, it benefits from contributions made of late in other areas of knowledge such as linguistics, semiotics, anthropology and sociology.

[41] Applied to the Bible, the new rhetoric aims to penetrate to the very core of the language of revelation precisely as persuasive religious discourse and to measure the impact of such discourse in the social context of the communication thus begun.

Because of the enrichment it brings to the critical study of texts, such rhetorical analysis is worthy of high regard, above all in view of the greater depth achieved in more recent work. It makes up for a negligence of long standing and can lead to the rediscovery or clarification of original perspectives that had been lost or obscured.

The new rhetoric is surely right in its drawing attention to the capacity of language to persuade and convince. The Bible is not simply a statement of truths. It is a message that carries within itself a function of communication within a particular context, a message which carries with it a certain power of argument and a rhetorical strategy.

[42] Rhetorical analysis does have, however, its limitations. When it remains simply on the level of description, its results often reflect a concern for style only. Basically synchronic in nature, it cannot claim to be an independent method which would be sufficient by itself. Its application to biblical texts raises several questions. Did the authors of these texts belong to the more educated levels of society? To what extent did they follow the rules of rhetoric in their work of composition? What kind of rhetoric is relevant for the analysis of any given text: Greco-Roman or Semitic? Is there sometimes the risk of attributing to certain biblical texts a rhetorical structure that is really too sophisticated? These questions—and there are others—ought not in any way cast doubt upon the use of this kind of analysis; they simply suggest that it is not something to which recourse ought be had without some measure of discernment.

2. NARRATIVE ANALYSIS

[43] Narrative exegesis offers a method of understanding and communicating the biblical message which corresponds to the form of story and personal testimony, something characteristic of holy Scripture and, of course, a fundamental modality of communication between human persons. The Old Testament in fact presents a story of salvation, the powerful recital of which provides the substance of the profession of faith, liturgy and catechesis (cf. Psalms 78:3–4; Exodus 12:24–27; Deuteronomy 6:20–25; 26:5–11). For its own part, the proclamation of the Christian kerygma amounts in essentials to a sequence telling the story of the life, death and resurrection of Jesus Christ, events of which the Gospels offer us a detailed account. Catechesis itself also appears in narrative form (cf. 1 Corinthians 11:23–25).

With respect to the narrative approach, it helps to distinguish methods of analysis, on the one hand, and theological reflection, on the other.

[44] Many analytic methods are in fact proposed today. Some start from the study of ancient models of narrative. Others base themselves upon present-day "narratology" in one or other of its forms, in which case there can often be points of contact with semiotics. Particularly attentive to elements in the text which have to do with plot, characterization and the point of view taken by a narrator, narrative analysis studies how a text tells a story in such a way as to engage the reader in its "narrative world" and the system of values contained therein.

[45] Several methods introduce a distinction between *real author* and *implied author, real reader* and *implied reader.* The *real author* is the person who actually composed the story. By *implied author* one means the image of the author which the text progressively creates in the course of the reading (with his or her own culture, character, inclinations, faith, etc.). The *real reader* is any person

who has access to the text—from those who first read it or heard it read, right down to those who read or hear it today. By *implied reader* one means the reader which the text presupposes and in effect creates, the one who is capable of performing the mental and affective operations necessary for entering into the narrative world of the text and responding to it in the way envisaged by the real author through the instrumentality of the implied author.

A text will continue to have an influence in the degree to which real readers (e.g., ourselves in the late 20th century) can identify with the implied reader. One of the major tasks of exegesis is to facilitate this process of identification.

[46] Narrative analysis involves a new way of understanding how a text works. While the historical-critical method considers the text as a "window" giving access to one or other period (not only to the situation which the story relates but also to that of the community for whom the story is told), narrative analysis insists that the text also functions as a "mirror" in the sense that it projects a certain image—a "narrative world"—which exercises an influence upon readers' perceptions in such a way as to bring them to adopt certain values rather than others.

[47] Connected with this kind of study primarily literary in character, is a certain mode of theological reflection as one considers the implications the "story" (and also the "witness") character of Scripture has with respect to the consent of faith and as one derives from this a hermeneutic of a more practical and pastoral nature. There is here a reaction against the reduction of the inspired text to a series of theological theses, often formulated in nonscriptural categories and language. What is asked of narrative exegesis is that it rehabilitate in new historical contexts the modes of communicating and conveying meaning proper to the biblical account in order to open up more effectively its saving power. Narrative analysis insists upon the need both to tell the story of salvation (the "informative" aspect) and to tell the story in view of salvation (the "performative" aspect). The biblical account, in effect, whether explicitly or implicitly as the case may be, contains an existential appeal addressed to the reader.

[48] The usefulness of narrative analysis for the exegesis of the Bible is clear. It is well suited to the narrative character which so many biblical texts display. It can facilitate the transition, often so difficult, from the meaning of the text in its historical context (the proper object of the historical-critical method) to its significance for the reader of today. On the other hand, the distinction between the real author and the implied author does tend to make problems of interpretation somewhat more complex.

[49] When applied to texts of the Bible, narrative analysis cannot rest content with imposing upon them certain pre-established models. It must strive to adapt itself to their own proper character. The synchronic approach which it brings to texts needs to be supplemented by diachronic studies as well. It must, moreover, beware of a tendency that can arise to exclude any kind of doctrinal elaboration in the content of biblical narratives. In such a case it would find itself out of step with the biblical tradition itself, which practices precisely this kind

of elaboration, and also with the tradition of the church, which has continued further along the same way. Finally, it is worth noting that the existential subjective effectiveness of the impact of the word of God in its narrative transmission cannot be considered to be in itself a sufficient indication that its full truth has been adequately grasped.

3. SEMIOTIC ANALYSIS

[50] Ranged among the methods identified as synchronic, those namely which concentrate on the study of the biblical text as it comes before the reader in its final state, is semiotic analysis. This has experienced a notable development in certain quarters over the last 20 years. Originally known by the more general term *structuralism*, this method can claim as forefather the Swiss linguist Ferdinand de Saussure, who at the beginning of the present century worked out the theory according to which all language is a system of relationships obeying fixed laws. Several linguists and literary critics have had a notable influence in the development of the method. The majority of biblical scholars who make use of semiotics in the study of the Bible take as their authority Algirdas J. Greimas and the School of Paris, which he founded. Similar approaches and methods, based upon modern linguistics, have developed elsewhere. But it is Greimas' method which we intend to present and analyze briefly here.

[51] Semiotics is based upon three main principles or presuppositions:

—The principle of immanence: Each text forms a unit of meaning complete in itself; the analysis considers the entire text but only the text it does not look to any date "external" to the text such as the author, the audience, any events it describes or what might have been its process of composition.

—The principle of the structure of meaning: There is no meaning given except in and through relationship, in particular the relationship of "difference"; the analysis of the text consists then in establishing the network of relationships (of opposition, confirmation, etc.) between the various elements; out of this the meaning of the text is constructed.

—The principle of the grammar of the text: Each text follows a "grammar," that is to say, a certain number of rules or structures; in the collection of sentences that we call discourse there are various levels, each of which has its own distinct grammar.

[52] The overall content of a text can be analyzed at three different levels.

—The narrative level. Here one studies in the story the transformations which move the action from the initial to the final state. Within the course of the narrative, the analysis seeks to retrace the different phases, logically bound to each other, which mark the transformation from one state to another. In each of these phases it establishes the relationships between the "roles" played by the "actants" which determine the various stages of development and bring about transformation.

—The level of discourse. The analysis here consists of three operations: (a) the fixing and classification of figures, that is to say, the elements of meaning in a text (actors, times, places); (b) the tracking of the course of each figure in the text in order to determine just how the text uses each one; (c) inquiry into the thematic value of the figures. This last operation consists in discerning "in the name of what" (= what value) the figures follow such a path in the text determined in this way.

—The logico-semantic level. This is the so-called deep level. It is also the most abstract. It proceeds from the assumption that certain forms of logic and meaning underlie the narrative and discursive organization of all discourse. The analysis at this level consists in identifying the logic which governs the basic articulations of the narrative and figurative flow of a text. To achieve this, recourse is often had to an instrument called the "semiotic square" (carré semiotique), a figure which makes use of the relationships between two "contrary" terms and two "contradictory" terms (for example, black and white; white and non-white; black and not-black).

[53] The exponents of the theory behind the semiotic method continue to produce new developments. Present research centers most particularly upon enunciation and intertextuality. Applied in the first instance to the narrative texts of Scripture, to which it is most readily applicable, the use of the method has been more and more extended to other kinds of biblical discourse as well.

[54] The description of semiotics that has been given and above all the formulation of its presuppositions should have already served to make clear the advantages and the limitations of this method. By directing greater attention to the fact that each biblical text is a coherent whole, obedient to a precise linguistic mechanic of operation, semiotics contributes to our understanding of the Bible as word of God expressed in human language.

[55] Semiotics can be usefully employed in the study of the Bible only insofar as the method is separated from certain assumptions developed in structuralist philosophy, namely the refusal to accept individual personal identity within the text and extratextual reference beyond it. The Bible is a word that bears upon reality, a word which God has spoken in a historical context and which God addresses to us today through the mediation of human authors. The semiotic approach must be open to history: first of all to the history of those who play a part in the texts; then to that of the authors and readers. The great risk run by those who employ semiotic analysis is that of remaining at the level of a formal study of the content of texts, failing to draw out the message.

[56] When it does not become lost in remote and complex language and when its principal elements are taught in simple terms, semiotic analysis can give Christians a taste for studying the biblical text and discovering certain of its dimensions, without their first having to acquire a great deal of instruction in historical matters relating to the production of the text and its sociocultural world. It can thus prove useful in pastoral practice itself, providing a certain appropriation of Scripture among those who are not specialized in the area.

C. APPROACHES BASED ON TRADITION

[57] The literary methods which we have just reviewed, although they differ from the historical-critical method in that they pay greater attention to the internal unity of the texts studied, remain nonetheless insufficient for the interpretation of the Bible because they consider each of its writings in isolation. But the Bible is not a compilation of texts unrelated to each other; rather, it is a gathering together of a whole array of witnesses from one great tradition. To be fully adequate to the object of its study, biblical exegesis must keep this truth firmly in mind. Such in fact is the perspective adopted by a number of approaches which are being developed at present.

1. CANONICAL APPROACH

[58] The "canonical" approach, which originated in the United States some 20 years ago, proceeds from the perception that the historical-critical method experiences at times considerable difficulty in arriving, in its conclusions, at a truly theological level. It aims to carry out the theological task of interpretation more successfully by beginning from within an explicit framework of faith: the Bible as a whole.

To achieve this, it interprets each biblical text in the light of the canon of Scriptures, that is to say, of the Bible as received as the norm of faith by a community of believers. It seeks to situate each text within the single plan of God, the goal being to arrive at a presentation of Scripture truly valid for our time. The method does not claim to be a substitute for the historical-critical method; the hope is, rather, to complete it.

[59] Two different points of view have been proposed:

Brevard S. Childs centers his interest on the final canonical form of the text (whether book or collection), the form accepted by the community as an authoritative expression of its faith and rule of life.

James A. Sanders, rather than looking to the final and fixed form of the text, devotes his attention to the "canonical process" or progressive development of the Scriptures which the believing community has accepted as a normative authority. The critical study of this process examines the way in which older traditions have been used again and again in new contexts before finally coming to constitute a whole that is at once stable and yet adaptable, coherent while holding together matter that is diverse—in short, a complete whole in which the faith community can find its identity. In the course of this process various hermeneutic procedures have been at work, and this continues to be the case even after the fixing of the canon. These procedures are often midrashic in nature, serving to make the biblical text relevant for a later time. They encourage a constant interaction between the community and the Scriptures, calling for an interpretation which ever seeks to bring the tradition up to date.

[60] The canonical approach rightly reacts against placing an exaggerated value upon what is supposed to be original and early, as if this alone were authentic.

Inspired Scripture is precisely Scripture in that it has been recognized by the church as the rule of faith. Hence the significance, in this light, of both the final form in which each of the books of the Bible appears and of the complete whole which all together make up as canon. Each individual book only becomes biblical in the light of the canon as a whole.

[61] It is the believing community that provides a truly adequate context for interpreting canonical texts. In this context faith and the Holy Spirit enrich exegesis; church authority, exercised as a service of the community, must see to it that this interpretation remains faithful to the great tradition which has produced the texts (cf. *Dei Verbum*, 10).

[62] The canonical approach finds itself grappling with more than one problem when it seeks to define the "canonical process." At what point in time precisely does a text become canonical? It seems reasonable to describe it as such from the time that the community attributes to it a normative authority, even if this should be before it has reached its final, definitive form. One can speak of a "canonical" hermeneutic once the repetition of the traditions, which comes about through the taking into account of new aspects of the situation (be they religious, cultural or theological), begins to preserve the identity of the message. But a question arises: Should the interpretive process which led to the formation of the canon be recognized as the guiding principle for the interpretation of Scripture today?

[63] On the other hand, the complex relationships that exist between the Jewish and Christian canons of Scripture raise many problems of interpretation. The Christian church has received as "Old Testament" the writings which had authority in the Hellenistic Jewish community, but some of these are either lacking in the Hebrew Bible or appear there in somewhat different form. The corpus is therefore different. From this it follows that the canonical interpretation cannot be identical in each case, granted that each text must be read in relation to the whole corpus. But, above all, the church reads the Old Testament in the light of the paschal mystery—the death and resurrection of Jesus Christ—who brings a radical newness and, with sovereign authority, gives a meaning to the Scriptures that is decisive and definitive (cf. *Dei Verbum*, 4). This new determination of meaning has become an integral element of Christian faith. It ought not, however, mean doing away with all attempt to be consistent with that earlier canonical interpretation which preceded the Christian Passover. One must respect each stage of the history of salvation. To empty out of the Old Testament its own proper meaning would be to deprive the New of its roots in history.

2. APPROACH THROUGH RECOURSE TO JEWISH TRADITIONS OF INTERPRETATION

[64] The Old Testament reached its final form in the Jewish world of the four or five centuries preceding the Christian era. Judaism of this time also provided the matrix for the origin of the New Testament and the infant church. Numerous studies of the history of ancient Judaism and notably the manifold research stimulated by the discoveries at Qumran have highlighted the complexity of the Jewish world, both in the land of Israel and in the Diaspora, throughout this period.

[65] It is in this world that the interpretation of Scripture had its beginning. One of the most ancient witnesses to the Jewish interpretation of the Bible is the Greek translation known as the Septuagint. The Aramaic Targums represent a further witness to the same activity which has carried on down to the present, giving rise in the process to an immense mass of learned procedures for the preservation of the text of the Old Testament and for the explanation of the meaning of biblical texts. At all stages, the more astute Christian exegetes, from Origen and Jerome onward, have sought to draw profit from the Jewish biblical learning in order to acquire a better understanding of Scripture. Many modern exegetes follow this example.

[66] The ancient Jewish traditions allow for a better understanding particularly of the Septuagint, the Jewish Bible which eventually became the first part of the Christian Bible for at least the first four centuries of the church and has remained so in the East down to the present day. The extracanonical Jewish literature, called apocryphal or intertestamental, in its great abundance and variety, is an important source for the interpretation of the New Testament. The variety of exegetical procedures practiced by the different strains of Judaism can actually be found within the Old Testament itself, for example in Chronicles with reference to the books of Samuel and Kings, and also within the New Testament, as for example in certain ways Paul goes about argument from Scripture. A great variety of forms—parables, allegories, anthologies and *florilegia*, rereadings *(relectures)*, *pesher* technique, methods of associating otherwise unrelated texts, psalms and hymns, vision, revelation and dream sequences, wisdom compositions—all are common to both the Old and the New Testaments as well as in Jewish circles before and after the time of Jesus. The Targums and the Midrashic literature illustrate the homiletic tradition and mode of biblical interpretation practiced by wide sectors of Judaism in the first centuries.

[67] Many Christian exegetes of the Old Testament look besides to the Jewish commentators, grammarians and lexicographers of the medieval and more recent period as a resource for understanding difficult passages or expressions that are either rare or unique. References to such Jewish works appear in current exegetical discussion much more frequently than was formerly the case.

[68] Jewish biblical scholarship in all its richness, from its origins in antiquity down to the present day, is an asset of the highest value for the exegesis of both Testaments, provided that it be used with discretion. Ancient Judaism took many diverse forms. The Pharisaic form which eventually came to be the most prevalent, in the shape of rabbinic Judaism, was by no means the only one. The range of ancient Jewish texts extends across several centuries; it is important to rank them in chronological order before proceeding to make comparisons. Above all, the overall pattern of the Jewish and Christian communities is very different: On the Jewish side, in very varied ways, it is a question of a religion which defines a people and a way of life based upon written revelation and an oral tradition; whereas, on the Christian side, it is faith in the Lord Jesus—the one who died, was raised and lives still, Messiah and Son of God; it is around faith in his person that the community is gathered. These two diverse starting points create, as

regards the interpretation of the Scriptures, two separate contexts, which for all their points of contact and similarity are in fact radically diverse.

3. APPROACH BY THE HISTORY OF THE INFLUENCE OF THE TEXT (wirkungsgeschichte)

[69] This approach rests upon two principles: a) a text only becomes a literary work insofar as it encounters readers who give life to it by appropriating it to themselves; b) this appropriation of the text, which can occur either on the individual or community level and can take shape in various spheres (literary, artistic, theological, ascetical and mystical), contributes to a better understanding of the text itself.

[70] Without being entirely unknown in antiquity, this approach was developed in literary studies between 1960 and 1970, a time when criticism became interested in the relation between a text and its readers. Biblical studies can only draw profit from research of this kind, all the more so since the philosophy of hermeneutics for its own part stresses the necessary distance between a work and its author as well as between a work and its readers. Within this perspective, the history of the effect produced by a book or a passage of Scripture (wirkungsgeschichte) begins to enter into the work of interpretation. Such an inquiry seeks to assess the development of interpretation over the course of time under the influence of the concerns readers have brought to the text. It also attempts to evaluate the importance of the role played by tradition in finding meaning in biblical texts.

[71] The mutual presence to each other of text and readers creates its own dynamic, for the text exercises an influence and provokes reactions. It makes a resonant claim that is heard by readers whether as individuals or as members of a group. The reader is in any case never an isolated subject. He or she belongs to a social context and lives within a tradition. Readers come to the text with their own questions, exercise a certain selectivity, propose an interpretation and, in the end, are able either to create a further work or else take initiatives inspired directly from their reading of Scripture.

[72] Numerous examples of such an approach are already evident. The history of the reading of the Song of Songs offers an excellent illustration: It would show how this book was received in the patristic period, in monastic circles of the medieval church and then again how it was taken up by a mystical writer such as St. John of the Cross. The approach thus offers a better chance of uncovering all the dimensions of meaning contained in such a writing. Similarly, in the New Testament it is both possible and useful to throw light upon the meaning of a passage (for example, that of the rich young man in Matthew 19:16–26) by pointing out how fruitful its influence has been throughout the history of the church.

[73] At the same time, history also illustrates the prevalence from time to time of interpretations that are tendentious and false, baneful in their effect— such as, for example, those that have promoted anti-Semitism or other forms

of racial discrimination or, yet again, various kinds of millennarian delusions. This serves to show that this approach cannot constitute a discipline that would be purely autonomous. Discernment is required. Care must be exercised not to privilege one or other stage of the history of the text's influence to such an extent that it becomes the sole norm of its interpretation for all time.

D. APPROACHES THAT USE THE HUMAN SCIENCES

[74] In order to communicate itself, the word of God has taken root in the life of human communities (cf. Sirach 24:12), and it has been through the psychological dispositions of the various persons who composed the biblical writings that it has pursued its path. It follows, then, that the human sciences—in particular sociology, anthropology and psychology—can contribute toward a better understanding of certain aspects of biblical texts. It should be noted, however, that in this area there are several schools of thought, with notable disagreement among them on the very nature of these sciences. That said, a good number of exegetes have drawn considerable profit in recent years from research of this kind.

1. SOCIOLOGICAL APPROACH

[75] Religious texts are bound in reciprocal relationship to the societies in which they originate. This is clearly the case as regards biblical texts. Consequently, the scientific study of the Bible requires as exact a knowledge as is possible of the social conditions distinctive of the various milieus in which the traditions recorded in the Bible took shape. This kind of sociohistorical information needs then to be completed by an accurate sociological explanation, which will provide a scientific interpretation of the implications for each case of the prevailing social conditions.

[76] The sociological point of view has had a role in the history of exegesis for quite some time. The attention which form-criticism devoted to the social circumstances in which various texts arose (sitz im leben) is already an indication of this: It recognized that biblical traditions bore the mark of the socio-cultural milieu which transmitted them. In the first third of the 20th century, the Chicago School studied the socio-historical situation of early Christianity, thereby giving historical criticism a notable impulse in this direction. In the course of the last 20 years (1970–1990), the sociological approach to biblical texts has become an integral part of exegesis.

[77] The questions which arise in this area for the exegesis of the Old Testament are manifold. One should ask, for example, concerning the various forms of social and religious organization which Israel has known in the course of its history. For the period before the formation of a nation-state, does the ethnological model of a society which is segmentary and lacking a unifying head (acephalous) provide a satisfactory base from which to work? What has been the process whereby a loosely organized tribal league became, first of all, an organized monarchical state and, after that, a community held together simply by bonds of religion and common descent? What economic, military and other

transformations were brought about by the movement toward political and religious centralization that led to the monarchy? Does not the study of the laws regulating social behavior in the ancient Near East and in Israel make a more useful contribution to the understanding of the Decalogue than purely literary attempts to reconstruct the earliest form of the text?

[78] For the exegesis of the New Testament, the questions will clearly be somewhat different. Let us mention some: to account for the way of life adopted by Jesus and his disciples before Easter, what value can be accorded to the theory of a movement of itinerant charismatic figures, living without fixed home, without family, without money and other goods? In the matter of the call to follow in the steps of Jesus, can we speak of a genuine relationship of continuity between the radical detachment involved in following Jesus in his earthly life and what was asked of members of the Christian movement after Easter in the very different social conditions of early Christianity? What do we know of the social structure of the Pauline communities, taking account in each case of the relevant urban culture?

[79] In general, the sociological approach broadens the exegetical enterprise and brings to it many positive aspects. Knowledge of sociological data which help us understand the economic, cultural and religious functioning of the biblical world is indispensable for historical criticism. The task incumbent upon the exegete to gain a better understanding of the early church's witness to faith cannot be achieved in a fully rigorous way without the scientific research which studies, the strict relationship that exists between the texts of the New Testament and life as actually lived by the early church. The employment of models provided by sociological science offers historical studies into the biblical period a notable potential for renewal—though it is necessary, of course, that the models employed be modified in accordance with the reality under study.

[80] Here let us signal some of the risks involved in applying the sociological approach to exegesis. It is surely the case that, if the work of sociology consists in the study of currently existing societies, one can expect difficulty when seeking to apply its methods to historical societies belonging to a very distant past. Biblical and extrabiblical texts do not necessarily provide the sort of documentation adequate to give a comprehensive picture of the society of the time. Moreover, the sociological method does tend to pay rather more attention to the economic and institutional aspects of human life than to its personal and religious dimensions.

2. THE APPROACH THROUGH CULTURAL ANTHROPOLOGY

[81] The approach to biblical texts which makes use of the study of cultural anthropology stands in close relationship with the sociological approach. The distinction between the two approaches exists, at one and the same time, on the level of perception, on that of method and on that of the aspect of reality under consideration. While the sociological approach—as we have just mentioned—studies economic and institutional aspects above all, the anthropological approach is interested in a wide assortment of other aspects, reflected in language, art,

religion, but also in dress, ornament, celebration, dance, myth, legend and all that concerns ethnography.

[82] In general, cultural anthropology seeks to define the characteristics of different kinds of human beings in their social context—as, for example the "Mediterranean person"—with all that this involves by way of studying the rural or urban context and with attention paid to the values recognized by the society in question (honor and dishonor, secrecy, keeping faith, tradition, kinds of education and schooling), to the manner in which social control is exercised, to the ideas which people have of family house, kin, to the situation of women, to institutionalized dualities (patron-client, owner-tenant, benefactor-benefi-ciary, free person-slave), taking into account also the prevailing conception of the sacred and the profane, taboos, rites of passage from one state to another, magic, the source of wealth, of power, of information, etc. On the basis of these diverse elements, typologies and "models" are constructed, which are claimed to be common to a number of cultures.

[83] Clearly this kind of study can be useful for the interpretation of biblical texts. It has been effectively applied to the study of the ideas of kinship in the Old Testament, of the position of women in Israelite society, of the influence of agrarian rituals, etc. In the texts which report the teaching of Jesus, for example the parables, many details can be explained thanks to this approach. This is also the case with regard to fundamental ideas, such as that of the reign of God or of the way of conceiving time with respect to the history of salvation, as well as of the processes by which the first Christians came to gather in communities. This approach allows one to distinguish more clearly those elements of the bib-lical message that are permanent, as having their foundation in human nature, and those which are more contingent, being due to the particular features of certain cultures. Nevertheless, no more than is the case with respect to other particularized approaches, this approach is not qualified simply by itself to determine what is specifically the content of revelation. It is important to keep this in mind when appreciating the valuable results it has brought.

3. PSYCHOLOGICAL AND PSYCHOANALYTICAL APPROACHES

[84] Psychology and theology continue their mutual dialogue. The modern extension of psychological research to the study of the dynamic structures of the subconscious has given rise to fresh attempts at interpreting ancient texts, including the Bible. Whole works have been devoted to the psychoanalytic interpretation of biblical texts, which has led to vigorous discussion: In what measure and under what conditions can psychological and psychoanalytical research contribute to a deeper understanding of sacred Scripture?

[85] Psychological and psychoanalytical studies do bring a certain enrichment to biblical exegesis in that, because of them, the texts of the Bible can be better understood in terms of experience of life and norms of behavior. As is well known religion is always in a relationship of conflict or debate with the uncon-scious. It plays a significant role in the proper orientation of human drives. The stages through which historical criticism passes in its methodical study of texts

need to be complemented by study of the different levels of reality they display. Psychology and psychoanalysis attempt to show the way in this respect. They lead to a multidimensional understanding of Scripture and help decode the human language of revelation.

[86] Psychology and, in a somewhat different way, psychoanalysis have led, in particular, to a new understanding of symbol. The language of symbol makes provision for the expression of areas of religious experience that are not accessible to purely conceptual reasoning but which have a genuine value for the expression of truth. For this reason, interdisciplinary study conducted in common by exegetes and psychologists or psychoanalysts offers particular advantages, especially when objectively grounded and confirmed by pastoral experience.

[87] Numerous examples could be cited showing the necessity of a collaborative effort on the part of exegetes and psychologists: to ascertain the meaning of cultic ritual, of sacrifice, of bans, to explain the use of imagery in biblical language, the metaphorical significance of miracle stories, the wellsprings of apocalyptic visual and auditory experiences. It is not simply a matter of describing the symbolic language of the Bible but of grasping how it functions with respect to the revelation of mystery and the issuing of challenge—where the "numinous" reality of God enters into contact with the human person.

[88] The dialogue between exegesis and psychology or psychoanalysis, begun with a view to a better understanding of the Bible, should clearly be conducted in a critical manner, respecting the boundaries of each discipline. Whatever the circumstances, a psychology or psychoanalysis of an atheistic nature disqualifies itself from giving proper consideration to the data of faith. Useful as they may be to determine more exactly the extent of human responsibility, psychology and psychoanalysis should not serve to eliminate the reality of sin and of salvation. One should moreover take care not to confuse spontaneous religiosity and biblical revelation or impugn the historical character of the Bible's message, which bestows upon it the value of a unique event.

[89] Let us note moreover that one cannot speak of "psychoanalytical exegesis" as though it existed in one single form. In fact, proceeding from the different fields of psychology and from the various schools of thought, there exists a whole range of approaches capable of shedding helpful light upon the human and theological interpretation of the Bible. To absolutize one or other of the approaches taken by the various schools of psychology and psychoanalysis would not serve to make collaborative effort in this area more fruitful but rather render it harmful.

[90] The human sciences are not confined to sociology, cultural anthropology and psychology. Other disciplines can also be very useful for the interpretation of the Bible. In all these areas it is necessary to take good account of competence in the particular field and to recognize that only rarely will one and the same person be fully qualified in both exegesis and one or other of the human sciences.

E. CONTEXTUAL APPROACHES

[91] The interpretation of a text is always dependent on the mindset and concerns of its readers. Readers give privileged attention to certain aspects and, without even being aware of it, neglect others. Thus it is inevitable that some exegetes bring to their work points of view that are new and responsive to contemporary currents of thought which have not up till now been taken sufficiently into consideration. It is important that they do so with critical discernment. The movements in this regard which claim particular attention today are those of liberation theology and feminism.

1. THE LIBERATIONIST APPROACH

[92] The theology of liberation is a complex phenomenon, which ought not be oversimplified. It began to establish itself as a theological movement in the early 1970s. Over and beyond the economic, social and political circumstances of Latin America, its starting point is to be found in two great events in the recent life of the church: the Second Vatican Council, with its declared intention of *aggiornamento* and of orienting the pastoral work of the church toward the needs of the contemporary world, and the Second General Conference of the Episcopate of Latin America held at Medellin in 1968, which applied the teachings of the council to the needs of Latin America. The movement has since spread also to other parts of the world (Africa, Asia, the black population of the United States).

[93] It is not all that easy to discern if there truly exists "one theology of liberation and to define what its methodology might be. It is equally difficult to determine adequately its manner of reading the Bible, in a way which would lead to an accurate assessment of advantages and limitations. One can say that liberation theology adopts no particular methodology. But starting from its own socio-cultural and political point of view, it practices a reading of the Bible which is oriented to the needs of the people, who seek in the Scriptures nourishment for their faith and their life.

[94] Liberation theology is not content with an objectifying interpretation which concentrates on what the text said in its original context. It seeks a reading drawn from the situation of people as it is lived here and now. If a people lives in circumstances of oppression, one must go to the Bible to find there nourishment capable of sustaining the people in its struggles and its hopes. The reality of the present time should not be ignored but, on the contrary, met head on, with a view to shedding upon it the light of the word. From this light will come authentic Christian praxis, leading to the transformation of society through works of justice and love. Within the vision of faith Scripture is transformed into a dynamic impulse for full liberation.

[95] The main principles guiding this approach are the following:

God is present in the history of his people, bringing them salvation. He is the God of the poor and cannot tolerate oppression or injustice.

It follows that exegesis cannot be neutral, but must, in imitation of God, take sides on behalf of the poor and be engaged in the struggle to liberate the oppressed.

It is precisely participation in this struggle that allows those interpretations to surface which are discovered only when the biblical texts are read in a context of solidarity with the oppressed.

Because the liberation of the oppressed is a communal process, the community of the poor is the privileged addressee of the Bible as word of liberation. Moreover, since the biblical texts were written for communities, it is to communities in the first place that the reading of the Bible has been entrusted. The word of God is fully relevant—above all because of the capacity inherent in the "foundational events" (the exodus from Egypt, the passion and resurrection of Jesus) for finding fresh realization again and again in the course of history.

[96] Liberation theology includes elements of undoubted value: the deep awareness of the presence of God who saves; the insistence on the communal dimension of faith; the pressing sense of need for a liberating praxis rooted in justice and love; a fresh reading of the Bible which seeks to make of the word of God the light and the nourishment of the people of God in the midst of its struggles and hopes. In all these ways it underlines the capacity of the inspired text to speak to the world of today.

[97] But a reading of the Bible from a stance of such commitment also involves some risks. Since liberation theology is tied to a movement that is still in a process of development, the remarks which follow can only be provisional.

This kind of reading is centered on narrative and prophetic texts which highlight situations of oppression and which inspire a praxis leading to social change. At times such a reading can be limited, not giving enough attention to other texts of the Bible. It is true that exegesis cannot be neutral, but it must also take care not to become one-sided. Moreover, social and political action is not the direct task of the exegete.

In their desire to insert the biblical message into a socio-political context some theologians and exegetes have made use of various instruments for the analysis of social reality. Within this perspective certain streams of liberation theology have conducted an analysis inspired by materialist doctrines, and it is within such frame of reference that they have also read the Bible, a practice which is very questionable, especially when it involves the Marxist principle of the class struggle.

Under the pressure of enormous social problems, there has understandably been more emphasis on an earthly eschatology. Sometimes this has been to the detriment of the more transcendent dimensions of Scriptural eschatology.

[98] More recent social and political changes have led this approach to ask itself new questions and to seek new directions. For its further development and fruitfulness within the church, a decisive factor will be the clarification of

its hermeneutical presuppositions, its methods and its coherence with the faith and the tradition of the church as a whole.

2. THE FEMINIST APPROACH

[99] The feminist biblical hermeneutic had its origin in the United States toward the end of the 19th century. In the sociocultural context of the struggle for the rights of women, the editorial board of a committee charged with the revision of the Bible produced "The Woman's Bible" in two volumes (New York 1885, 1898).

This movement took on fresh life in the 1970s and has since undergone an enormous development in connection with the movement for the liberation of women, especially in North America. To be precise, several forms of feminist biblical hermeneutics have to be distinguished, for the approaches taken are very diverse. All unite around a common theme, woman, and a common goal: the liberation of women and the acquisition on their part of rights equal to those enjoyed by men.

[100] We can here mention three principal forms of feminist biblical hermeneutics: the radical form, the neo-orthodox form and the critical form.

The *radical* form denies all authority to the Bible, maintaining that it has been produced by men simply with a view to confirming man's age-old domination of woman (androcentrism).

The *neo-orthodox* form accepts the Bible as prophetic and as potentially of service, at least to the extent that it takes sides on behalf of the oppressed and thus also of women; this orientation is adopted as a "canon within the canon," so as to highlight whatever in the Bible favors the liberation of women and the acquisition of their rights.

The *critical* form, employing a subtle methodology, seeks to rediscover the status and role of women disciples within the life of Jesus and in the Pauline churches. At this period, it maintains, a certain equality prevailed. But this equality has for the most part been concealed in the writings of the New Testament, something which came to be more and more the case as a tendency toward patriarchy and androcentrism became increasingly dominant.

[101] Feminist hermeneutic has not developed a new methodology. It employs the current methods of exegesis, especially the historical-critical method. But it does add two criteria of investigation.

The first is the feminist criterion, borrowed from the women's liberation movement, in line with the more general direction of liberation theology. This criterion involves a hermeneutic of suspicion: Since history was normally written by the victors, establishing the full truth requires that one does not simply trust texts as they stand but look for signs which may reveal something quite different.

The second criterion is sociological; it is based on the study of societies in the biblical times, their social stratification and the position they accorded to women.

[102] With respect to the New Testament documents, the goal of study, in a word is not the idea of woman as expressed in the New Testament but the historical reconstruction of two different situations of woman in the first century: that which was the norm in Jewish and Greco-Roman society and that which represented the innovation that took shape in the public life of Jesus and in the Pauline churches, where the disciples of Jesus formed "a community of equals." Galatians 3:28 is a text often cited in defense of this view. The aim is to rediscover for today the forgotten history of the role of women in the earliest stages of the church.

[103] Feminist exegesis has brought many benefits. Women have played a more active part in exegetical research. They have succeeded, often better than men, in detecting the presence, the significance and the role of women in the Bible, in Christian origins and in the church. The worldview of today, because of its greater attention to the dignity of women and to their role in society and in the church, ensures that new questions are put to the biblical text, which in turn occasions new discoveries. Feminine sensitivity helps to unmask and correct certain commonly accepted interpretations which were tendentious and sought to justify the male domination of women.

[104] With regard to the Old Testament, several studies have striven to come to a better understanding of the image of God. The God of the Bible is not a projection of a patriarchal mentality. He is Father, but also the God of tenderness and maternal love.

[105] Feminist exegesis, to the extent that it proceeds from a preconceived judgment, runs the risk of interpreting the biblical texts in a tendentious and thus debatable manner. To establish its positions it must often, for want of something better, have recourse to arguments *ex silentio*. As is well known, this type of argument is generally viewed with much reserve: It can never suffice to establish a conclusion on a solid basis. On the other hand, the attempt made on the basis of fleeting indications in the texts to reconstitute a historical situation which these same texts are considered to have been designed to hide—this does not correspond at all to the work of exegesis properly so called. It entails rejecting the content of the inspired texts in preference for a hypothetical construction, quite different in nature.

[106] Feminist exegesis often raises questions of power within the church, questions which, as is obvious, are matters of discussion and even of confrontation. In this area, feminist exegesis can be useful to the church only to the degree that it does not fall into the very traps it denounces and that it does not lose sight of the evangelical teaching concerning power as service, a teaching addressed by Jesus to all disciples, men and women.[2]

F. FUNDAMENTALIST INTERPRETATION

[107] Fundamentalist interpretation starts from the principle that the Bible, being the word of God, inspired and free from error, should be read and interpreted literally in all its details. But by "literal interpretation" it understands a naively literalist interpretation, one, that is to say, which excludes every effort at understanding the Bible that takes account of its historical origins and development. It is opposed, therefore, to the use of the historical-critical method, as indeed to the use of any other scientific method for the interpretation of Scripture.

[108] The fundamentalist interpretation had its origin at the time of the Reformation, arising out of a concern for fidelity to the literal meaning of Scripture. After the century of the Enlightenment it emerged in Protestantism as a bulwark against liberal exegesis.

The actual term *fundamentalist* is connected directly with the American Biblical Congress held at Niagara, N.Y., in 1895. At this meeting, conservative Protestant exegetes defined "five points of fundamentalism": the verbal inerrancy of Scripture, the divinity of Christ, his virginal birth, the doctrine of vicarious expiation and the bodily resurrection at the time of the second coming of Christ. As the fundamentalist way of reading the Bible spread to other parts of the world, it gave rise to other ways of interpretation, equally "literalist," in Europe, Asia, Africa and South America. As the 20th century comes to an end, this kind of interpretation is winning more and more adherents, in religious groups and sects, as also among Catholics.

[109] Fundamentalism is right to insist on the divine inspiration of the Bible, the inerrancy of the word of God and other biblical truths included in its five fundamental points. But its way of presenting these truths is rooted in an ideology which is not biblical, whatever the proponents of this approach might say. For it demands an unshakable adherence to rigid doctrinal points of view and imposes, as the only source of teaching for Christian life and salvation, a reading of the Bible which rejects all questioning and any kind of critical research.

[110] The basic problem with fundamentalist interpretation of this kind is that, refusing to take into account the historical character of biblical revelation, it makes itself incapable of accepting the full truth of the incarnation itself. As regards relationships with God, fundamentalism seeks to escape any closeness of the divine and the human. It refuses to admit that the inspired word of God has been expressed in human language and that this word has been expressed, under divine inspiration, by human authors possessed of limited capacities and resources. For this reason, it tends to treat the biblical text as if it had been dictated word for word by the Spirit. It fails to recognize that the word of God has been formulated in language and expression conditioned by various periods. It pays no attention to the literary forms and to the human ways of thinking to be found in the biblical texts, many of which are the result of a process extending over long periods of time and bearing the mark of very diverse historical situations.

[111] Fundamentalism also places undue stress upon the inerrancy of certain details in the biblical texts, especially in what concerns historical events or supposedly scientific truth. It often historicizes material which from the start never claimed to be historical. It considers historical everything that is reported or recounted with verbs in the past tense, failing to take the necessary account of the possibility of symbolic or figurative meaning.

[112] Fundamentalism often shows a tendency to ignore or to deny the problems presented by the biblical text in its original Hebrew, Aramaic or Greek form. It is often narrowly bound to one fixed translation, whether old or present-day. By the same token it fails to take account of the "rereadings" *(relectures)* of certain texts which are found within the Bible itself.

[113] In what concerns the Gospels, fundamentalism does not take into account the development of the Gospel tradition, but naively confuses the final stage of this tradition (what the evangelists have written) with the initial (the words and deeds of the historical Jesus). At the same time fundamentalism neglects an important fact: The way in which the first Christian communities themselves understood the impact produced by Jesus of Nazareth and his message. But it is precisely there that we find a witness to the apostolic origin of the Christian faith and its direct expression. Fundamentalism thus misrepresents the call voiced by the Gospel itself.

[114] Fundamentalism likewise tends to adopt very narrow points of view. It accepts the literal reality of an ancient, out-of-date cosmology simply because it is found expressed in the Bible; this blocks any dialogue with a broader way of seeing the relationship between culture and faith. Its relying upon a non-critical reading of certain texts of the Bible serves to reinforce political ideas and social attitudes that are marked by prejudices—racism, for example—quite contrary to the Christian Gospel.

[115] Finally, in its attachment to the principle "Scripture alone," fundamentalism separates the interpretation of the Bible from the tradition, which, guided by the Spirit, has authentically developed in union with Scripture in the heart of the community of faith. It fails to realize that the New Testament took form within the Christian church and that it is the Holy Scripture of this church, the existence of which preceded the composition of the texts. Because of this, fundamentalism is often anti-church, it considers of little importance the creeds, the doctrines and liturgical practices which have become part of church tradition, as well as the teaching function of the church itself. It presents itself as a form of private interpretation which does not acknowledge that the church is founded on the Bible and draws its life and inspiration from Scripture.

[116] The fundamentalist approach is dangerous, for it is attractive to people who look to the Bible for ready answers to the problems of life. It can deceive these people, offering them interpretations that are pious but illusory, instead of telling them that the Bible does not necessarily contain an immediate answer to

each and every problem. Without saying as much in so many words, fundamentalism actually invites people to a kind of intellectual suicide. It injects into life a false certitude, for it unwittingly confuses the divine substance of the biblical message with what are in fact its human limitations.

II. HERMENEUTICAL QUESTIONS

A. PHILOSOPHICAL HERMENEUTICS

[117] In its recent course exegesis has been challenged to some rethinking in the light of contemporary philosophical hermeneutics, which has stressed the involvement of the knowing subject in human understanding, especially as regards historical knowledge. Hermeneutical reflection took new life with the publication of the works of Friedrich Schleiermacher, Wilhelm Dilthey and above all, Martin Heidegger. In the footsteps of these philosophers, but also to some extent moving away from them, various authors have more deeply developed contemporary hermeneutical theory and its applications to Scripture. Among them we will mention especially Rudolf Bultmann, Hans Georg Gadamer and Paul Ricoeur. It is not possible to give a complete summary of their thought here. It will be enough to indicate certain central ideas of their philosophies which have had their impact on the interpretation of biblical texts.[3]

1. MODERN PERSPECTIVES

[118] Conscious of the cultural distance between the world of the first century and that of the 20th, Bultmann was particularly anxious to make the reality of which the Bible treats speak to his contemporaries. He insisted upon the "pre-understanding" necessary for all understanding and elaborated the theory of the existential interpretation of the New Testament writings. Relying upon the thinking of Heidegger, Bultmann insisted that it is not possible to have an exegesis of a biblical text without presuppositions which guide comprehension. "Pre-understanding" ("vorverständnis") is founded upon the life-relationship ("lebensverhältnis") of the interpreter to the reality of which the text speaks. To avoid subjectivism, however, one must allow pre-understanding to be deepened and enriched—even to be modified and corrected—by the reality of the text.

Bultmann asked what might be the most appropriate frame of thought for defining the sort of questions that would render the texts of Scripture understandable to people of today. He claimed to have found the answer in the existential analysis of Heidegger, maintaining that Heideggerian existential principles have a universal application and offer structures and concepts most appropriate for the understanding of human existence as revealed in the New Testament message.

[119] Gadamer likewise stresses the historical distance between the text and its interpreter. He takes up and develops the theory of the hermeneutical circle. Anticipations and preconceptions affecting our understanding stem from the tradition which carries us. This tradition consists in a mass of historical and

cultural data which constitute our life context and our horizon of understanding. The interpreter is obliged to enter into dialogue with the reality at stake in the text. Understanding is reached in the fusion of the differing horizons of text and reader ("*horizontverschmelzung*"). This is possible only to the extent that there is a "belonging" ("*zugehörigkeit*"), that is, a fundamental affinity between the interpreter and his or her object. Hermeneutics is a dialectical process: The understanding of a text always entails an enhanced understanding of oneself.

[120] With regard to the hermeneutical thought of Ricoeur, the principal thing to note is the highlighting of the function of distantiation. This is the necessary prelude to any correct appropriation of a text. A first distancing occurs between the text and its author, for, once produced, the text takes on a certain autonomy in relation to its author; it begins its own career of meaning. Another distancing exists between the text and its successive readers; these have to respect the world of the text in its otherness.

[121] Thus the methods of literary and historical analysis are necessary for interpretation. Yet the meaning of a text can be fully grasped only as it is actualized in the lives of readers who appropriate it. Beginning with their situation, they are summoned to uncover new meanings, along the fundamental line of meaning indicated by the text. Biblical knowledge should not stop short at language, it must seek to arrive at the reality of which the language speaks. The religious language of the Bible is a symbolic language which "gives rise to thought" ("*donne à penser*"), a language the full richness of which one never ceases to discover, a language which points to a transcendent reality and which, at the same time, awakens human beings to the deepest dimensions of personal existence.

2. USEFULNESS FOR EXEGESIS

[122] What is to be said about these contemporary theories of the interpretation of texts? The Bible is the word of God for all succeeding ages. Hence the absolute necessity of a hermeneutical theory which allows for the incorporation of the methods of literary and historical criticism within a broader model of interpretation. It is a question of overcoming the distance between the time of the authors and first addressees of the biblical texts, and our own contemporary age, and of doing so in a way that permits a correct actualization of the Scriptural message so that the Christian life of faith may find nourishment. All exegesis of texts is thus summoned to make itself fully complete through a "hermeneutics" understood in this modern sense.

[123] The Bible itself and the history of its interpretation point to the need for a hermeneutics—for an interpretation, that is, that proceeds from and addresses our world today. The whole complex of the Old and New Testament writings show themselves to be the product of a long process where founding events constantly find reinterpretation through connection with the life of communities of faith. In church tradition, the fathers, as first interpreters of Scripture, considered that their exegesis of texts was complete only when it had found a meaning relevant to the situation of Christians in their own day. Exegesis is truly faithful to proper intention of biblical texts when it goes not only to the heart of their

formulation to find the reality of faith there expressed but also seeks to link this reality to the experience of faith in our present world.

[124] Contemporary hermeneutics is a healthy reaction to historical positivism and to the temptation to apply to the study of the Bible the purely objective criteria used in the natural sciences. On the one hand, all events reported in the Bible are interpreted events. On the other, all exegesis of the accounts of these events necessarily involves the exegete's own subjectivity. Access to a proper understanding of biblical texts is only granted to the person who has an affinity with what the text is saying on the basis of life experience. The question which faces every exegete is this: Which hermeneutical theory best enables a proper grasp of the profound reality of which Scripture speaks and its meaningful expression for people today?

[125] We must frankly accept that certain hermeneutical theories are inadequate for interpreting Scripture. For example, Bultmann's existentialist interpretation tends to enclose the Christian message within the constraints of a particular philosophy. Moreover, by virtue of the presuppositions insisted upon in this hermeneutic, the religious message of the Bible is for the most part emptied of its objective reality (by means of an excessive "demythologization") and tends to be reduced to an anthropological message only. Philosophy becomes the norm of interpretation, rather than an instrument for understanding the central object of all interpretation: the person of Jesus Christ and the saving events accomplished in human history. An authentic interpretation of Scripture, then, involves in the first place a welcoming of the meaning that is given in the events and, in a supreme way, in the person of Jesus Christ.

This meaning is expressed in the text. To avoid, then, purely subjective readings, an interpretation valid for contemporary times will be founded on the study of the text, and such an interpretation will constantly submit its presuppositions to verification by the text.

[126] Biblical hermeneutics, for all that it is a part of the general hermeneutics applying to every literary and historical text, constitutes at the same time a unique instance of general hermeneutics. Its specific characteristics stem from its object. The events of salvation and their accomplishment in the person of Jesus Christ give meaning to all human history. New interpretations in the course of time can only be the unveiling or unfolding of this wealth of meaning. Reason alone cannot fully comprehend the account of these events given in the Bible. Particular presuppositions, such as the faith lived in ecclesial community and the light of the Spirit, control its interpretation. As the reader matures in the life of the Spirit, so there grows also his or her capacity to understand the realities of which the Bible speaks.

B. THE MEANING OF INSPIRED SCRIPTURE

[127] The contribution made by modern philosophical hermeneutics and the recent development of literary theory allows biblical exegesis to deepen its

understanding of the task before it, the complexity of which has become ever more evident. Ancient exegesis, which obviously could not take into account modern scientific requirements, attributed to every text of Scripture several levels of meaning. The most prevalent distinction was that between the literal sense and the spiritual sense. Medieval exegesis distinguished within the spiritual sense three different aspects, each relating, respectively, to the truth revealed, to the way of life commended and to the final goal to be achieved. From this came the famous couplet of Augustine of Denmark (13th century):

> "Littera gesta docet, quid credas allegoria,
> moralis quid agas, quid speras anagogia."

[The literal sense teaches you what happened, the allegorical what you believe, the moral sense how you are to act, the anagogical how you are to hope.]

[128] In reaction to this multiplicity of senses, historical-critical exegesis adopted, more or less overtly, the thesis of the one single meaning: A text cannot have at the same time more than one meaning. All the effort of historical-critical exegesis goes into defining "the" precise sense of this or that biblical text seen within the circumstances in which it was produced.

But this thesis has now run aground on the conclusions of theories of language and of philosophical hermeneutics, both of which affirm that written texts are open to a plurality of meaning.

The problem is not simple, and it arises in different ways in regard to different types of texts: historical accounts, parables, oracular pronouncements, laws, proverbs, prayers, hymns, etc. Nevertheless, while keeping in mind that considerable diversity of opinion also prevails, some general principles can be stated.

1. THE LITERAL SENSE

[129] It is not only legitimate, it is also absolutely necessary to seek to define the precise meaning of texts as produced by their authors—what is called the "literal" meaning. St. Thomas Aquinas had already affirmed the fundamental importance of this sense (S. Th. I, q. 1, a. 10, ad 1).

[130] The literal sense is not to be confused with the "literalist" sense to which fundamentalists are attached. It is not sufficient to translate a text word for word in order to obtain its literal sense. One must understand the text according to the literary conventions of the time. When a text is metaphorical, its literal sense is not that which flows immediately from a word-to-word translation (e.g. "Let your loins be girt": Luke 12:35), but that which corresponds to the metaphorical use of these terms ("Be ready for action"). When it is a question of a story, the literal sense does not necessarily imply belief that the facts recounted actually took place, for a story need not belong to the genre of history but be instead a work of imaginative fiction.

[131] The literal sense of Scripture is that which has been expressed directly by the inspired human authors. Since it is the fruit of inspiration, this sense is also intended by God, as principal author. One arrives at this sense by means of

a careful analysis of the text, within its literary and historical context. The principal task of exegesis is to carry out this analysis, making use of all the resources of literary and historical research, with a view to defining the literal sense of the biblical texts with the greatest possible accuracy (cf. *Divino Afflante Spiritu: Ench. Bibl.*, 550). To this end, the study of ancient literary genres is particularly necessary (ibid. 560).

[132] Does a text have only one literal sense? In general, yes; but there is no question here of a hard and fast rule, and this for two reasons. First, a human author can intend to refer at one and the same time to more than one level of reality. This is in fact normally the case with regard to poetry. Biblical inspiration does not reject this capacity of human psychology and language; the fourth Gospel offers numerous examples of it. Second, even when a human utterance appears to have only one meaning, divine inspiration can guide the expression in such way as to create more than one meaning. This is the case with the saying of Caiaphas in John 11:50: At one and the same time it expresses both an immoral political ploy and a divine revelation. The two aspects belong, both of them, to the literal sense, for they are both made clear by the context. Although this example may be extreme, it remains significant, providing a warning against adopting too narrow a conception of the inspired text's literal sense.

[133] One should be especially attentive to the dynamic aspect of many texts. The meaning of the royal psalms, for example, should not be limited strictly to the historical circumstances of their production. In speaking of the king, the psalmist evokes at one and the same time both the institution as it actually was and an idealized vision of kingship as God intended it to be; in this way the text carries the reader beyond the institution of kingship in its actual historical manifestation. Historical-critical exegesis has too often tended to limit the meaning of texts by tying it too rigidly to precise historical circumstances. It should seek rather to determine the direction of thought expressed by the text; this direction, far from working toward a limitation of meaning, will on the contrary dispose the exegete to perceive extensions of it that are more or less foreseeable in advance.

[134] One branch of modern hermeneutics has stressed that human speech gains an altogether fresh status when put in writing. A written text has the capacity to be placed in new circumstances, which will illuminate it in different ways, adding new meanings to the original sense. This capacity of written texts is especially operative in the case of the biblical writings, recognized as the word of God. Indeed, what encouraged the believing community to preserve these texts was the conviction that they would continue to be bearers of light and life for generations of believers to come. The literal sense is, from the start, open to further developments, which are produced through the "rereading" (*"relectures"*) of texts in new contexts.

It does not follow from this that we can attribute to a biblical text whatever meaning we like, interpreting it in a wholly subjective way. On the contrary, one must reject as unauthentic every interpretation alien to the meaning expressed by the human authors in their written text. To admit the possibility of such alien meanings would be equivalent to cutting off the biblical message from its root, which is the word of God in its historical communication; it would also mean opening the door to interpretations of a wildly subjective nature.

2. THE SPIRITUAL SENSE

[135] There are reasons, however, for not taking alien in so strict a sense as to exclude all possibility of higher fulfillment. The paschal event, the death and resurrection of Jesus, has established a radically new historical context, which sheds fresh light upon the ancient texts and causes them to undergo a change in meaning. In particular, certain texts which in ancient times had to be thought of as hyperbole (e.g. the oracle where God, speaking of a son of David, promised to establish his throne "forever": 2 Samuel 7:12–13; 1 Chronicles 17:11–14), these texts must now be taken literally, because "Christ, having been raised from the dead, dies no more" (Romans 6:9). Exegetes who have a narrow, "historicist" idea about the literal sense will judge that here is an example of an interpretation alien to the original. Those who are open to the dynamic aspect of a text will recognize here a profound element of continuity as well as a move to a different level: Christ rules forever, but not on the earthly throne of David (cf. also Psalms 2:7–8; 110: 1–4).

In such cases one speaks of "the spiritual sense." As a general rule we can define the spiritual sense, as understood by Christian faith, as the meaning expressed by the biblical texts when read under the influence of the Holy Spirit, in the context of the paschal mystery of Christ and of the new life which flows from it. This context truly exists. In it the New Testament recognizes the fulfillment of the Scriptures. It is therefore quite acceptable to reread the Scriptures in the light of this new context, which is that of life in the Spirit.

[136] The above definition allows us to draw some useful conclusions of a more precise nature concerning the relationship between the spiritual and literal senses:

Contrary to a current view, there is not necessarily a distinction between the two senses. When a biblical text relates directly to the paschal mystery of Christ or to the new life which results from it, its literal sense is already a spiritual sense. Such is regularly the case in the New Testament. It follows that it is most often in dealing with the Old Testament that Christian exegesis speaks of the spiritual sense. But already in the Old Testament there are many instances where texts have a religious or spiritual sense as their literal sense. Christian faith recognizes in such cases an anticipatory relationship to the new life brought by Christ.

[137] While there is a distinction between the two senses, the spiritual sense can never be stripped of its connection with the literal sense. The latter remains the indispensable foundation. Otherwise one could not speak of the "fulfillment" of Scripture. Indeed, in order that there be fulfillment, a relationship of continuity and of conformity is essential. But it is also necessary that there be transition to a higher level of reality.

[138] The spiritual sense is not to be confused with subjective interpretations stemming from the imagination or intellectual speculation. The spiritual sense results from setting the text in relation to real facts which are not foreign to it: the paschal event, in all its inexhaustible richness, which constitutes the summit of the divine intervention in the history of Israel, to the benefit of all mankind.

Spiritual interpretation, whether in community or in private, will discover the authentic spiritual sense only to the extent that it is kept within these perspectives. One then holds together three levels of reality: the biblical text, the paschal mystery and the present circumstances of life in the Spirit.

[139] Persuaded that the mystery of Christ offers the key to interpretation of all Scripture, ancient exegesis labored to find a spiritual sense in the minutest details of the biblical text—for example, in every prescription of the ritual law—making use of rabbinic methods or inspired by Hellenistic allegorical exegesis. Whatever its pastoral usefulness might have been in the past, modern exegesis cannot ascribe true interpretative value to this kind of procedure (cf. *Divino Afflante Spiritu: Ench. Bibl.* 553).

[140] One of the possible aspects of the spiritual sense is the typological. This is usually said to belong not to Scripture itself but to the realities expressed by Scripture: Adam as the figure of Christ (cf. Romans 5:14), the flood as the figure of baptism (1 Peter 3:20–21), etc. Actually, the connection involved in typology is ordinarily based on the way in which Scripture describes the ancient reality (cf. the voice of Abel: Genesis 4:10; Hebrews 11:4; 12:24) and not simply on the reality itself. Consequently, in such a case one can speak of a meaning that is truly Scriptural.

3. THE FULLER SENSE

[141] The term *fuller sense (sensus plenior)*, which is relatively recent, has given rise to discussion. The fuller sense is defined as a deeper meaning of the text, intended by God but not clearly expressed by the human author. Its existence in the biblical text comes to be known when one studies the text in the light of other biblical texts which utilize it or in its relationship with the internal development of revelation.

It is then a question either of the meaning that a subsequent biblical author attributes to an earlier biblical text, taking it up in a context which confers upon it a new literal sense, or else it is a question of the meaning that an authentic doctrinal tradition or a conciliar definition gives to a biblical text. For example, the context of Matthew 1:23 gives a fuller sense to the prophecy of Isaiah 7:14 in regard to the *almah* who will conceive, by using the translation of the Septuagint *(parthenos)*: "The *virgin* will conceive." The patristic and conciliar teaching about the Trinity expresses the fuller sense of the teaching of the New Testament regarding God the Father, the Son and the Holy Spirit. The definition of original sin by the Council of Trent provided the fuller sense of Paul's teaching in Romans 5:12–21 about the consequences of the sin of Adam for humanity. But when this kind of control—by an explicit biblical text or by an authentic doctrinal tradition—is lacking, recourse to a claimed fuller sense could lead to subjective interpretations deprived of validity.

[142] In a word, one might think of the "fuller sense" as another way of indicating the spiritual sense of a biblical text in the case where the spiritual sense is distinct from the literal sense. It has its foundation in the fact that the Holy Spirit, principal author of the Bible, can guide human authors in the choice of expressions in such a way that the latter will express a truth the fullest depths of which the authors themselves do not perceive. This deeper truth will be more fully revealed in the course of time—on the one hand, through further divine interventions which clarify the meaning of texts and, on the other, through the insertion of texts into the canon of Scripture. In these ways there is created a new context, which brings out fresh possibilities of meaning that had lain hidden in the original context.

III. CHARACTERISTICS OF CATHOLIC INTERPRETATION

[143] Catholic exegesis does not claim any particular scientific method as its own. It recognizes that one of the aspects of biblical texts is that they are the work of human authors, who employed both their own capacities for expression and the means which their age and social context put at their disposal. Consequently Catholic exegesis freely makes use of the scientific methods and approaches which allow a better grasp of the meaning of texts in their linguistic, literary, sociocultural, religious and historical contexts, while explaining them as well through studying their sources and attending to the personality of each author (cf. *Divino Afflante Spiritu: Ench. Bibl.* 557). Catholic exegesis actively contributes to the development of new methods and to the progress of research.

[144] What characterizes Catholic exegesis is that it deliberately places itself within the living tradition of the church, whose first concern is fidelity to the revelation attested by the Bible. Modern hermeneutics has made clear, as we have noted, the impossibility of interpreting a text without starting from a "pre-understanding" of one type or another.

[145] Catholic exegetes approach the biblical text with a pre-understanding which holds closely together modern scientific culture and the religious tradition emanating from Israel and from the early Christian community. Their interpretation stands thereby in continuity with a dynamic pattern of interpretation that is found within the Bible itself and continues in the life of the church. This dynamic pattern corresponds to the requirement that there be a lived affinity between the interpreter and the object, an affinity which constitutes, in fact, one of the conditions that makes the entire exegetical enterprise possible.

[146] All pre-understanding, however, brings dangers with it. As regards Catholic exegesis, the risk is that of attributing to biblical texts a meaning which they do not contain but which is the product of a later development within the tradition. The exegete must beware of such a danger.

A. INTERPRETATION IN THE BIBLICAL TRADITION

[147] The texts of the Bible are the expression of religious traditions which existed before them. The mode of their connection with these traditions is different in each case, with the creativity of the authors shown in various degrees. In the course of time, multiple traditions have flowed together little by little to form one great common tradition. The Bible is a privileged expression of this process: It has itself contributed to the process and continues to have controlling influence upon it.

[148] The subject, "interpretation in the biblical tradition," can be approached in very many ways. The expression can be taken to include the manner in which the Bible interprets fundamental human experiences or the particular events of the history of Israel, or again the manner in which the biblical texts make use of their sources, written or oral, some of which may well come from other religions or cultures—through a process of reinterpretation. But our subject is the interpretation of the Bible; we do not want to treat here these very broad questions but simply to make some observations about the interpretation of biblical texts that occurs within the Bible itself.

1. REREADINGS (*RELECTURES*)

[149] One thing that gives the Bible an inner unity, unique of its kind, is the fact that later biblical writings often depend upon earlier ones. These more recent writings allude to older ones, create "rereadings" *(relectures)* which develop new aspects of meaning, sometimes quite different from the original sense. A text may also make explicit reference to older passages, whether it is to deepen their meaning or to make known their fulfillment.

Thus it is that the inheritance of the land, promised by God to Abraham for his offspring (Genesis 15:7,18), becomes entrance into the sanctuary of God (Exodus 15:17), a participation in God's "rest" (Psalms 132:7–8) reserved for those who truly have faith (Psalms 95:8–11; Hebrews 3:7—4:11) and, finally, entrance into the heavenly sanctuary (Hebrews 6:12, 18–20), "the eternal inheritance" (Hebrews 9:15).

The prophecy of Nathan, which promised David a "house," that is a dynastic succession, "secure forever" (2 Samuel 7:12–16), is recalled in a number of rephrasings (2 Samuel 23:5; 1 Kings 2:4; 3:6; 1 Chronicles 17:11–14), arising especially out of times of distress (Psalms 89:20–38), not without significant changes; it is continued by other prophecies (Psalms 2:7–8; 110: 1,4; Amos 9: 11; Isaiah 7: 13-14; Jeremiah 23:56, etc.), some of which announce the return of the kingdom of David itself (Hosea 3:5, Jeremiah 30:9, Ezra 34:24, 37:24–25; cf. Mark 11:10). The promised kingdom becomes universal (Psalms 2:8; Daniel 2:35, 44; 7:14; cf. Matthew 28:18). It brings to fullness the vocation of human beings (Genesis 1:28; Psalms 8:6–9; Wisdom 9:2-3; 10:2).

The prophecy of Jeremiah concerning the 70 years of chastisement incurred by Jerusalem and Juda (Jeremiah 25:11–12; 29:10) is recalled in 2 Chronicles

25:20–23 which affirms that this punishment has actually occurred. Nonetheless, much later, the author of Daniel returns to reflect upon it once more, convinced that this word of God still conceals a hidden meaning that could throw light upon the situation of his own day (Daniel 9:24–27).

The basic affirmation of the retributive justice of God, rewarding the good and punishing the evil (Psalms 1:1–6; 112:1–10; Leviticus 26:3–33; etc.), flies in the face of much immediate experience, which often fails to bear it out. In the face of this, Scripture allows strong voices of protestation and argument to be heard (Psalms 44; Job 10:1–7; 13:3–28; 23–24), as little by little it plumbs more profoundly the full depths of the mystery (Psalms 37; Job 38–42; Isaiah 53; Wisdom 3–5).

2. RELATIONSHIPS BETWEEN THE OLD TESTAMENT AND THE NEW

[150] Intertextual relationships become extremely dense in the writings of the New Testament, thoroughly imbued as it is with the Old Testament through both multiple allusion and explicit citation. The authors of the New Testament accorded to the Old Testament the value of divine revelation. They proclaimed that this revelation found its fulfillment in the life, in the teaching and above all in the death and resurrection of Jesus, source of pardon and of everlasting life. "Christ died for our sins *according to the Scriptures* and was buried; he was raised on the third day *according to the Scriptures* and appeared" (1 Corinthians 15:3–5): Such is the center and core of the apostolic preaching (1 Corinthians 15:11).

[151] As always, the relationship between Scripture and the events which bring it to fulfillment is not one of simple material correspondence. On the contrary, there is mutual illumination and a progress that is dialectic: What becomes clear is that Scripture reveals the meaning of events and that events reveal the meaning of Scripture, that is, they require that certain aspects of the received interpretation be set aside and a new interpretation adopted.

[152] Right from the start of his public ministry, Jesus adopted a personal and original stance different from the accepted interpretation of his age, that "of the scribes and Pharisees" (Matthew 5:20). There is ample evidence of this: The antitheses of his Sermon on the Mount (Matthew 5:21–48); his sovereign freedom with respect to Sabbath observance (Mark 2:27–28 and parallels); his way of relativizing the precepts of ritual purity (Mark 7: 1–23 and parallels); on the other hand, the radicality of his demand in other areas (Matthew 10:2–12 and parallels; 10:17–27 and parallels), and, above all, his attitude of welcome to "the tax-collectors and sinners" (Mark 2: 15–17 and parallels). All this was in no sense the result of a personal whim to challenge the established order. On the contrary, it represented a most profound fidelity to the will of God expressed in Scripture (cf. Matthew 5:17; 9:13; Mark 7:8–13 and parallels; 10:5–9 and parallels).

Jesus' death and resurrection pushed to the very limit the interpretative development he had begun, provoking on certain points a complete break with the past, alongside unforeseen new openings. The death of the Messiah, "king of the Jews" (Mark 15:26 and parallels), prompted a transformation of the purely earthly interpretation of the royal psalms and messianic prophecies. The resurrection and heavenly glorification of Jesus as Son of God lent these texts a fullness of meaning previously unimaginable. The result was that some expressions which had seemed to be hyperbole had now to be taken literally. They came to be seen as divine preparations to express the glory of Christ Jesus, for Jesus is truly "Lord" (Psalms 110:1), in the fullest sense of the word (Acts 2:36; Philippians 2:10–11; Hebrews 1:10–12); he is Son of God (Psalms 2:7; Mark 14:62; Romans 1:3–4), God with God (Psalms 45:7; Hebrews 1:8; John 1:1; 20:28); "his reign will have no end" (Luke 1:32–33; cf. 1 Chronicles 17: 11–14; Psalms 45:7; Hebrews 1:8) and he is at the same time "priest forever" (Psalms 110:4; Hebrews 5:6–10; 7:23–24).

[153] It is in the light of the events of Easter that the authors of the New Testament read anew the Scriptures of the Old. The Holy Spirit, sent by the glorified Christ (cf. John 15:26; 16:7), led them to discover the spiritual sense. While this meant that they came to stress more than ever the prophetic value of the Old Testament, it also had the effect of relativizing very considerably its value as a system of salvation. This second point of view, which already appears in the Gospels (cf. Matthew 11:11–13 and parallels; 12:41–42 and parallels; John 4:12–14; 5:37; 6:32), emerges strongly in certain Pauline letters as well as in the Letter to the Hebrews. Paul and the author of the Letter to the Hebrews show that the Torah itself, insofar as it is revelation, announces its own proper end as a legal system (cf. Galatians 2:15—5:1; Romans 3:20–21; 6:14; Hebrews 7:11–19; 10:8–9). It follows that the pagans who adhere to faith in Christ need not be obliged to observe all the precepts of biblical law, from now on reduced in its entirety simply to the status of a legal code of a particular people. But in the Old Testament as the word of God they have to find the spiritual sustenance that will assist them to discover the full dimensions of the paschal mystery which now governs their lives (cf. Luke 24:25–27, 44–45; Romans 1: 1–2).

[154] All this serves to show that within the one Christian Bible the relationships that exist between the New and the Old Testament are quite complex. When it is a question of the use of particular texts, the authors of the New Testament naturally have recourse to the ideas and procedures for interpretation current in their time. To require them to conform to modern scientific methods would be anachronistic. Rather, it is for the exegete to acquire a knowledge of ancient techniques of exegesis so as to be able to interpret correctly the way in which a Scriptural author has used them. On the other hand, it remains true that the exegete need not put absolute value in something which simply reflects limited human understanding.

[155] Finally, it is worth adding that within the New Testament, as already within the Old, one can see the juxtaposing of different perspectives that sit sometimes in tension with one another: For example, regarding the status of Jesus (John 8:29; 16:32 and Mark 15:34) or the value of the Mosaic Law (Matthew 5:17–19 and Romans 6:14) or the necessity of works for justification (James 2:24 and Romans 3:28; Ephesians 2:8–9). One of the characteristics of the Bible is

precisely the absence of a sense of systematization and the presence, on the contrary, of things held in dynamic tension. The Bible is a repository of many ways of interpreting the same events and reflecting upon the same problems. In itself it urges us to avoid excessive simplification and narrowness of spirit.

3. SOME CONCLUSIONS

[156] From what has just been said one can conclude that the Bible contains numerous indications and suggestions relating to the art of interpretation. In fact, from its very inception the Bible has been itself a work of interpretation. Its texts were recognized by the communities of the Former Covenant and by those of the apostolic age as the genuine expression of the common faith. It is in accordance with the interpretative work of these communities and together with it that the texts were accepted as sacred Scripture (thus, e.g. the Song of Songs was recognized as sacred Scripture when applied to the relation between God and Israel). In the course of the Bible's formation, the writings of which it consists were in many cases reworked and reinterpreted so as to make them respond to new situations previously unknown.

[157] The way in which sacred Scripture reveals its own interpretation of texts suggests the following observations:

Sacred Scripture has come into existence on the basis of a consensus in the believing communities recognizing in the texts the expression of revealed faith. This means that, for the living faith of the ecclesial communities, the interpretation of Scripture should itself be a source of consensus on essential matters.

Granted that the expression of faith, such as it is found in the sacred Scripture acknowledged by all, has had to renew itself continually in order to meet new situations, which explains the "rereadings" of many of the biblical texts, the interpretation of the Bible should likewise involve an aspect of creativity; it ought also to confront new questions so as to respond to them out of the Bible.

Granted that tensions can exist in the relationship between various texts of sacred Scripture, interpretation must necessarily show a certain pluralism. No single interpretation can exhaust the meaning of the whole, which is a symphony of many voices. Thus the interpretation of one particular text has to avoid seeking to dominate at the expense of others.

[158] Sacred Scripture is in dialogue with communities of believers: It has come from their traditions of faith. Its texts have been developed in relation to these traditions and have contributed, reciprocally, to the development of the traditions. It follows that interpretation of Scripture takes place in the heart of the church: in its plurality and its unity, and within its tradition of faith.

[159] Faith traditions formed the living context for the literary activity of the authors of sacred Scripture. Their insertion into this context also involved a sharing in both the liturgical and external life of the communities, in their

intellectual world, in their culture and in the ups and downs of their shared history. In like manner, the interpretation of sacred Scripture requires full participation on the part of exegetes in the life and faith of the believing community of their own time.

[160] Dialogue with Scripture in its entirety, which means dialogue with the understanding of the faith prevailing in earlier times, must be matched by a dialogue with the generation of today. Such dialogue will mean establishing a relationship of continuity. It will also involve acknowledging differences. Hence the interpretation of Scripture involves a work of sifting and setting aside; it stands in continuity with earlier exegetical traditions, many elements of which it preserves and makes its own; but in other matters it will go its own way, seeking to make further progress.

B. INTERPRETATION IN THE TRADITION OF THE CHURCH

[161] The church, as the people of God, is aware that it is helped by the Holy Spirit in its understanding and interpretation of Scripture. The first disciples of Jesus knew that they did not have the capacity right away to understand the full reality of what they had received in all its aspects. As they persevered in their life as a community, they experienced an ever-deepening and progressive clarification of the revelation they had received. They recognized in this the influence and the action of "the Spirit of truth," which Christ had promised them to guide them to the fullness of the truth (John 16:12–13). Likewise the church today journeys onward, sustained by the promise of Christ: "The Paraclete, the Holy Spirit, which the Father will send in my name, will teach you all things and will make you recall all that I have said to you" (John 14:26).

1. FORMATION OF THE CANON

[162] Guided by the Holy Spirit and in the light of the living tradition which it has received, the church has discerned the writings which should be regarded as sacred Scripture in the sense that, "having been written under the inspiration of the Holy Spirit, they have God for author and have been handed on as such to the church" (Dei Verbum, 11) and contain "that truth which God wanted put into the sacred writings for the sake of our salvation" (ibid.).

[163] The discernment of a "canon" of sacred Scripture was the result of a long process. The communities of the Old Covenant (ranging from particular groups, such as those connected with prophetic circles or the priesthood to the people as a whole) recognized in a certain number of texts the word of God capable of arousing their faith and providing guidance for daily life; they received these texts as a patrimony to be preserved and handed on. In this way these texts ceased to be merely the expression of a particular author's inspiration; they became the common property of the whole people of God. The New Testament attests its own reverence for these sacred texts, received as a precious heritage passed on by the Jewish people. It regards these texts as "sacred Scripture" (Romans 1:2), "inspired" by the Spirit of God (2 Timothy 3:16; cf. 2 Peter 1:20–21), which "can never be annulled" (John 10:35).

To these texts, which form "the Old Testament" (cf. 2 Corinthians 3:14), the church has closely associated other writings: first those in which it recognized the authentic witness, coming from the apostles (cf. Luke 1:2; 1 John 1:1–3) and guaranteed by the Holy Spirit (cf. 1 Peter 1:12), concerning "all that Jesus began to do and teach" (Acts 1:1) and, second, the instructions given by the apostles themselves and other disciples for the building up of the community of believers. This double series of writings subsequently came to be known as "the New Testament."

[164] Many factors played a part in this process: the conviction that Jesus—and the apostles along with him—had recognized the Old Testament as inspired Scripture and that the paschal mystery is its true fulfillment; the conviction that the writings of the New Testament were a genuine reflection of the apostolic preaching (which does not imply that they were all composed by the apostles themselves); the recognition of their conformity with the rule of faith and of their use in the Christian liturgy; finally, the experience of their affinity with the ecclesial life of the communities and of their potential for sustaining this life.

[165] In discerning the canon of Scripture, the church was also discerning and defining her own identity. Henceforth Scripture was to function as a mirror in which the church could continually rediscover her identity and assess, century after century, the way in which she constantly responds to the Gospel and equips herself to be an apt vehicle of its transmission (cf. *Dei Verbum*, 7). This confers on the canonical writings a salvific and theological value completely different from that attaching to other ancient texts. The latter may throw much light on the origins of the faith. But they can never substitute for the authority of the writings held to be canonical and thus fundamental for the understanding of the Christian faith.

2. PATRISTIC EXEGESIS

[166] From earliest times it has been understood that the same Holy Spirit, who moved the authors of the New Testament to put in writing the message of salvation (*Dei Verbum*, 7; 18), likewise provided the church with continual assistance for the interpretation of its inspired writings (cf. Irenaeus, *Adv. Haer.*, 3 24.1; cf. 3.1.1; 4 33 8; Origen, *De Princ.*, 2.7.2; Tertullian, *De Praescr.*, 22).

The fathers of the church, who had a particular role in the process of the formation of the canon, likewise have a foundational role in relation to the living tradition which unceasingly accompanies and guides the church's reading and interpretation of Scripture (cf. *Providentissimus Deus: Ench. Bibl.* 110–111; *Divino Afflante Spiritu*, 28–30: *Ench. Bibl.* 554; *Dei Verbum*, 23; PCB, *Instr. de Evang. Histor.*, 1). Within the broader current of the great tradition, the particular contribution of patristic exegesis consists in this: to have drawn out from the totality of Scripture the basic orientations which shaped the doctrinal tradition of the church and to have provided a rich theological teaching for the instruction and spiritual sustenance of the faithful.

[167] The fathers of the church placed a high value upon the reading of Scripture and its interpretation. This can be seen, first of all, in works directly linked to the understanding of Scripture, such as homilies and commentaries. But it is also evident in works of controversy and theology, where appeal is made to Scripture in support of the main argument.

[168] For the fathers the chief occasion for reading the Bible is in church, in the course of the liturgy. This is why the interpretations they provide are always of a theological and pastoral nature, touching upon relationship with God, so as to be helpful both for the community and the individual believer.

[169] The fathers look upon the Bible above all as the Book of God, the single work of a single author. This does not mean, however, that they reduce the human authors to nothing more than passive instruments; they are quite capable, also, of according to a particular book its own specific purpose. But their type of approach pays scant attention to the historical development of revelation. Many fathers of the church present the *Logos*, the Word of God, as author of the Old Testament and in this way insist that all Scripture has a Christological meaning.

[170] Setting aside certain exegetes of the School of Antioch (Theodore of Mopsuestia, in particular), the fathers felt themselves at liberty to take a sentence out of its context in order to bring out some revealed truth which they found expressed within it. In apologetic directed against Jewish positions or in theological dispute with other theologians, they did not hesitate to rely on this kind of interpretation.

Their chief concern being to live from the Bible in communion with their brothers and sisters, the fathers were usually content to use the text of the Bible current in their own context. What led Origen to take a systematic interest in the Hebrew Bible was a concern to conduct arguments with Jews from texts which the latter found acceptable. Thus, in his praise for the *hebraica veritas*, St. Jerome appears, in this respect, a somewhat untypical figure.

[171] As a way of eliminating the scandal which particular passages of the Bible might provide for certain Christians, not to mention pagan adversaries of Christianity, the fathers had recourse fairly frequently to the allegorical method. But they rarely abandoned the literalness and historicity of texts. The fathers' recourse to allegory transcends for the most part a simple adaptation to the allegorical method in use among pagan authors.

Recourse to allegory stems also from the conviction that the Bible, as God's book, was given by God to his people, the church. In principle, there is nothing in it which is to be set aside as out of date or completely lacking meaning. God is constantly speaking to his Christian people a message that is ever relevant for their time. In their explanations of the Bible, the fathers mix and weave together typological and allegorical interpretations in a virtually inextricable way. But they do so always for a pastoral and pedagogical purpose, convinced that everything that has been written has been written for our instruction (cf. 1 Corinthians 10:11).

[172] Convinced that they are dealing with the Book of God and therefore with something of inexhaustible meaning, the fathers hold that any particular passage is open to any particular interpretation on an allegorical basis. But they also consider that others are free to offer something else, provided only that what is offered respects the analogy of faith.

[173] The allegorical interpretation of Scripture so characteristic of patristic exegesis runs the risk of being something of an embarrassment to people today. But the experience of the church expressed in this exegesis makes a contribution that is always useful (cf. *Divino Afflante Spiritu*, 31–32; *Dei Verbum*, 23). The fathers of the church teach to read the Bible theologically, within the heart of a living tradition, with an authentic Christian spirit.

3. ROLES OF VARIOUS MEMBERS OF THE CHURCH IN INTERPRETATION

[173] The Scriptures, as given to the church, are the communal treasure of the entire body of believers: "Sacred tradition and sacred Scripture form one sacred deposit of the word of God, entrusted to the church. Holding fast to this deposit, the entire holy people, united with its pastors, remains steadfastly faithful to the teaching of the apostles" (*Dei Verbum*, 10; cf. also 21). It is true that the familiarity with the text of Scripture has been more notable among the faithful at some periods of the church's history than in others. But Scripture has been at the forefront of all the important moments of renewal in the life of the church, from the monastic movement of the early centuries to the recent era of the Second Vatican Council.

This same council teaches that all the baptized, when they bring their faith in Christ to the celebration of the eucharist, recognize the presence of Christ also in his word, "for it is he himself who speaks when the holy Scriptures are read in the church" (*Sacrosanctum Concilium*, 7). To this hearing of the word, they bring that "sense of the faith *(sensus fidei)* which characterizes the entire people (of God) . . . . For by this sense of faith aroused and sustained by the Spirit of truth, the people of God, guided by the sacred magisterium which it faithfully follows, accepts not a human word but the very Word of God (cf. 1 Thessalonians 2:13). It holds fast unerringly to the faith once delivered to the saints (cf. Jude 3), it penetrates it more deeply with accurate insight and applies it more thoroughly to Christian life" (*Lumen Gentium*, 12).

[174] Thus all the members of the church have a role in the interpretation of Scripture. In the exercise of their pastoral ministry, *bishops*, as successors of the apostles, are the first witnesses and guarantors of the living tradition within which Scripture is interpreted in every age. "Enlightened by the Spirit of truth, they have the task of guarding faithfully the word of God, of explaining it and through their preaching making it more widely known" (*Dei Verbum*, 9; cf. *Lumen Gentium*, 25). As co-workers with the bishops, priests have as their primary duty the proclamation of the word (*Presbyterorum Ordinis*, 4). They are gifted with a particular charism for the interpretation of Scripture, when, transmitting not their own ideas but the word of God, they apply the eternal truth of the Gospel to the concrete circumstances of daily life (ibid.). It belongs to priests

and to *deacons*, especially when they administer the sacraments, to make clear the unity constituted by word and sacrament in the ministry of the church.

[175] As those who preside at the eucharistic community and as educators in the faith, the ministers of the word have as their principal task not simply to impart instruction, but also to assist the faithful to understand and discern what the word of God is saying to them in their hearts when they hear and reflect upon the Scriptures. Thus the *local church* as a whole, on the pattern of Israel, the people of God (Exodus 19:5–6), becomes a community which knows that it is addressed by God (cf. John 6:45), a community that listens eagerly to the word with faith, love and docility (Deuteronomy 6:4–6). Granted that they remain ever united in faith and love with the wider body of the church, such truly listening communities become in their own context vigorous sources of evangelization and of dialogue, as well as agents for social change (*Evangelii Nuntiandi*, 57–58; CDF, "Instruction Concerning Christian Freedom and Liberation," 69–70).

[176] The Spirit is, assuredly, also given to *individual Christians*, so that their hearts can "burn within them" (Luke 24:32) as they pray and prayerfully study the Scripture within the context of their own personal lives. This is why the Second Vatican Council insisted that access to Scripture be facilitated in every possible way (*Dei Verbum*, 22; 25). This kind of reading, it should be noted, is never completely private, for the believer always reads and interprets Scripture within the faith of the church and then brings back to the community the fruit of that reading for the enrichment of the common faith.

[177] The entire biblical tradition and, in a particular way, the teaching of Jesus in the Gospels indicates as privileged hearers of the word of God those whom the world considers *people of lowly status*. Jesus acknowledged that things hidden from the wise and learned have been revealed to the simple (Matthew 11:25, Luke 10:21) and that the kingdom of God belongs to those who make themselves like little children (Mark 10:14 and parallels).

Likewise, Jesus proclaimed: "Blessed are you poor, because the kingdom of God is yours" (Luke 6:20; cf. Matthew 5:3). One of the signs of the Messianic era is the proclamation of the good news to the poor (Luke 4:18; 7:22; Matthew 11:5, cf. CDF, "Instruction Concerning Christian Freedom and Liberation," 47–48). Those who in their powerlessness and lack of human resources find themselves forced to put their trust in God alone and in his justice have a capacity for hearing and interpreting the word of God which should be taken into account by the whole church, it demands a response on the social level as well.

[178] Recognizing the diversity of gifts and functions which the Spirit places at the service of the community, especially the gift of teaching (1 Corinthians 12:28–30; Romans 12:6–7; Ephesians 4:11–16), the church expresses its esteem for those who display a particular ability to contribute to the building up of the body of Christ through their expertise in interpreting Scripture (*Divino Afflante Spiritu*, 4648: *Ench. Bibl.* 564–565; *Dei Verbum*, 23; PCB, "Instruction Concerning the Historical Truth of the Gospels," Introduction). Although their

labors did not always receive in the past the encouragement that is given them today, *exegetes* who offer their learning as a service to the church find that they are part of a rich tradition which stretches from the first centuries, with Origen and Jerome, up to more recent times, with Pére Lagrange and others, and continues right up to our time. In particular, the discovery of the literal sense of Scripture, upon which there is now so much insistence, requires the combined efforts of those who have expertise in the fields of ancient languages, of history and culture, of textual criticism and the analysis of literary forms, and who know how to make good use of the methods of scientific criticism.

[179] Beyond this attention to the text in its original historical context, the church depends on exegetes, animated by the same Spirit as inspired Scripture, to ensure that "there be as great a number of servants of the word of God as possible capable of effectively providing the people of God with the nourishment of the Scriptures (*Divino Afflante Spiritu*, 24; 53–55: *Ench. Bibl.*, 551, 567; *Dei Verbum*, 23; Paul VI, *Sedula Cura* [1971]). A particular cause for satisfaction in our times is the growing number of *women exegetes*; they frequently contribute new and penetrating insights to the interpretation of Scripture and rediscover features which had been forgotten.

[180] If, as noted above, the Scriptures belong to the entire church and are part of "the heritage of the faith," which all, pastors and faithful, "preserve, profess and put into practice in a communal effort," it nevertheless remains true that "responsibility for authentically interpreting the word of God, as transmitted by Scripture and tradition, has been entrusted solely to the living magisterium of the church, which exercises its authority in the name of Jesus Christ" (*Dei Verbum*, 10).

Thus, in the last resort it is the magisterium which has the responsibility of guaranteeing the authenticity of interpretation and, should the occasion arise, of pointing out instances where any particular interpretation is incompatible with the authentic Gospel. It discharges this function within the *koinonia* of the body, expressing officially the faith of the church, as a service to the church; to this end it consults theologians, exegetes and other experts, whose legitimate liberty it recognizes and with whom it remains united by reciprocal relationship in the common goal of "preserving the people of God in the truth which sets them free" (CDF, "Instruction Concerning the Ecclesial Vocation of the Theologian," 21).

C. THE TASK OF THE EXEGETE

[181] The task of Catholic exegetes embraces many aspects. It is an ecclesial task, for it consists in the study and explanation of holy Scripture in a way that makes all its riches available to pastors and the faithful. But it is at the same time a work of scholarship, which places the Catholic exegete in contact with non-Catholic colleagues and with many areas of scholarly research. Moreover, this task includes at the same time both research and teaching. And each of these normally leads to publication.

1. PRINCIPAL GUIDELINES

[182] In devoting themselves to their task, Catholic exegetes have to pay due account to the *historical character* of biblical revelation. For the two testaments express in human words bearing the stamp of their time the historical revelation communicated by God in various ways concerning himself and his plan of salvation. Consequently, exegetes have to make use of the historical-critical method. They cannot, however, accord to it a sole validity. All methods pertaining to the interpretation of texts are entitled to make their contribution to the exegesis of the Bible.

[183] In their work of interpretation Catholic exegetes must never forget that what they are interpreting is the *word of God*. Their common task is not finished when they have simply determined sources, defined forms or explained literary procedures. They arrive at the true goal of their work only when they have explained the meaning of the biblical text as God's word for today. To this end, they must take into consideration the various hermeneutical perspectives which help toward grasping the contemporary meaning of the biblical message and which make it responsive to the needs of those who read Scripture today.

[184] Exegetes should also explain the Christological, canonical and ecclesial meanings of the biblical texts.

The *Christological* significance of biblical texts is not always evident, it must be made clear whenever possible. Although Christ established the New Covenant in his blood, the books of the First Covenant have not lost their value. Assumed into the proclamation of the Gospel, they acquire and display their full meaning in the "mystery of Christ" (Ephesians 3:4); they shed light upon multiple aspects of this mystery, while in turn being illuminated by it themselves. These writings, in fact, served to prepare the people of God for his coming (cf. *Dei Verbum*, 14–16).

Although each book of the Bible was written with its own particular end in view and has its own specific meaning, it takes on a deeper meaning when it becomes part of the *canon* as a whole. The exegetical task includes therefore bringing out the truth of Augustine's dictum: *Novum Testamentum in Vetere latet, et in Novo Vetus patet* ("The New Testament lies hidden in the Old, and the Old becomes clear in the New") (cf. *Quaest. in Hept.*, 2, 73: *Collected Works of Latin Church Writers*, 28, III, 3, p. 141).

Exegetes have also to explain the relationship that exists between the Bible and the *church*. The Bible came into existence within believing communities. In it the faith of Israel found expression, later that of the early Christian communities. United to the living tradition which preceded it, which accompanies it and is nourished by it (cf. *Dei Verbum*, 21), the Bible is the privileged means which God uses yet again in our own day to shape the building up and the growth of the church as the people of God. This ecclesial dimension necessarily involves an openness to ecumenism.

Moreover, since the Bible tells of God's offer of salvation to all people, the exegetical task necessarily includes a universal dimension. This means taking account of other religions and of the hopes and fears of the world of today.

2. RESEARCH

[185] The exegetical task is far too large to be successfully pursued by individual scholars working alone. It calls for a division of labor, especially in *research*, which demands specialists in different fields. Interdisciplinary collaboration will help overcome any limitations that specialization may tend to produce.

[186] It is very important for the good of the entire church, as well as for its influence in the modern world, that a sufficient number of well-prepared persons be committed to research in the various fields of exegetical study. In their concern for the more immediate needs of the ministry, bishops and religious superiors are often tempted not to take sufficiently seriously the responsibility incumbent upon them to make provision for this fundamental need. But a lack in this area exposes the church to serious harm, for pastors and the faithful then run the risk of being at the mercy of an exegetical scholarship which is alien to the church and lacks relationship to the life of faith.

[187] In stating that "the study of sacred Scripture" should be "as it were the soul of theology" (*Dei Verbum*, 24), the Second Vatican Council has indicated the crucial importance of exegetical research. By the same token, the council has also implicitly reminded Catholic exegetes that their research has an essential relationship to theology, their awareness of which must also be evident.

3. TEACHING

[188] The declaration of the council made equally clear the fundamental role which belongs to the teaching of exegesis in the faculties of theology, the seminaries and the religious houses of studies. It is obvious that the level of these studies will not be the same in all cases. It is desirable that the teaching of exegesis be carried out by both men and women. More technical in university faculties, this teaching will have a more directly pastoral orientation in seminaries. But it can never be without an intellectual dimension that is truly serious. To proceed otherwise would be to show disrespect toward the word of God.

[189] Professors of exegesis should communicate to their students a profound appreciation of sacred Scripture, showing how it deserves the kind of attentive and objective study which will allow a better appreciation of its literary, historical, social and theological value. They cannot rest content simply with the conveying of a series of facts to be passively absorbed, but should give a genuine introduction to exegetical method, explaining the principal steps, so that students will be in a position to exercise their own personal judgment.

[190] Given the limited time at a teacher's disposal, it is appropriate to make use of two alternative modes of teaching: on the one hand, a synthetic exposition to introduce the student to the study of whole books of the Bible, omitting no

important area of the Old or New Testament; on the other hand, in-depth analyses of certain well-chosen texts, which will provide at the same time an introduction to the practice of exegesis. In either case, care must be taken to avoid a one-sided approach that would restrict itself, on the one hand, to a spiritual commentary empty of historical-critical grounding or, on the other, to a historical-critical commentary lacking doctrinal or spiritual content (cf. *Divino Afflante Spiritu: Ench. Bibl.* 551–552, PCB, *De Sacra Scriptura Recte Docenda: Ench. Bibl.* 598). Teaching should at one and the same time show forth the historical roots of the biblical writings, the way in which they constitute the personal word of the heavenly Father addressing his children with love (cf. *Dei Verbum*, 21) and their indispensable role in the pastoral ministry (cf 2 Timothy 3:16).

4. PUBLICATIONS

[191] As the fruit of research and a complement to teaching, publications play a highly important role in the advancement and spread of exegetical work. Beyond printed texts, publication today embraces other more powerful and more rapid means of communication (radio, television, other electronic media); it is very advantageous to know how to make use of these things.

[192] For those engaged in research, publication at a high academic level is the principal means of dialogue, discussion and cooperation. Through it, Catholic exegesis can interact with other centers of exegetical research as well as with the scholarly world in general.

[193] There is another form of publication, more short-term in nature, which renders a very great service by its ability to adapt itself to a variety of readers, from the well-educated to children of catechism age, reaching biblical groups, apostolic movements and religious congregations. Exegetes who have a gift for popularization provide an extremely useful and fruitful work, one that is indispensable if the fruit of exegetical studies is to be dispersed as widely as need demands. In this area, the need to make the biblical message something real for today is ever more obvious. This requires that exegetes take into consideration the reasonable demands of educated and cultured persons of our time, clearly distinguishing for their benefit what in the Bible is to be regarded as secondary detail conditioned by a particular age, what must be interpreted as the language of myth and what is to be regarded as the true historical and inspired meaning. The biblical writings were not composed in modern language nor in the style of the 20th century. The forms of expression and literary genres employed in the Hebrew, Aramaic or Greek text must be made meaningful to men and women of today, who otherwise would be tempted to lose all interest in the Bible or else to interpret it in a simplistic way that is literalist or simply fanciful.

[194] In all this variety of tasks, the Catholic exegete has no other purpose than the service of the word of God. The aim of the exegete is not to substitute for the biblical texts the results of his or her work, whether that involves the reconstruction of ancient sources used by the inspired authors or up-to-date presentation of the latest conclusions of exegetical science. On the contrary, the aim of

the exegete is to shed more and more light on the biblical texts themselves, help-ing them to be better appreciated for what they are in themselves and understood with ever more historical accuracy and spiritual depth.

D. RELATIONSHIP WITH OTHER THEOLOGICAL DISCIPLINES

[195] Being itself a theological discipline, *"fides quaerens intellectum,"* exegesis has close and complex relationships with other fields of theological learning. On the one hand, systematic theology has an influence upon the presupposi-tions with which exegetes approach biblical texts. On the other hand, exegesis provides the other theological disciplines with data fundamental for their opera-tion. There is, accordingly, a relationship of dialogue between exegesis and the other branches of theology, granted always a mutual respect for that which is specific to each.

1. THEOLOGY AND PRESUPPOSITIONS REGARDING BIBLICAL TEXTS

[196] Exegetes necessarily bring certain presuppositions (Fr., *precomprehen-sion*) to biblical writings. In the case of the Catholic exegete, it is a question of presuppositions based on the certainties of faith: The Bible is a text inspired by God, entrusted to the church for the nurturing of faith and guidance of the Christian life. These certainties of faith do not come to an exegete in an unre-fined, raw state, but only as developed in the ecclesial community through the process of theological reflection. The reflection undertaken by systematic the-ologians upon the inspiration of Scripture and the function it serves in the life of the church provides in this way direction for exegetical research.

But correspondingly, the work of exegetes on the inspired texts provides them with an experience which systematic theologians should take into account as they seek to explain more clearly the theology of Scriptural inspiration and the interpretation of the Bible within the church. Exegesis creates, in particular, a more lively and precise awareness of the historical character of biblical inspi-ration. It shows that the process of inspiration is historical, not only because it took place over the course of the history of Israel and of the early church, but also because it came about through the agency of human beings, all of them con-ditioned by their time and all, under the guidance of the Spirit, playing an active role in the life of the people of God.

Moreover, theology's affirmation of the strict relationship between inspired Scripture and tradition has been both confirmed and made more precise through the advance of exegetical study, which has led exegetes to pay increasing atten-tion to the influence upon texts of the life-setting *(sitz im leben)* out of which they were formed.

2. EXEGESIS AND SYSTEMATIC THEOLOGY

[197] Without being the sole *locus theologicus*, sacred Scripture provides the privileged foundation of theological studies. In order to interpret Scripture with scholarly accuracy and precision, theologians need the work of exegetes. From their side, exegetes must orient their research in such fashion that "the

study of sacred Scripture can be in reality "as it were the soul of theology" (*Dei Verbum*, 24). To achieve this, they ought pay particular attention to the religious content of the biblical writings.

[198] Exegetes can help systematic theologians avoid two extremes: on the one hand, a dualism, which would completely separate a doctrinal truth from its linguistic expression, as though the latter were of no importance; on the other hand, a fundamentalism, which, confusing the human and the divine, would consider even the contingent features of human discourse to be revealed truth.

To avoid these two extremes, it is necessary to make distinctions without at the same time making separations—thus to accept a continuing tension. The word of God finds expression in the work of human authors. The thought and the words belong at one and the same time both to God and to human beings, in such a way that the whole Bible comes at once from God and from the inspired human author. This does not mean, however, that God has given the historical conditioning of the message a value which is absolute. It is open both to interpretation and to being brought up to date—which means being detached, to some extent, from its historical conditioning in the past and being transplanted into the historical conditioning of the present. The exegete performs the groundwork for this operation, which the systematic theologian continues by taking into account the other *loci theologici* which contribute to the development of dogma.

3. EXEGESIS AND MORAL THEOLOGY

[199] Similar observations can be made regarding the relationship between exegesis and moral theology. The Bible closely links many instructions about proper conduct—commandments, prohibitions, legal prescriptions, prophetic exhortations and accusations, counsels of wisdom, and so forth—to the stories concerning the history of salvation. One of the tasks of exegesis consists in preparing the way for the work of moralists by assessing the significance of this wealth of material.

This task is not simple, for often the biblical texts are not concerned to distinguish universal moral principles from particular prescriptions of ritual purity and legal ordinances. All is mixed together. On the other hand, the Bible reflects a considerable moral development, which finds its completion in the New Testament. It is not sufficient therefore that the Old Testament should indicate a certain moral position (e.g. the practice of slavery or of divorce, or that of extermination in the case of war) for this position to continue to have validity. One has to undertake a process of discernment. This will review the issue in the light of the progress in moral understanding and sensitivity that has occurred over the years.

The writings of the Old Testament contain certain "imperfect and provisional" elements (*Dei Verbum*, 15), which the divine pedagogy could not eliminate right away. The New Testament itself is not easy to interpret in the area of morality, for it often makes use of imagery, frequently in a way that is paradoxical or even provocative; moreover, in the New Testament area the relationship between Christians and the Jewish Law is the subject of sharp controversy.

Moral theologians therefore have a right to put to exegetes many questions which will stimulate exegetical research. In many cases the response may be that no biblical text explicitly addresses the problem proposed. But even when such is the case, the witness of the Bible, taken within the framework of the forceful dynamic that governs it as a whole, will certainly indicate a fruitful direction to follow. On the most important points the moral principles of the Decalogue remain basic. The Old Testament already contains the principles and the values which require conduct in full conformity with the dignity of the human person, created "in the image of God" (Genesis 1:27). Through the revelation of God's love that comes in Christ, the New Testament sheds the fullest light upon these principles and values.

4. DIFFERING POINTS OF VIEW AND NECESSARY INTERACTION

[200] In its 1988 document on the interpretation of theological truths, the International Theological Commission recalled that a conflict has broken out in recent times between exegesis and dogmatic theology; it then notes the positive contribution modern exegesis has made to systematic theology ("The Interpretation of Theological Truths,"1988, C.I, 2). To be more precise, it should be said that the conflict was provoked by liberal exegesis. There was no conflict in a generalized sense between Catholic exegesis and dogmatic theology, but only some instances of strong tension. It remains true, however, that tension can degenerate into conflict when, from one side or the other, differing points of view, quite legitimate in themselves, become hardened to such an extent that they become in fact irreconcilable opposites.

The points of view of both disciplines are in fact different and rightly so. The primary task of the exegete is to determine as accurately as possible the meaning of biblical texts in their own proper context, that is, first of all, in their particular literary and historical context and then in the context of the wider canon of Scripture. In the course of carrying out this task, the exegete expounds the theological meaning of texts when such a meaning is present. This paves the way for a relationship of continuity between exegesis and further theological reflection. But the point of view is not the same, for the work of the exegete is fundamentally historical and descriptive and restricts itself to the interpretation of the Bible.

[201] Theologians as such have a role that is more speculative and more systematic in nature. For this reason, they are really interested only in certain texts and aspects of the Bible and deal, besides, with much other data which is not biblical—patristic writings, conciliar definitions, other documents of the magisterium, the liturgy—as well as systems of philosophy and the cultural, social and political situation of the contemporary world. Their task is not simply to interpret the Bible; their aim is to present an understanding of the Christian faith that bears the mark of a full reflection upon all its aspects and especially that of its crucial relationship to human existence.

Because of its speculative and systematic orientation, theology has often yielded to the temptation to consider the Bible as a store of *dicta probantia* serving to confirm doctrinal theses. In recent times theologians have become more keenly conscious of the importance of the literary and historical context for the correct interpretation of ancient texts, and they are much more ready to work in collaboration with exegetes.

[202] Inasmuch as it is the word of God set in writing, the Bible has a richness of meaning that no one systematic theology can ever completely capture or confine. One of the principal functions of the Bible is to mount serious challenges to theological systems and to draw attention constantly to the existence of important aspects of divine revelation and human reality which have at times been forgotten or neglected in efforts at systematic reflection. The renewal that has taken place in exegetical methodology can make its own contribution to awareness in these areas.

In a corresponding way, exegesis should allow itself to be informed by theological research. This will prompt it to put important questions to texts and so discover their full meaning and richness. The critical study of the Bible cannot isolate itself from theological research, nor from spiritual experience and the discernment of the church. Exegesis produces its best results when it is carried out in the context of the living faith of the Christian community, which is directed toward the salvation of the entire world.

IV. INTERPRETATION OF THE BIBLE IN THE LIFE OF THE CHURCH

[203] Exegetes may have a distinctive role in the interpretation of the Bible but they do not exercise a monopoly. This activity within the church has aspects which go beyond the academic analysis of texts. The church, indeed, does not regard the Bible simply as a collection of historical documents dealing with its own origins; it receives the Bible as word of God, addressed both to itself and to the entire world at the present time. This conviction, stemming from the faith, leads in turn to the work of actualizing and inculturating the biblical message, as well as to various uses of the inspired text in liturgy, in "lectio divina," in pastoral ministry and in the ecumenical movement.

A. ACTUALIZATION

[204] Already within the Bible itself—as we noted in the previous chapter—one can point to instances of actualization: very early texts have been reread in the light of new circumstances and applied to the contemporary situation of the people of God. The same basic conviction necessarily stimulates believing communities of today to continue the process of actualization.

1. PRINCIPLES

[205] Actualization rests on the following basic principles:

Actualization is possible because the richness of meaning contained in the biblical text gives it a value for all time and all cultures (cf. Isaiah 40:8; 66:18–21; Matthew 28: 19–20). The biblical message can at the same time both relativize and enrich the value systems and norms of behavior of each generation.

Actualization is necessary because, although their message is of lasting value, the biblical texts have been composed with respect to circumstances of the past and in language conditioned by a variety of times and seasons. To reveal their significance for men and women of today, it is necessary to apply their message to contemporary circumstances and to express it in language adapted to the present time. This presupposes a hermeneutical endeavor, the aim of which is to go beyond the historical conditioning so as to determine the essential points of the message.

The work of actualization should always be conscious of the complex relationships that exist in the Christian Bible between the two testaments, since the New Testament presents itself, at one and the same time, as both the fulfillment and the surpassing of the Old. Actualization takes place in line with the dynamic unity thus established.

[206] It is the living tradition of the community of faith that stimulates the task of actualization. This community places itself in explicit continuity with the communities which gave rise to Scripture and which preserved and handed it on. In the process of actualization, tradition plays a double role: On the one hand, it provides protection against deviant interpretations; on the other hand, it ensures the transmission of the original dynamism.

[207] Actualization, therefore, cannot mean manipulation of the text. It is not a matter of projecting novel opinions or ideologies upon the biblical writings, but of sincerely seeking to discover what the text has to say at the present time. The text of the Bible has authority over the Christian church at all times, and, although centuries have passed since the time of its composition, the text retains its role of privileged guide not open to manipulation. The magisterium of the church "is not above the word of God, but serves it, teaching only what has been handed on, by divine commission, with the help of the Holy Spirit, the church listens to the text with love, watches over it in holiness and explains it faithfully" (*Dei Verbum*, 10).

2. METHODS

[208] Based on these principles, various methods of actualization are available.

Actualization, already practiced within the Bible itself, was continued in the Jewish tradition through procedures found in the Targums and Midrashim: searching for parallel passages *(gezerah shawah)*, modification in the reading of the text *('al tiqrey)*, appropriation of a second meaning *(tartey mishma')*, etc.

In their turn, the fathers of the church made use of typology and allegory in order to actualize the biblical text in a manner appropriate to the situation of Christians of their time.

Modern attempts at actualization should keep in mind both changes in ways of thinking and the progress made in interpretative method.

[209] Actualization presupposes a correct exegesis of the text, part of which is the determining of its *literal sense*. Persons engaged in the work of actualization who do not themselves have training in exegetical procedures should have recourse to good introductions to Scripture, this will ensure that their interpretation proceeds in the right direction.

[210] The most sure and promising method for arriving at a successful actualization is the interpretation of Scripture by Scripture, especially in the case of the texts of the Old Testament which have been reread in the Old Testament itself (e.g., the manna of Exodus 16 in Wisdom 16:20–29) and/or in the New Testament (John 6). The actualization of a biblical text in Christian life will proceed correctly only in relation to the mystery of Christ and of the church. It would be inappropriate, for example, to propose to Christians as models of a struggle for liberation episodes drawn solely from the Old Testament (Exodus, 1–2 Maccabees).

[211] Based upon various forms of the philosophy of hermeneutics, the task of interpretation involves, accordingly, three steps: 1. to hear the word from within one's own concrete situation; 2. to identify the aspects of the present situation highlighted or put in question by the biblical text; 3. to draw from the fullness of meaning contained in the biblical text those elements capable of advancing the present situation in a way that is productive and consonant with the saving will of God in Christ.

[212] By virtue of actualization, the Bible can shed light upon many current issues: for example, the question of various forms of ministry, the sense of the church as communion, the preferential option for the poor, liberation theology, the situation of women. Actualization can also attend to values of which the modern world is more and more conscious, such as the rights of the human person, the protection of human life, the preservation of nature, the longing for world peace.

3. LIMITS

[213] So as to remain in agreement with the saving truth expressed in the Bible, the process of actualization should keep within certain limits and be careful not to take wrong directions.

While every reading of the Bible is necessarily selective, care should be taken to avoid tendentious interpretations, that is, readings which, instead of being docile to the text make use of it only for their own narrow purposes (as is the case in the actualization practiced by certain sects, for example Jehovah's Witnesses).

Actualization loses all validity if it is grounded in theoretical principles which are at variance with the fundamental orientations of the biblical text, as, for example, a rationalism which is opposed to faith or an atheistic materialism.

[214] Clearly to be rejected also is every attempt at actualization set in a direction contrary to evangelical justice and charity, such as, for example, the use of the Bible to justify racial segregation, anti-Semitism or sexism whether on the part of men or of women. Particular attention is necessary, according to the spirit of the Second Vatican Council (*Nostra Aetate*, 4), to avoid absolutely any actualization of certain texts of the New Testament which could provoke or reinforce unfavorable attitudes to the Jewish people. The tragic events of the past must, on the contrary, impel all to keep unceasingly in mind that, according to the New Testament, the Jews remain "beloved" of God, "since the gifts and calling of God are irrevocable" (Romans 11:28–29).

[215] False paths will be avoided if actualization of the biblical message begins with a correct interpretation of the text and continues within the stream of the living tradition, under the guidance of the church's magisterium.

In any case, the risk of error does not constitute a valid objection against performing what is a necessary task: that of bringing the message of the Bible to the ears and hearts of people of our own time.

B. INCULTURATION

[216] While actualization allows the Bible to remain fruitful at different periods, inculturation in a corresponding way looks to the diversity of place: It ensures that the biblical message takes root in a great variety of terrains. This diversity is, to be sure, never total. Every authentic culture is, in fact, in its own way the bearer of universal values established by God.

[217] The theological foundation of inculturation is the conviction of faith that the word of God transcends the cultures in which it has found expression and has the capability of being spread in other cultures, in such a way as to be able to reach all human beings in the cultural context in which they live. This conviction springs from the Bible itself, which, right from the book of Genesis, adopts a universalist stance (Genesis 1:27–28), maintains it subsequently in the blessing promised to all peoples through Abraham and his offspring (Genesis 12:3; 18:18) and confirms it definitively in extending to "all nations" the proclamation of the Christian Gospel (Matthew 28:18–20; Romans 4:16–17; Ephesians 3:6).

[218] The first stage of inculturation consists in translating the inspired Scripture into another language. This step was taken already in the Old Testament period, when the Hebrew text of the Bible was translated orally into Aramaic (Nehemiah 8:8,12) and later in written form into Greek. A translation, of course, is always more than a simple transcription of the original text. The passage from

one language to another necessarily involves a change of cultural context: Concepts are not identical and symbols have a different meaning, for they come up against other traditions of thought and other ways of life.

[219] Written in Greek, the New Testament is characterized in its entirety by a dynamic of inculturation. In its transposition of the Palestinian message of Jesus into Judeo-Hellenistic culture it displays its intention to transcend the limits of a single cultural world.

[220] While it may constitute the basic step, the translation of biblical texts cannot, however, ensure by itself a thorough inculturation. Translation has to be followed by interpretation, which should set the biblical message in more explicit relationship with the ways of feeling, thinking, living and self-expression which are proper to the local culture. From interpretation, one passes then to other stages of inculturation, which lead to the formation of a local Christian culture, extending to all aspects of life (prayer, work, social life, customs, legislation, arts and sciences, philosophical and theological reflection). The word of God is, in effect, a seed, which extracts from the earth in which it is planted the elements which are useful for its growth and fruitfulness (cf. *Ad Gentes*, 22). As a consequence, Christians must try to discern "what riches God, in his generosity, has bestowed on the nations; at the same time they should try to shed the light of the Gospel on these treasures, to set them free and bring them under the dominion of God the Savior" (*Ad Gentes*, 11).

This is not, as is clear, a one-way process; it involves "mutual enrichment." On the one hand, the treasures contained in diverse cultures allow the word of God to produce new fruits and on the other hand, the light of the word allows for a certain selectivity with respect to what cultures have to offer: Harmful elements can be left aside and the development of valuable ones encouraged. Total fidelity to the person of Christ, to the dynamic of his paschal mystery and to his love for the church make it possible to avoid two false solutions: a superficial "adaptation" of the message, on the one hand, and a syncretistic confusion, on the other (*Ad Gentes*, 22).

[221] Inculturation of the Bible has been carried out from the first centuries, both in the Christian East and in the Christian West, and it has proved very fruitful. However, one can never consider it a task achieved. It must be taken up again and again, in relationship to the way in which cultures continue to evolve. In countries of more recent evangelization, the problem arises in somewhat different terms. Missionaries, in fact, cannot help bring the word of God in the form in which it has been inculturated in their own country of origin. New local churches have to make every effort to convert this foreign form of biblical inculturation into another form more closely corresponding to the culture of their own land.

C. USE OF THE BIBLE

1. IN THE LITURGY

[222] From the earliest days of the church, the reading of Scripture has been an integral part of the Christian liturgy, an inheritance to some extent from the liturgy of the synagogue. Today, too, it is above all through the liturgy that Christians come into contact with Scripture, particularly during the Sunday celebration of the Eucharist.

[223] In principle, the liturgy, and especially the sacramental liturgy, the high point of which is the eucharistic celebration, brings about the most perfect actualization of the biblical texts, for the liturgy places the proclamation in the midst of the community of believers, gathered around Christ so as to draw near to God. Christ is then "present in his word, because it is he himself who speaks when sacred Scripture is read in the church" (*Sacrosanctum Concilium*, 7). Written text thus becomes living word.

[224] The liturgical reform initiated by the Second Vatican Council sought to provide Catholics with rich sustenance from the Bible. The triple cycle of Sunday readings gives a privileged place to the Gospels, in such a way as to shed light on the mystery of Christ as principle of our salvation. By regularly associating a text of the Old Testament with the text of the Gospel, the cycle often suggests a Scriptural interpretation moving in the direction of typology. But, of course, such is not the only kind of interpretation possible.

The homily, which seeks to actualize more explicitly the word of God, is an integral part of the liturgy. We will speak of it later when we treat of the pastoral ministry.

The lectionary, issued at the direction of the council (*Sacrosanctum Concilium*, 35) is meant to allow for a reading of sacred Scripture that is "more abundant, more varied and more suitable." In its present state, it only partially fulfills this goal. Nevertheless even as it stands it has had positive ecumenical results. In certain countries it also has served to indicate the lack of familiarity with Scripture on the part of many Catholics.

[225] The Liturgy of the Word is a crucial element in the celebration of each of the sacraments of the church; it does not consist simply in a series of readings one after the other; it ought to involve as well periods of silence and of prayer. This liturgy, in particular the Liturgy of the Hours, makes selections from the book of Psalms to help the Christian community pray. Hymns and prayers are all filled with the language of the Bible and the symbolism it contains. How necessary it is, therefore, that participation in the liturgy be prepared for and accompanied by the practice of reading Scripture.

If in the readings "God addresses the word to his people" (Roman Missal, n. 33), the Liturgy of the Word requires that great care be taken both in the proclamation of the readings and in their interpretation. It is therefore desirable that the formation of those who are to preside at the assembly and of those who serve with them take full account of what is required for a liturgy of the word of God that is fully renewed. Thus, through a combined effort, the church will carry on the mission entrusted to it, "to take the bread of life from the table both of the word of God and of the body of Christ and offer it to the faithful" (*Dei Verbum*, 21).

2. LECTIO DIVINA

[226] *Lectio divina* is a reading, on an individual or communal level, of a more or less lengthy passage of Scripture, received as the word of God and leading, at the prompting of the Spirit, to meditation, prayer and contemplation.

[227] Concern for regular, even daily reading of Scripture reflects early church custom. As a group practice, it is attested in the third century, at the time of Origen; he used to give homilies based on a text of Scripture read continuously throughout a week. At that time there were daily gatherings devoted to the reading and explanation of Scripture. But the practice did not always meet with great success among Christians (Origen, *Hom. Gen.*, X.1) and was eventually abandoned.

[228] *Lectio divina*, especially on the part of the individual, is attested in the monastic life in its golden age. In modern times, an instruction of the biblical commission, approved by Pope Pius XII, recommended this *lectio* to all clerics, secular and religious (*De Scriptura Sacra*, 1950: *Ench. Bibl.*, 592). Insistence on lectio divina in both its forms, individual and communal, has therefore become a reality once more. The end in view is to create and nourish "an efficacious and constant love" of sacred Scripture, source of the interior life and of apostolic fruitfulness (*Ench. Bibl.*, 591 and 567), also to promote a better understanding of the liturgy and to assure the Bible a more important place in theological studies and in prayer.

[229] The conciliar constitution *Dei Verbum* (No. 25) is equally insistent on an assiduous reading of Scripture for priests and religious. Moreover—and this is something new—it also invites, "all the faithful of Christ" to acquire "through frequent reading of the divine Scripture 'the surpassing knowledge of Christ Jesus' (Philippians 3:8)." Different methods are proposed. Alongside private reading, there is the suggestion of reading in a group. The conciliar text stresses that prayer should accompany the reading of Scripture, for prayer is the response to the word of God encountered in Scripture under the inspiration of the Spirit. Many initiatives for communal reading have been launched among Christians, and one can only encourage this desire to derive from Scripture a better knowledge of God and of his plan of salvation in Jesus Christ.

3. IN PASTORAL MINISTRY

[230] The frequent recourse to the Bible in pastoral ministry, as recommended by *Dei Verbum* (No. 24), takes on various forms depending on the kind of interpretation that is useful to pastors and helpful for the understanding of the faithful. Three principal situations can be distinguished: catechesis, preaching and

the biblical apostolate. Many factors are involved, relating to the general level of Christian life.

[231] The explanation of the word of God in *catechesis* (*Sacrosanctum Concilium*, 35; General Catechetical Directory, 1971, 16) has sacred Scripture as first source. Explained in the context of the tradition, Scripture provides the starting point, foundation and norm of catechetical teaching. One of the goals of catechesis should be to initiate a person in a correct understanding and fruitful reading of the Bible. This will bring about the discovery of the divine truth it contains and evoke as generous a response as is possible to the message God addresses through his word to the whole human race.

Catechesis should proceed from the historical context of divine revelation so as to present persons and events of the Old and New Testaments in the light of God's overall plan.

To move from the biblical text to its salvific meaning for the present time various hermeneutic procedures are employed. These will give rise to different kinds of commentary. The effectiveness of the catechesis depends on the value of the hermeneutic employed. There is the danger of resting content with a superficial commentary, one which remains simply a chronological presentation of the sequence of persons and events in the Bible.

Clearly, catechesis can avail itself of only a small part of the full range of biblical texts. Generally speaking, it will make particular use of stories, both those of the New Testament and those of the Old. It will single out the Decalogue. It should also see that it makes use of the prophetic oracles, the wisdom teaching and the great discourses in the Gospels such as the Sermon on the Mount.

The presentation of the Gospels should be done in such a way as to elicit an encounter with Christ, who provides the key to the whole biblical revelation and communicates the call of God that summons each one to respond. The word of the prophets and that of the "ministers of the word" (Luke 1:2) ought to appear as something addressed to Christians now.

[232] Analogous remarks apply to the ministry of *preaching*, which should draw from the ancient texts spiritual sustenance adapted to the present needs of the Christian community. Today this ministry is exercised especially at the close of the first part of the eucharistic celebration, through the *homily* which follows the proclamation of the word of God.

The explanation of the biblical texts given in the course of the homily cannot enter into great detail. It is, accordingly, fitting to explain the central contribution of texts, that which is most enlightening for faith and most stimulating for the progress of the Christian life, both on the community and individual level. Presenting this central contribution means striving to achieve its actualization and inculturation, in accordance with what has been said above. Good hermeneutical principles are necessary to attain this end. Want of preparation in this area leads to the temptation to avoid plumbing the depths of the biblical readings and to being content simply to moralize or to speak of contemporary issues in a way that fails to shed upon them the light of God's word.

In some countries exegetes have helped produce publications designed to assist pastors in their responsibility to interpret correctly the biblical texts of the liturgy and make them properly meaningful for today. It is desirable that such efforts be repeated on a wider scale.

Preachers should certainly avoid insisting in a one-sided way on the obligations incumbent upon believers. The biblical message must preserve its principal characteristic of being the good news of salvation freely offered by God. Preaching will perform a task more useful and more conformed to the Bible if it helps the faithful above all to "know the gift of God" (John 4:10) as it has been revealed in Scripture; they will then understand in a positive light the obligations that flow from it.

[233] The *biblical apostolate* has as its objective to make known the Bible as the word of God and source of life. First of all, it promotes the translation of the Bible into every kind of language and seeks to spread these translations as widely as possible. It creates and supports numerous initiatives: the formation of groups devoted to the study of the Bible, conferences on the Bible, biblical weeks, the publication of journals and books, etc.

An important contribution is made by church associations and movements which place a high premium upon the reading of the Bible within the perspective of faith and Christian action. Many "basic Christian communities" focus their gatherings upon the Bible and set themselves a threefold objective: to know the Bible, to create community and to serve the people. Here also exegetes can render useful assistance in avoiding actualizations of the biblical message that are not well grounded in the text. But there is reason to rejoice in seeing the Bible in the hands of people of lowly condition and of the poor; they can bring to its interpretation and to its actualization a light more penetrating, from the spiritual and existential point of view, than that which comes from a learning that relies upon its own resources alone (cf. Matthew 11:25).

[234] The ever increasing importance of the instruments of mass communication ("mass media")—the press, radio, television—requires that proclamation of the word of God and knowledge of the Bible be propagated by these means. Their very distinctive features and, on the other hand, their capacity to influence a vast public require a particular training in their use. This will help to avoid paltry improvisations, along with striking effects that are actually in poor taste.

Whatever be the context—catechetics, preaching or the biblical apostolate—the text of the Bible should always be presented with the respect it deserves.

4. IN ECUMENISM

[235] If the ecumenical movement as a distinct and organized phenomenon is relatively recent, the idea of the unity of God's people, which this movement seeks to restore, is profoundly based in Scripture. Such an objective was the

constant concern of the Lord (John 10:16; 17:11, 20–23). It looks to the union of Christians in faith, hope and love (Ephesians 4:2–5), in mutual respect (Philippians 2: 1–5) and solidarity (1 Corinthians 12:14–27; Romans 12:45), but also and above all an organic union in Christ, after the manner of vine and branches (John 15:4–5), head and members (Ephesians 1:22–23; 4:12–16). This union should be perfect, in the likeness of the union of the Father and the Son (John 17:11, 22). Scripture provides its theological foundation (Ephesians 4:4–6; Galatians 3:27–28), the first apostolic community its concrete, living model (Acts 2:44; 4:32).

[236] Most of the issues which ecumenical dialogue has to confront are related in some way to the interpretation of biblical texts. Some of the issues are theological: eschatology, the structure of the church, primacy and collegiality, marriage and divorce, the admission of women to the ministerial priesthood and so forth. Others are of a canonical and juridical nature: They concern the administration of the universal church and of local churches. There are others, finally, that are strictly biblical: the list of the canonical books, certain hermeneutical questions, etc.

[237] Although it cannot claim to resolve all these issues by itself, biblical exegesis is called upon to make an important contribution in the ecumenical area. A remarkable degree of progress has already been achieved. Through the adoption of the same methods and analogous hermeneutical points of view, exegetes of various Christian confessions have arrived at a remarkable level of agreement in the interpretation of Scripture, as is shown by the text and notes of a number of ecumenical translations of the Bible, as well as by other publications.

Indeed, it is clear that on some points differences in the interpretation of Scripture are often stimulating and can be shown to be complementary and enriching. Such is the case when these differences express values belonging to the particular tradition of various Christian communities and so convey a sense of the manifold aspects of the mystery of Christ.

[238] Since the Bible is the common basis of the rule of faith, the ecumenical imperative urgently summons all Christians to a rereading of the inspired text, in docility to the Holy Spirit, in charity, sincerity and humility; it calls upon all to meditate on these texts and to live them in such a way as to achieve conversion of heart and sanctity of life. These two qualities, when united with prayer for the unity of Christians, constitute the soul of the entire ecumenical movement (cf. *Unitatis Redintegratio*, No. 8). To achieve this goal, it is necessary to make the acquiring of a Bible something within the reach of as many Christians as possible, to encourage ecumenical translations—since having a common text greatly assists reading and understanding together—and also ecumenical prayer groups, in order to contribute, by an authentic and living witness, to the achievement of unity within diversity (cf. Romans 12:4–5).

CONCLUSION

[239] From what has been said in the course of this long account—admittedly far too brief on a number of points—the first conclusion that emerges is that biblical exegesis fulfills, in the church and in the world, an *indispensable task*. To attempt to bypass it when seeking to understand the Bible would be to create an illusion and display lack of respect for the inspired Scripture.

[240] When fundamentalists relegate exegetes to the role of translators only (failing to grasp that translating the Bible is already a work of exegesis) and refuse to follow them further in their studies, these same fundamentalists do not realize that for all their very laudable concern for total fidelity to the word of God, they proceed in fact along ways which will lead them far away from the true meaning of the biblical texts, as well as from full acceptance of the consequences of the incarnation. The eternal Word became incarnate at a precise period of history, within a clearly defined cultural and social environment. Anyone who desires to understand the word of God should humbly seek it out there where it has made itself visible and accept to this end the necessary help of human knowledge. Addressing men and women, from the beginnings of the Old Testament onward, God made use of all the possibilities of human language, while at the same time accepting that his word be subject to the constraints caused by the limitations of this language. Proper respect for inspired Scripture requires undertaking all the labors necessary to gain a thorough grasp of its meaning. Certainly, it is not possible that each Christian personally pursue all the kinds of research which make for a better understanding of the biblical text. This task is entrusted to exegetes, who have the responsibility in this matter to see that all profit from their labor.

[241] A second conclusion is that the very nature of biblical texts means that interpreting them will require continued use of the *historical-critical method*, at least in its principal procedures. The Bible, in effect, does not present itself as a direct revelation of timeless truths but as the written testimony to a series of interventions in which God reveals himself in human history. In a way that differs from tenets of other religions, the message of the Bible is solidly grounded in history. It follows that the biblical writings cannot be correctly understood without an examination of the historical circumstances that shaped them. "Diachronic" research will always be indispensable for exegesis. Whatever be their own interest and value, "synchronic" approaches cannot replace it. To function in a way that will be fruitful, synchronic approaches should accept the conclusions of the diachronic, at least according to their main lines.

[242] But granted this basic principle, the synchronic approaches (the rhetorical, narrative, semiotic and others) are capable, to some extent at least, of bringing about a renewal of exegesis and making a very useful contribution. The historical-critical method, in fact, cannot lay claim to enjoying a monopoly in this area. It must be conscious of *its limits*, as well as of the dangers to which it is exposed. Recent developments in philosophical hermeneutics and, on the other hand, the observations which we have been able to make concerning interpretation within the biblical tradition and the tradition of the church have shed light upon many

aspects of the problem of interpretation that the historical-critical method has tended to ignore. Concerned above all to establish the meaning of texts by situating them in their original historical context, this method has at times shown itself insufficiently attentive to the dynamic aspect of meaning and to the possibility that meaning can continue to develop. When historical-critical exegesis does not go as far as to take into account the final result of the editorial process but remains absorbed solely in the issues of sources and stratification of texts, it fails to bring the exegetical task to completion.

[243] Through fidelity to the great tradition, of which the Bible itself is a witness, Catholic exegesis should avoid as much as possible this kind of professional bias and maintain its identity as a *theological discipline*, the principal aim of which is the deepening of faith. This does not mean a lesser involvement in scholarly research of the most rigorous kind, nor should it provide excuse for abuse of methodology out of apologetic concern. Each sector of research (textual criticism, linguistic study, literary analysis, etc.) has its own proper rules, which it ought follow with full autonomy. But no one of these specializations is an end in itself. In the organization of the exegetical task as a whole, the orientation toward the principal goal should remain paramount and thereby serve to obviate any waste of energy. Catholic exegesis does not have the right to become lost, like a stream of water, in the sands of a hypercritical analysis. Its task is to fulfill, in the church and in the world, a vital function, that of contributing to an ever more authentic transmission of the content of the inspired Scriptures.

The work of Catholic exegesis already tends toward this end, hand in hand with the renewal of other theological disciplines and with the pastoral task of the actualizing and inculturating of the word of God. In examining the present state of the question and expressing some reflections on the matter, the present essay hopes to have made some contribution toward the gaining, on the part of all, of a clearer awareness of the role of the Catholic exegete.

NOTES

1. By an exegetical *method,* we understand a group of scientific procedures employed in order to explain texts. We speak of an *approach* when it is a question of an inquiry proceeding from a particular point of view.

2. Out of 19 votes cast, the text of this last paragraph received 11 in favor, four against and there were four abstentions. Those who voted against it asked that the result of the vote be published along with the text. The commission consented to this.

3. The hermeneutic of the word developed by Gerhard Ebeling and Ernst Fuchs adopts a different approach and proceeds from another field of thought. It involves more a theological rather than a philosophical hermeneutic. Ebeling agrees however with such authors as Bultmann and Ricoeur in affirming that the word of God finds its true meaning only in the encounter with those to whom it is addressed.

CATECHISM OF
THE CATHOLIC CHURCH

PARAGRAPHS 74–141
1992

OVERVIEW OF *CATECHISM OF THE CATHOLIC CHURCH* (#74–141)

Michael Cameron

INTRODUCTION

It is important to read the *Catechism of the Catholic Church* (CCC) in terms of its purpose. A catechism is a tool of catechesis—literally, "echoing on down"—which is the process of faithfully transmitting to new generations of believers the same faith given to the apostles. Catechesis preserves and delivers, but does not exhaust, the mystery of salvation. While "we do not believe in formulas, but in those realities they express, which faith allows us to touch" (CCC, 170), verbal formulas are critical to expressing the knowledge inherent in the wisdom given to the church; they put spiritual mystery into teachable form. Such compact summaries of faith date to the earliest days of the church (see 1 Corinthians 12:3, Romans 10:9–10, 1 Timothy 3:16); indeed they reach back deep into the history of ancient Israel (Deuteronomy 26:5–10).

The declared intent of CCC is to present "an organic synthesis of the essential and fundamental contents of Catholic doctrine, as regards both faith and morals, in light of the Second Vatican Council and the whole of the Church's Tradition" (#11). So we do not expect scripture exegesis, theological essays or mystical reflection, but an outline and exposition of the salient points necessary for basic formation in the faith.

A look at the context of the section of CCC on tradition and scripture (#74–141) will help the reader grasp its importance. CCC is divided into four parts and this overall fourfold approach treats in order the content of Christian belief (Part One, "The Profession of Faith"), its liturgical expression (Part Two, "The Celebration of the Christian Mystery"), the practice of discipleship (Part Three, "Life in Christ"), and the spiritual life (Part Four, "Christian Prayer"). Each part culminates in an exposition of one of the central symbols of the faith arising from the history of salvation, namely: in Part One, the Apostles' Creed; in Part Two, the seven sacraments; in Part Three, the Ten Commandments; and in Part Four, the Lord's Prayer. It is in the midst of the discussion on the Apostles' Creed, in the chapter entitled "God Comes to Meet Man," that the material on tradition and scripture, paragraphs 74 to 141, appears.

Early on, the chapter characterizes the Christian profession of faith as a response to God's self-revelation in a history of salvation that continues to the present day. The stages of salvation history from Adam to Christ that unveil God's "plan of loving goodness" are then outlined in paragraphs 50–73. Our material comes next: paragraphs 74–100 dealing with the transmission of revelation in tradition, scripture and the magisterium; and paragraphs 101–141 on sacred scripture. If we think of these sections as an ever-narrowing series of concentric circles focusing on a central theme, then the final material on scripture represents the chapter's ultimate concern.

One unusual feature of this material should be noted. Forty-two of its sixty-eight numbered paragraphs consist—sometimes entirely—of quotations or paraphrases of the Second Vatican Council's 1965 Dogmatic Constitution on Divine Revelation (*Dei verbum*, abbreviated as DV). Of the 421 lines in the official English edition, 187 are taken verbatim from DV, fully 44% of the text. Apart from the "In Brief" summaries, only paragraphs 83, 87–93, 102, 108, 115–118, 123, and 127–130 are original to CCC.

This strong reliance on DV has a number of implications. First, it indicates DV's historic status; the church's understanding of tradition and scripture has never been so fully articulated at this level of authority. Second, it reflects the crucial importance that the church attaches to an informed understanding of the historical dynamic at work in tradition and scripture (a strong theme of DV), and not only their doctrinal content. Third, it shows the urgency of the church's call to incorporate scripture at every level of reflection, from the writings of professional theologians to the daily meditations of ordinary believers. Fourth, the pedagogic frame of CCC sets DV's value for the work of catechesis into bold relief. Correspondingly, the material original to CCC underscores the way it unfolds or nuances DV's teaching in particular directions.

TRANSMISSION OF DIVINE REVELATION

The apostolic tradition (#74–79)

Paragraphs 74–79 deal with the way revelation is transmitted through the ages. Some see no problem here: "God said it—I believe it—that settles it." But the issue is more complex than that. Revelation is not primarily a set of words, but a history of salvation, a "divine pedagogy" gradually leading the ancient chosen people to God's saving love and culminating in the paschal mystery of Jesus Christ. This history is conveyed and explained by means of language borrowed from our rough-and-tumble world where peoples, ideas, movements and empires continually rise and fall. Things *do* change, and all language and meaning is subject to the flux of time and human imperfection, and thus to the risk of corruption, distortion and memory loss. So it is necessary to certify the continuing trustworthiness of God's self-communication. The Catholic faith insists that the message of God's love was not unveiled and then left to the winds of chance for its propagation, but that its handing on was made part of the process of revelation itself. God preserves the truth and purity of the message through time by means of tradition and scripture.

The character of revelation indicates the kind of transmission that was needed. We were not left with a laundry list of so many things to believe. Rather, as DV strongly stressed, revelation was a personal act of divine self-disclosure (#79). This self-disclosure of God happened in various and fragmentary ways in the history of Israel until Jesus Christ appeared as the unequivocal center and pinnacle of revelation, the origin and destination of the church's faith (#65). The salvation foreseen by the prophets was fulfilled in Jesus and announced from his lips.

When the Lord Jesus entrusted the gospel to the apostles, it was both the first moment of transmission and the paradigm for its preservation. Oral proclamation was its original form, the form that tradition takes even today in preaching and catechesis (#76). This underscores the fact that the gospel is not impersonal, but is essentially interpersonal. It emerges from a living conversation appropriate to the fact that its substance is not a set of doctrines, but a living person, "the Person of Jesus of Nazareth, the only Son of the Father" (#426). The faith is essentially preserved in this act of handing itself over by word of mouth. Just as love is not love while it remains unexpressed, the gospel is not the gospel until it breaks forth from the mouths and lives of believers. Among ancient peoples the breath of the mouth brought forth the essence of the person, as when God breathed life into humanity (Genesis 2:7), and Jesus breathed the Spirit upon the disciples (John 20:22). Thus, in tradition "the Church brings forth all that she is, everything she believes" (#78), and realizes itself most fully in evangelization and catechesis. We have a model for this in the work of the early church Fathers, who hold a special place in the church as instructors in the faith.

What the apostles received from the Lord, the magisterium of the church protects and interprets. CCC teaches that the revelation that was accomplished in history, given to the apostles, and is cherished in the church, is one and the same, and the Holy Spirit has superintended the process from beginning to end (#77–78). Tradition is a spiritually living, breathing, growing entity that extends from the mouth of the Lord to the apostles and their successors through time into the hearts of all believers to this day (#9).

The relationship between tradition and sacred scripture (#80–83)

In keeping with the outlook of the ancient culture from which it emerged, the church sees oral tradition as the matrix of written tradition. The tradition embodied in apostolic preaching existed prior to the writing of the scriptures. Scripture hands on this tradition, but is not its only source or expression. Tradition is the source of scripture, and scripture is the intelligible form of tradition, but "both of them, flowing out from the same divine well-spring, come together in some fashion to form one thing and move toward the same goal" (#80; DV, 9). How they originate and separate, form one thing and move in concert, is not explained. Use of the water metaphor in paragraph 80 shows that, at least for now, the church is unwilling to define logically how this is so. But the teaching is clear that they embody the *same* deposit of faith that the apostles received from the Lord, and function together for its transmission: Tradition depends on scripture to be expressed, and scripture depends on tradition to be understood.

This discussion echoes the debates of the sixteenth century over the status of tradition and scripture in the church. To the Protestants of the Reformation, the church seemed to make an idol of tradition, making it independent and more authoritative than scripture, and implicitly exalting the church over revelation. Their reaction produced the doctrine of *sola scriptura*—"by scripture alone"—emphasizing the Bible's uniqueness in mediating revelation as well as its critical function over against the church. Against this standoff between Holy Writ or Holy Church, the Second Vatican Council (1962–1965) affirmed the unity of revelation, tradition, scripture and church as a single movement of God's self-communication in the world. On account of this unity, the church "does not derive her certainty about all revealed truths from the holy Scriptures alone" (#82). Some disagreement about the nature and authority of tradition remains.

But the Reformation churches now mostly agree that a living apostolic tradition did give rise to scripture and has always been essential to its proper interpretation, while for its part the Catholic church agrees that the church stands under revelation as its servant (#86).

The interpretation of the heritage of the faith (#84–93)

God cares for the faithful transmission of the "deposit of faith" *(depositum fidei)*; God has also ensured that it is also rightly understood. Paragraphs 84–93 cover the process of coming to an understanding of what the church has received, from its official teaching office (the magisterium) to the subjective appropriation of the word in the hearts of the members of the church.

The magisterium guards the authentic understanding of the faith by measuring individual teachings or practices against the integrity of the whole message of salvation. Its task is to keep in focus the essentials deriving from the hierarchy of truths and to ensure that all the parts of doctrine and life in the church are ordered to it (#90). When lines of understanding become distorted or unclear, the magisterium searches out the truth, or the lines along which such truth should be sought. (In passing, it may be noted that, historically, the magisterium has clearly defined the central elements of the Catholic faith, but has spoken definitively on relatively few particular parts of the Bible.) Paragraphs 87–90 treat the magisterium's exercise of teaching authority in the church when defining church dogma, that is, the central truths that form part of revelation itself or are closely connected to it. Against too strong a separation between the cognitive and experiential aspects of the faith, the section characterizes church dogmas as "lights along the path of faith" (#89). Paragraphs 91–93 offer instruction on "the supernatural sense of the faith" *(sensus fidei)*, by which the people of God as a collective whole enjoy freedom from error in matters of faith.

SACRED SCRIPTURE

Christ—the unique word of sacred scripture (#101–104)

Modern critical biblical study begins its work by focusing on the Bible's roots in the historical phenomena of ancient speech and culture, a scientific approach that was officially encouraged by DV. CCC repeats the affirmation while setting this piecemeal study in the context of scripture's unity. The words and lives of people who lived long ago still bring forth the word of God who lives today (see 1 Thessalonians 2:13; Hebrews 4:12). Each part of the Bible, sometimes in ways not easy to discern, reinforces every other part, and all the parts cohere around its core message of salvation. But scripture is a single book not only because it has one source and a central message: The written word's far-flung diversity comes into discernible unity as it mediates the living Word of God who became flesh in Jesus Christ. In an idea going back to the third-century scholar and martyr Origen of Alexandria, the church sees a likeness and bond between the human expression of scripture and the flesh of the Lord in the paschal mystery. "For this reason the Church has always venerated the Scriptures as she venerates the Lord's Body," and, rejecting any separation between word and sacrament, presents both to the faithful as living bread from "the one table of God's Word and Christ's Body" (#103; DV, 21).

Inspiration and truth of sacred scripture (#105–108)

The theological name for the divine authorship of the scriptures is "inspiration." But this idea must be carefully separated from the notion—held wittingly or unwittingly by some Christians even in our own day—that God dictated the words of the Bible to human scribes. Here CCC reflects the nuanced judgment that, in authoring the word, God neither bypassed the human authors' native abilities and habits of thought and speech, nor canceled their cultural formation and attention to their communities' immediate needs. God's word comes forth, not despite, but in and through these human elements, just as the divinity of the living word meets us through the humanity of Jesus (see #106).

Furthermore, CCC reaffirms the teaching of the Second Vatican Council that the books of scripture "without error teach that truth which God, for the sake of our salvation, wished to see confided to the Sacred Scriptures" (#107; DV, 11). This careful wording—"for the sake of our salvation"—excludes any idea that untenable factual representations used by the ancient writers should be considered part of revelation. It also institutes an interpretive "salvation principle" that means every text must ultimately be seen in the light of God's desire that everyone "might be saved and come to the knowledge of the truth" (1 Timothy 2:4; see CCC, 74). This is important for interpreting difficult passages such as the judgment of Sodom, the imprecatory psalms or the book of Revelation (see below).

While Christianity is a religion of the word, CCC reminds us that it is not a religion of the book (#108). That is to say, in scriptures we do not seek a "dead letter," lifeless shapes on a page that recount past deeds and impose abstract ideals. Rather, our reading of scripture is part of a living relationship with an ever-present God who engages us in a living, growing conversation. The perfect image of this is found in the story of the risen Christ opening the minds of the disciples to the depths of the scriptures on Easter Day (see #108; Luke 24:45).

The Holy Spirit, interpreter of scripture (#109–119)

With this section CCC moves to treat the process of understanding scripture's relevance for today, a process sometimes called "actualization." In order to receive the word of God in all its particularity and richness, interpreters must hold together two perspectives—the human and the divine—as depth and texture comes from seeing with two eyes instead of one.

The human perspective searches out the intention of the historical author(s), studying all the various historical, cultural and linguistic characteristics of the texts, while recognizing that ancient literary genres and scientific categories differ from our own, sometimes radically. It recognizes that people who did not reduce truth to mere factuality produced these documents. This saves the church from naively interpreting as literal fact the outmoded—and ultimately incidental—historical and scientific knowledge that the ancient authors used to convey spiritual truth. The essential story of salvation being rooted in real events, the ancient authors used modes of knowledge and writing current in their day to bring out the profound meaning of the stories of salvation. So we need not be concerned about the sun stopping over Joshua's army (see Joshua 10), or that Psalm 104 borrows heavily from Egyptian poetry, or that historical records contradict Luke's account of the census when Jesus was born. Israel still entered the Promised Land, the praise of God our creator remains fruitful, and Christ remains the Son of David born for our salvation.

The divine perspective insists that scripture must be interpreted in the light of the same Spirit who inspired it (see #111; DV, 12), that is to say, with attention to the essential movement toward salvation accomplished in Jesus Christ. In what amounts to a summary of DV 12, paragraphs 112–114 of CCC state that the "light of the Spirit" confers a unity on scripture that is the context for sound interpretation. This is a major theme of this portion of CCC. This unity derives in the first place from Christ, whose death looked backward to all the prophecies that anticipated the coming of his kingdom, and looked forward to its fulfillment yet to come. Unity emerges secondly in the sense of spiritual meaning that the church has discerned by the gift of the Spirit throughout its living tradition. The tradition of the church is not the arbitrary imposition of the viewpoints of a few, but the cumulative wisdom of many women and men prayerfully reading scripture through the centuries; we read best in their company. Finally, unity appears in the principle called the "analogy of faith," which refers to the coherence among the truths of faith within the whole plan of revelation. These three principles articulate what it means to read the scriptures with the mind and the heart of the church.

Against the backdrop of the Second Vatican Council's approval of historical methods of research, paragraphs 115–118 recall the church's ancient teaching on the literal and spiritual senses of scripture. All interpretation begins by using the rules of sound interpretation in order to establish the literal sense; from this, the spiritual sense emerges. The spiritual sense is subdivided into several interrelated strains: the allegorical (stressing the unity of salvation history culminating in Christ), the moral (indicating the life of discipleship lived in light of salvation) and the anagogical (literally, "leading up," pointing to communion in God's life in the eternal kingdom). Scripture study remains incomplete without the movement into spiritual understanding and conversion. These perspectives from deep within the church's tradition keep the study of the Bible from being reduced to a mere archaeological dig among antique ideas.

The canon of scripture (#120–130)

After summarizing the canonical list of sacred books as defined by the Council of Trent (1545–1563) (#120), CCC recounts the essential thrust of the Old and New Testaments considered individually and in their interrelationship. The "old" in "Old Testament" does not imply cancellation, since "the Old Covenant has never been revoked" (#121). Rather, it underscores the fulfillment of salvation history in Christ and emphasizes the Old Testament's forward-looking character. Its incompleteness takes nothing away from the intrinsic value of these writings as inspired documents, which continue to function authoritatively also for Jews. The temptation to exclude the Old Testament from the canon of scripture—either by overemphasis on the fulfillment in Christ, as in the case of some early heresies, or by uncomprehending neglect, as in much of the rest of Christian history—is decisively rejected (#123).

Because they deal directly with the center of salvation history in the words and deeds of the incarnate Word, the writings of the New Testament and particularly the gospels provide the privileged vantage point from which all the scriptures are understood. CCC rehearses the teaching of DV on the three stages of formation of the gospels (#126), a teaching that DV itself took over from the Pontifical Biblical Commission's (PBC) historic 1964 instruction *Sancta mater ecclesia*, on the historicity of the gospels. The PBC, the Second Vatican Council, and now CCC affirm the freedom of the ancient writers to shape their stories, while declaring the reliability of the gospels. CCC then goes on to describe the dynamic unity between the two Testaments in the divine plan. The church's perception of fulfillment in Christ explains the constant interplay of prophecy and fulfillment that is evident not only in the New Testament but also in the church's liturgy and catechesis (#128–130).

Sacred scripture in the life of the church (#131–133)

This last section recaps with verbatim quotes from DV the church's desire that scripture should become a constant source of nourishment and instruction for all the Christian faithful. The appeal is addressed to professionally trained theologians, for whom "study of the sacred page should be the very soul of sacred theology" (#132; DV, 24), and to everyone involved in the ministry of the word. But it is also addressed to the all the baptized, many of whom are unfortunate victims of the wrongheaded view, still common both inside and outside the church, that reading the Bible is discouraged or even forbidden for Catholics. Against this, CCC echoes the Second Vatican Council's insistence that "access to Sacred Scripture ought to be open wide to the Christian faithful" (#131; DV, 22). The reason for this is summed up memorably by the early church's greatest scripture scholar, Saint Jerome: "Ignorance of the Scriptures is ignorance of Christ" (#133).

OUTLINE

CATECHISM OF THE CATHOLIC CHURCH

(PARAGRAPHS 74–141)

PART ONE—THE PROFESSION OF FAITH

SECTION 1, CHAPTER 2, ARTICLE 2—
THE TRANSMISSION OF DIVINE REVELATION

74. God "desires all men to be saved and to come to the knowledge of the truth":[29] that is, of Christ Jesus.[30] Christ must be proclaimed to all nations and individuals, so that this revelation may reach to the ends of the earth:

God graciously arranged that the things he had once revealed for the salvation of all peoples should remain in their entirety, throughout the ages, and be transmitted to all generations.[31]

I. THE APOSTOLIC TRADITION

75. "Christ the Lord, in whom the entire Revelation of the most high God is summed up, commanded the apostles to preach the Gospel, which had been promised beforehand by the prophets, and which he fulfilled in his own person and promulgated with his own lips. In preaching the Gospel, they were to communicate the gifts of God to all men. This Gospel was to be the source of all saving truth and moral discipline."[32]

IN THE APOSTOLIC PREACHING . . .

76. In keeping with the Lord's command, the Gospel was handed on in two ways:

—*orally* "by the apostles who handed on, by the spoken word of their preaching, by the example they gave, by the institutions they established, what they themselves had received—whether from the lips of Christ, from his way of life and his works, or whether they had learned it at the prompting of the Holy Spirit";[33]

—*in writing* "by those apostles and other men associated with the apostles who, under the inspiration of the same Holy Spirit, committed the message of salvation to writing".[34]

. . . CONTINUED IN APOSTOLIC SUCCESSION

77. "In order that the full and living Gospel might always be preserved in the Church the apostles left bishops as their successors. They gave them 'their own

position of teaching authority.'"[35] Indeed, "the apostolic preaching, which is expressed in a special way in the inspired books, was to be preserved in a continuous line of succession until the end of time."[36]

78. This living transmission, accomplished in the Holy Spirit, is called Tradition, since it is distinct from Sacred Scripture, though closely connected to it. Through Tradition, "the Church, in her doctrine, life and worship, perpetuates and transmits to every generation all that she herself is, all that she believes."[37] "The sayings of the holy Fathers are a witness to the life-giving presence of this Tradition, showing how its riches are poured out in the practice and life of the Church, in her belief and her prayer."[38]

79. The Father's self-communication made through his Word in the Holy Spirit, remains present and active in the Church: "God, who spoke in the past, continues to converse with the Spouse of his beloved Son. And the Holy Spirit, through whom the living voice of the Gospel rings out in the Church—and through her in the world—leads believers to the full truth, and makes the Word of Christ dwell in them in all its richness."[39]

II. THE RELATIONSHIP BETWEEN TRADITION AND SACRED SCRIPTURE

ONE COMMON SOURCE . . .

80. "Sacred Tradition and Sacred Scripture, then, are bound closely together, and communicate one with the other. For both of them, flowing out from the same divine well-spring, come together in some fashion to form one thing, and move towards the same goal."[40] Each of them makes present and fruitful in the Church the mystery of Christ, who promised to remain with his own "always, to the close of the age."[41]

. . . TWO DISTINCT MODES OF TRANSMISSION

81. "*Sacred Scripture* is the speech of God as it is put down in writing under the breath of the Holy Spirit."[42]

"And [Holy] *Tradition* transmits in its entirety the Word of God which has been entrusted to the apostles by Christ the Lord and the Holy Spirit. It transmits it to the successors of the apostles so that, enlightened by the Spirit of truth, they may faithfully preserve, expound and spread it abroad by their preaching."[43]

82. As a result the Church, to whom the transmission and interpretation of Revelation is entrusted, "does not derive her certainty about all revealed truths from the holy Scriptures alone. Both Scripture and Tradition must be accepted and honored with equal sentiments of devotion and reverence."[44]

83.   The Tradition here in question comes from the apostles and hands on what they received from Jesus' teaching and example and what they learned from the Holy Spirit. The first generation of Christians did not yet have a written New Testament, and the New Testament itself demonstrates the process of living Tradition.

Tradition is to be distinguished from the various theological, disciplinary, liturgical or devotional traditions, born in the local churches over time. These are the particular forms, adapted to different places and times, in which the great Tradition is expressed. In the light of Tradition, these traditions can be retained, modified or even abandoned under the guidance of the Church's magisterium.

III. THE INTERPRETATION OF THE HERITAGE OF FAITH

THE HERITAGE OF FAITH ENTRUSTED TO THE WHOLE OF THE CHURCH

84.   The apostles entrusted the "Sacred deposit" of the faith (the *depositum fidei*),[45] contained in Sacred Scripture and Tradition, to the whole of the Church. "By adhering to [this heritage] the entire holy people, united to its pastors, remains always faithful to the teaching of the apostles, to the brotherhood, to the breaking of bread and the prayers. So, in maintaining, practicing, and professing the faith that has been handed on, there should be a remarkable harmony between the bishops and the faithful."[46]

THE MAGISTERIUM OF THE CHURCH

85.   "The task of giving an authentic interpretation of the Word of God, whether in its written form or in the form of Tradition, has been entrusted to the living, teaching office of the Church alone. Its authority in this matter is exercised in the name of Jesus Christ."[47] This means that the task of interpretation has been entrusted to the bishops in communion with the successor of Peter, the Bishop of Rome.

86.   "Yet this Magisterium is not superior to the Word of God, but is its servant. It teaches only what has been handed on to it. At the divine command and with the help of the Holy Spirit, it listens to this devotedly, guards it with dedication and expounds it faithfully. All that it proposes for belief as being divinely revealed is drawn from this single deposit of faith."[48]

87.   Mindful of Christ's words to his apostles: "He who hears you, hears me,"[49] the faithful receive with docility the teachings and directives that their pastors give them in different forms.

THE DOGMAS OF THE FAITH

88.   The Church's Magisterium exercises the authority it holds from Christ to the fullest extent when it defines dogmas, that is, when it proposes truths contained in divine Revelation or having a necessary connection with them, in a form obliging the Christian people to an irrevocable adherence of faith.

89.   There is an organic connection between our spiritual life and the dogmas. Dogmas are lights along the path of faith; they illuminate it and make it secure. Conversely, if our life is upright, our intellect and heart will be open to welcome the light shed by the dogmas of faith.[50]

90.   The mutual connections between dogmas, and their coherence, can be found in the whole of the Revelation of the mystery of Christ.[51] "In Catholic doctrine there exists an order or 'hierarchy' of truths, since they vary in their relation to the foundation of the Christian faith."[52]

THE SUPERNATURAL SENSE OF FAITH

91.   All the faithful share in understanding and handing on revealed truth. They have received the anointing of the Holy Spirit, who instructs them[53] and guides them into all truth.[54]

92.   "The whole body of the faithful . . . cannot err in matters of belief. This characteristic is shown in the supernatural appreciation of faith *(sensus fidei)* on the part of the whole people, when, 'from the bishops to the last of the faithful,' they manifest a universal consent in matters of faith and morals."[55]

93.   "By this appreciation of the faith, aroused and sustained by the Spirit of truth, the People of God, guided by the sacred teaching authority *(Magisterium),* . . . receives . . . the faith, once for all delivered to the saints . . . . The People unfailingly adheres to this faith, penetrates it more deeply with right judgment, and applies it more fully in daily life."[56]

GROWTH IN UNDERSTANDING THE FAITH

94.   Thanks to the assistance of the Holy Spirit, the understanding of both the realities and the words of the heritage of faith is able to grow in the life of the Church:

    —"through the contemplation and study of believers who ponder these things in their hearts";[57] it is in particular "theological research [which] deepens knowledge of revealed truth".[58]

    —"from the intimate sense of spiritual realities which [believers] experience",[59] the sacred Scriptures "grow with the one who reads them."[60]

    —"from the preaching of those who have received, along with their right of succession in the episcopate, the sure charism of truth".[61]

95.   "It is clear therefore that, in the supremely wise arrangement of God, sacred Tradition, Sacred Scripture and the Magisterium of the Church are so connected and associated that one of them cannot stand without the others. Working together, each in its own way, under the action of the one Holy Spirit, they all contribute effectively to the salvation of souls."[62]

96.   What Christ entrusted to the apostles, they in turn handed on by their preaching and writing, under the inspiration of the Holy Spirit, to all generations, until Christ returns in glory.

97.   "Sacred Tradition and Sacred Scripture make up a single sacred deposit of the Word of God" (*DV*, 10) in which, as in a mirror, the pilgrim Church contemplates God, the source of all her riches.

98.   "The Church, in her doctrine, life and worship, perpetuates and transmits to every generation all that she herself is, all that she believes" (*DV*, 8 § 1).

99.   Thanks to its supernatural sense of faith, the People of God as a whole never ceases to welcome, to penetrate more deeply and to live more fully from the gift of divine Revelation.

100. The task of interpreting the Word of God authentically has been entrusted solely to the Magisterium of the Church, that is, to the Pope and to the bishops in communion with him.

ARTICLE 3—SACRED SCRIPTURE

I. CHRIST—THE UNIQUE WORD OF SACRED SCRIPTURE

101. In order to reveal himself to men, in the condescension of his goodness God speaks to them in human words: "Indeed the words of God, expressed in the words of men, are in every way like human language, just as the Word of the eternal Father, when he took on himself the flesh of human weakness, became like men."[63]

102. Through all the words of Sacred Scripture, God speaks only one single Word, his one Utterance in whom he expresses himself completely:[64]

> You recall that one and the same Word of God extends throughout Scripture, that it is one and the same Utterance that resounds in the mouths of all the sacred writers, since he who was in the beginning God with God has no need of separate syllables; for he is not subject to time.[65]

103. For this reason, the Church has always venerated the Scriptures as she venerates the Lord's Body. She never ceases to present to the faithful the bread of life, taken from the one table of God's Word and Christ's Body.[66]

104. In Sacred Scripture, the Church constantly finds her nourishment and her strength, for she welcomes it not as a human word, "but as what it really is, the word of God".[67] "In the sacred books, the Father who is in heaven comes lovingly to meet his children, and talks with them."[68]

II. INSPIRATION AND TRUTH OF SACRED SCRIPTURE

105. *God is the author of Sacred Scripture.* "The divinely revealed realities, which are contained and presented in the text of Sacred Scripture, have been written down under the inspiration of the Holy Spirit."[69]

"For Holy Mother Church, relying on the faith of the apostolic age, accepts as sacred and canonical the books of the Old and the New Testaments, whole and entire, with all their parts, on the grounds that, written under the inspiration of the Holy Spirit, they have God as their author, and have been handed on as such to the Church herself."[70]

106. God inspired the human authors of the sacred books. "To compose the sacred books, God chose certain men who, all the while he employed them in this task, made full use of their own faculties and powers so that, though he acted in them and by them, it was as true authors that they consigned to writing whatever he wanted written, and no more."[71]

107. The inspired books teach the truth. "Since therefore all that the inspired authors or sacred writers affirm should be regarded as affirmed by the Holy Spirit, we must acknowledge that the books of Scripture firmly, faithfully, and without error teach that truth which God, for the sake of our salvation, wished to see confided to the Sacred Scriptures."[72]

108. Still, the Christian faith is not a "religion of the book". Christianity is the religion of the "Word" of God, "not a written and mute word, but incarnate and living".[73] If the Scriptures are not to remain a dead letter, Christ, the eternal Word of the living God, must, through the Holy Spirit, "open [our] minds to understand the Scriptures."[74]

III. THE HOLY SPIRIT, INTERPRETER OF SCRIPTURE

109. In Sacred Scripture, God speaks to man in a human way. To interpret Scripture correctly, the reader must be attentive to what the human authors truly wanted to affirm, and to what God wanted to reveal to us by their words.[75]

110. In order to discover the *sacred authors' intention,* the reader must take into account the conditions of their time and culture, the literary genres in use at that time, and the modes of feeling, speaking and narrating then current. "For the fact is that truth is differently presented and expressed in the various types of historical writing, in prophetical and poetical texts, and in other forms of literary expression."[76]

111. But since Sacred Scripture is inspired, there is another and no less important principle of correct interpretation, without which Scripture would remain a dead letter. "Sacred Scripture must be read and interpreted in the light of the same Spirit by whom it was written."[77]

The Second Vatican Council indicates three criteria for interpreting Scripture in accordance with the Spirit who inspired it.[78]

112. 1. *Be especially attentive "to the content and unity of the whole Scripture."* Different as the books which compose it may be, Scripture is a unity by reason of the unity of God's plan, of which Christ Jesus is the center and heart, open since his Passover.[79]

> The phrase "heart of Christ" can refer to Sacred Scripture, which makes known his heart, closed before the Passion, as the Scripture was obscure. But the Scripture has been opened since the Passion; since those who from then on have understood it, consider and discern in what way the prophecies must be interpreted.[80]

113. 2. *Read the Scripture within "the living Tradition of the whole Church."* According to a saying of the Fathers, Sacred Scripture is written principally in the Church's heart rather than in documents and records, for the Church carries in her Tradition the living memorial of God's Word, and it is the Holy Spirit who gives her the spiritual interpretation of the Scripture (". . . according to the spiritual meaning which the Spirit grants to the Church"[81]).

114. 3. *Be attentive to the analogy of faith.*[82] By "analogy of faith" we mean the coherence of the truths of faith among themselves and within the whole plan of Revelation.

THE SENSES OF SCRIPTURE

115. According to an ancient tradition, one can distinguish between two *senses* of Scripture: the literal and the spiritual, the latter being subdivided into the allegorical, moral and anagogical *senses*. The profound concordance of the four senses guarantees all its richness to the living reading of Scripture in the Church.

116. The *literal sense* is the meaning conveyed by the words of Scripture and discovered by exegesis, following the rules of sound interpretation: "All other senses of Sacred Scripture are based on the literal."[83]

117. The *spiritual sense.* Thanks to the unity of God's plan, not only the text of Scripture but also the realities and events about which it speaks can be signs.

   1. The *allegorical sense.* We can acquire a more profound understanding of events by recognizing their significance in Christ; thus the crossing of the Red Sea is a sign or type of Christ's victory and also of Christian Baptism.[84]

   2. The *moral sense.* The events reported in Scripture ought to lead us to act justly. As St. Paul says, they were written "for our instruction."[85]

   3. The *anagogical sense* (Greek: *anagoge*, "leading"). We can view realities and events in terms of their eternal significance, leading us toward our true homeland: thus the Church on earth is a sign of the heavenly Jerusalem.[86]

118. A medieval couplet summarizes the significance of the four senses:

> The Letter speaks of deeds; Allegory to faith;
> The Moral how to act; Anagogy our destiny.[87]

119. "It is the task of exegetes to work, according to these rules, toward a better understanding and explanation of the meaning of Sacred Scripture in order that their research may help the Church to form a firmer judgement. For, of course, all that has been said about the manner of interpreting Scripture is ultimately subject to the judgement of the Church which exercises the divinely conferred commission and ministry of watching over and interpreting the Word of God."[88]

But I would not believe in the Gospel, had not the authority of the Catholic Church already moved me.[89]

IV. THE CANON OF SCRIPTURE

120. It was by the apostolic Tradition that the Church discerned which writings are to be included in the list of the sacred books.[90] This complete list is called the canon of Scripture. It includes 46 books for the Old Testament (45 if we count Jeremiah and Lamentations as one) and 27 for the New.[91]

The Old Testament: Genesis, Exodus, Leviticus, Numbers, Deuteronomy, Joshua, Judges, Ruth, 1 *and* 2 Samuel, 1 *and* 2 Kings, 1 *and* 2 Chronicles, Ezra *and* Nehemiah, Tobit, Judith, Esther, 1 *and* 2 Maccabees, Job, Psalms, Proverbs, Ecclesiastes, *the* Song of Songs, *the* Wisdom of Solomon, Sirach (Ecclesiasticus), Isaiah, Jeremiah, Lamentations, Baruch, Ezekiel, Daniel, Hosea, Joel, Amos, Obadiah, Jonah, Micah, Nahum, Habakkuk, Zephaniah, Haggai, Zachariah *and* Malachi.

The New Testament: the Gospels *according to* Matthew, Mark, Luke *and* John, the Acts of the Apostles, *the* Letters of St. Paul to the Romans, 1 *and* 2 Corinthians, Galatians, Ephesians, Philippians, Colossians, 1 *and* 2 Thessalonians, 1 *and* 2 Timothy, Titus, Philemon, *the* Letter to the Hebrews, *the* Letters of James, 1 *and* 2 Peter, 1, 2 *and* 3 John, *and* Jude, *and* Revelation (the Apocalypse).

THE OLD TESTAMENT

121. The Old Testament is an indispensable part of Sacred Scripture. Its books are divinely inspired and retain a permanent value,[92] for the Old Covenant has never been revoked.

122. Indeed, "the economy of the Old Testament was deliberately oriented that it should prepare for and declare in prophecy the coming of Christ, redeemer of all men."[93] "Even though they contain matters imperfect and provisional,[94] the books of the Old Testament bear witness to the whole divine pedagogy of God's saving love: these writings "are a storehouse of sublime teaching on God and of sound wisdom on human life, as well as a wonderful treasury of prayers; in them, too, the mystery of our salvation is present in a hidden way."[95]

123. Christians venerate the Old Testament as true Word of God. The Church has always vigorously opposed the idea of rejecting the Old Testament under the pretext that the New has rendered it void (Marcionism).

124. "The Word of God, which is the power of God for salvation to everyone who has faith, is set forth and displays its power in a most wonderful way in the writings of the New Testament"[96] which hand on the ultimate truth of God's Revelation. Their central object is Jesus Christ, God's incarnate Son: his acts, teachings, Passion and glorification, and his Church's beginnings under the Spirit's guidance.[97]

125. The *Gospels* are the heart of all the Scriptures "because they are our principal source for the life and teaching of the Incarnate Word, our Saviour".[98]

126. We can distinguish three stages in the formation of the Gospels:

1. *The life and teaching of Jesus.* The Church holds firmly that the four Gospels, "whose historicity she unhesitatingly affirms, faithfully hand on what Jesus, the Son of God, while he lived among men, really did and taught for their eternal salvation, until the day when he was taken up."[99]

2. *The oral tradition.* "For, after the ascension of the Lord, the apostles handed on to their hearers what he had said and done, but with that fuller understanding which they, instructed by the glorious events of Christ and enlightened by the Spirit of truth, now enjoyed."[100]

3. *The written Gospels.* "The sacred authors, in writing the four Gospels, selected certain of the many elements which had been handed on, either orally or already in written form; others they synthesized or explained with an eye to the situation of the churches, the while sustaining the form of preaching, but always in such a fashion that they have told us the honest truth about Jesus."[101]

127. The fourfold Gospel holds a unique place in the Church, as is evident both in the veneration which the liturgy accords it and in the surpassing attraction it has exercised on the saints at all times:

> There is no doctrine which could be better, more precious and more splendid than the text of the Gospel. Behold and retain what our Lord and Master, Christ, has taught by his words and accomplished by his deeds.[102]

> But above all it's the gospels that occupy my mind when I'm at prayer; my poor soul has so many needs, and yet this is the one thing needful. I'm always finding fresh lights there; hidden meanings which had meant nothing to me hitherto.[103]

THE UNITY OF THE OLD AND NEW TESTAMENTS

128. The Church, as early as apostolic times,[104] and then constantly in her Tradition, has illuminated the unity of the divine plan in the two Testaments through typology, which discerns in God's works of the Old Covenant prefigurations of what he accomplished in the fullness of time in the person of his incarnate Son.

129. Christians therefore read the Old Testament in the light of Christ crucified and risen. Such typological reading discloses the inexhaustible content of the Old Testament; but it must not make us forget that the Old Testament retains its own intrinsic value as Revelation reaffirmed by our Lord himself.[105] Besides, the New Testament has to be read in the light of the Old. Early Christian catechesis made constant use of the Old Testament.[106] As an old saying put it, the New Testament lies hidden in the Old and the Old Testament is unveiled in the New.[107]

130. Typology indicates the dynamic movement toward the fulfilment of the divine plan when "God [will] be everything to everyone."[108] Nor do the calling of the patriarchs and the exodus from Egypt, for example, lose their own value in God's plan, from the mere fact that they were intermediate stages.

V. SACRED SCRIPTURE IN THE LIFE OF THE CHURCH

131. "And such is the force and power of the Word of God that it can serve the Church as her support and vigor, and the children of the Church as strength for their faith, food for the soul, and a pure and lasting fount of spiritual life."[109] Hence "access to Sacred Scripture ought to be open wide to the Christian faithful."[110]

132. "Therefore, the 'study of the sacred page' should be the very soul of sacred theology. The ministry of the Word, too—pastoral preaching, catechetics and all forms of Christian instruction, among which the liturgical homily should hold pride of place—is healthily nourished and thrives in holiness through the Word of Scripture."[111]

133. The Church "forcefully and specifically exhorts all the Christian faithful . . . to learn 'the surpassing knowledge of Jesus Christ,' by frequent reading of the divine Scriptures. 'Ignorance of the Scriptures is ignorance of Christ.'"[112]

IN BRIEF

134. "All Sacred Scripture is but one book, and that one book is Christ, because all divine Scripture speaks of Christ, and all divine Scripture is fulfilled in Christ" (Hugh of St. Victor, *De arca Noe* 2, 8: PL 176, 642).

135. "The Sacred Scriptures contain the Word of God and, because they are inspired, they are truly the Word of God" (*DV,* 24).

136. God is the author of Sacred Scripture because he inspired its human authors; he acts in them and by means of them. He thus gives assurance that their writings teach without error his saving truth (cf. *DV,* 11).

137. Interpretation of the inspired Scripture must be attentive above all to what God wants to reveal through the sacred authors for our salvation. What comes from the Spirit is not fully "understood except by the Spirit's action" (cf. Origen, *Hom. In Ex.* 4, 5: PG 12, 320).

138. The Church accepts and venerates as inspired the 46 books of the Old Testament and the 27 books of the New.

139. The four Gospels occupy a central place because Christ Jesus is their center.

140. The unity of the two Testaments proceeds from the unity of God's plan and his Revelation. The Old Testament prepares for the New and the New Testament fulfills the Old; the two shed light on each other; both are true Word of God.

141. "The Church has always venerated the divine Scriptures as she venerated the Body of the Lord" (*DV*, 21): both nourish and govern the whole Christian life. "Your word is a lamp to my feet and a light to my path" (*Ps* 119:105; cf. *Isa* 50:4).

NOTES

29. 1 *Timothy* 2:4.

30. cf. *John* 14:6.

31. *DV*, 7; cf. *2 Corinthians* 1:20; 3:16—4:6.

32. *DV*, 7; cf. *Matthew* 28:19–20; *Mark* 16:15.

33. *DV*, 7.

34. *DV*, 7.

35. *DV*, 7 § 2; St. Irenaeus, *Adv. haeres.* 3, 3, 1: PG 7/1, 848; Harvey, 2, 9.

36. *DV*, 8 § 1.

37. *DV*, 8 § 1.

38. *DV*, 8 § 3.

39. *DV*, 8 § 3; cf. *Colossians* 3:16.

40. *DV*, 9.

41. *Matthew* 28:20.

42. *DV*, 9.

43. *DV*, 9.

44. *DV*, 9.

45. *DV*, 10 § 1; cf. 1 *Timothy* 6:20; 2 *Timothy* 1:12–14 (Vulg.).

46. *DV*, 10 § 1; cf. *Acts* 2:42 (Gk.); Pius XII, apost. const. *Munificentissimus Deus*, 1 November 1950: AAS 42 (1950), 756, taken along with the words of St. Cyprian, *Epist.* 66, 8: CSEL 3/2, 733: "The Church is the people united to its Priests, the flock adhering to its Shepherd."

47. *DV*, 10 § 2.

48. *DV*, 10 § 2.

49. *Luke* 10:16; cf. LG, 20.

50. Cf. *John* 8:31–32.

51. Cf. Vatican Council I: DS 3016: *nexus mysteriorum*; LC 25.

52. *UR*, II.

53. Cf. *1 John* 2:20, 27.

54. Cf. *John* 16:13.

55. *LG*, 12; cf. St. Augustine, *De praed. sanct.* 14, 27: PL 44, 980.

56. *LG*, 12; cf. *Jude* 3.

57. *DV*, 8 § 2; cf. *Luke* 2:19, 51.

58. *GS*, 62 § 7; cf. *GS*, 44 § 2; *DV*, 23; 24; *UR*, 4.

59. *DV*, 8 § 2.

60. *DV*, 8 § 2.

61. St. Gregory the Great, Hom. in *Ezek.* 1, 7, 8: PL 76, 843D.

62. *DV*, 10 § 3.

63. *DV*, 13.

64. Cf. *Hebrews* 1:1–3.

65. St. Augustine, *En. in Ps.* 103, 4, 1: PL 37, 1378; cf. Ps 104; John 1:1.

66. Cf. *DV*, 21.

67. *Thessalonians* 2:13; cf. *DV*, 24.

68. *DV*, 21.

69. *DV*, 11;

70. *DV*, 11; cf. *John* 20:31; *2 Timothy* 3:16; *2 Peter* 1:19–21; 3:15–16.

71. *DV*, 11.

72. *DV*, 11.

73. St. Bernard, *S. missus est hom.* 4, 11: PL 183, 86.

74. Cf. *Luke* 24:45.

75. Cf. *DV*, 12 § 1.

76. *DV*, 12 § 2.

77. *DV*, 12 § 3.

78. Cf. *DV*, 12 § 4.

79. Cf. *Luke* 24:25–27, 44–46.

80. St. Thomas Aquinas, *Expos. in Ps.* 21, 11; cf. Psalms 22:14.

81. Origen, *Hom. in Lev.* 5, 5: PG 12, 454D.

82. Cf. *Romans* 12:6.

83. St. Thomas Aquinas, *S Th* I, 1, 10, *ad* I.

84. Cf. *1 Corinthians* 10:2.

85. *1 Corinthians* 10:11; cf. Hebrews 3—4:11.

86. Cf. Revelation 21:1–22:5.

87. *Lettera gesta docet, quid credas allegoria, moralis quid agas, quo tendas anagogia,* Augustine of Dacia, *Rotulus pugillaris,* I: ed. A. Walz: Angelicum 6 (1929) 256.

88. *DV,* 12 § 3.

89. St. Augustine, *Contra epistolam Manichaei* 5, 6: PL 42, 176.

90. Cf. *DV,* 8 § 3.

91. Cf. *DS* 179; 1334–1336; 1501–1504.

92. Cf. *DV,* 14.

93. *DV,* 15.

94. *DV,* 15.

95. *DV,* 15.

96. *DV,* 17; cf. *Romans* 1:16.

97. Cf. *DV,* 20.

98. *DV,* 18.

99. *DV,* 19; cf. *Acts* 1:1–2.

100. *DV,* 19.

101. *DV,* 19.

102. St. Caesaria the Younger to St. Richildis and St. Radegunde: *SCh* 345, 480.

103. St. Thérèse of Lisieux, *ms. autob.* A 83v.

104. Cf. *1 Corinthians* 10:6, 11; *Hebrews* 10:1; *1 Peter* 3:21.

105. Cf. *Mark* 12:29–31

106. Cf. *1 Corinthians* 5:6–8; 10:1–11.

107. Cf. St. Augustine, *Quaest. in Hept.* 2, 73: PL 34, 623; Cf. DU 16.

108. *1 Corinthians* 15:28.

109. *DV,* 21.

110. *DV,* 22.

111. *DV,* 24.

112. *DV,* 25; cf. Philippians 3:8 and St. Jerome, *Commentariorum in Isaiam libri xviii* prol.: PL 24, 17b.

AUTHORS

Michael Cameron, PHD, is a consultant for adult catechesis in the Office for Catechesis of the archdiocese of Chicago. He has published articles in *The Bible Today*, *Catechumenate* and *New Theology Review*, and has written scholarly pieces on Saint Augustine's interpretation of the Bible.

Eugene LaVerdiere, SSS, is a senior editor of *Emmanuel* magazine and a professor of New Testament at Mundelein Seminary and the Catholic Theological Union in Chicago. He holds a doctorate in New Testament and early Christian literature and is the author of numerous books, including *Dining in the Kingdom of God* and *The Breaking of the Bread* on the origins and development of the eucharist in Luke-Acts, both from LTP.

Marion Moeser, OSF, holds a doctorate in Christianity and Judaism in Antiquity from the University of Notre Dame. She is currently assistant professor of New Testament at the Franciscan School of Theology, Berkeley, California.

Joseph Prior is a priest of the archdiocese of Philadelphia, and academic dean at St. Charles Borromeo Seminary in Overbrook, Pennsylvania. He holds a licentiate in scripture and a doctorate in theology.

Gerard S. Sloyan is a priest of the diocese of Trenton and is distinguished lecturer in the department of religion and religious education at The Catholic University of America, Washington, D.C.

Murray Watson, a priest of the diocese of London, Ontario (Canada), is a member of the faculty of St. Peter's Seminary in London.

Ronald D. Witherup, SS, is provincial of the U.S. province of Sulpicians. He holds a doctorate in biblical studies and is the author of several books on the Bible, including the spiritual commentary, *Matthew* (New City Press, 2001).

INDEX

References are to paragraph or section numbers of individual documents. For a list of abbreviations of document names, see page vi.

PONTIFICAL BIBLICAL
INSTITUTE (ROME)
DAS 6, 7, 10

PREACHING
See Catechesis; Homilies

PROFESSION OF FAITH
LMIn 29

PROVIDENTISSIMUS DEUS
(LEO XIII)
DAS 1–2, 5, 11–12, 24; IBC 3

PSALMS, RESPONSORIAL
LMIn 19–22, 33, 56, 89

RICOEUR, PAUL
IBC 117, 120

SANDERS, JAMES A.
IBC 59

SCHLEIERMACHER, FRIEDRICH
IBC 117

SECOND VATICAN COUNCIL
DAS 1; DV 1; LMIn 1, 58–59; IBC 3, 92,
176, 214, 224; CCC 111

SEMINARIES, SCRIPTURAL
INSTRUCTION IN
DAS 53–55; SME 3; IBC 188–90

SIMON, RICHARD
IBC 13

SINGING, DURING LITURGY
OF THE WORD
LMIn 14, 17, 20–22, 23, 56, 89–91

SOCIETY OF SAINT JEROME
DAS 8–9

SONG OF SONGS
IBC 72

TEXTUAL CRITICISM, AND
SCRIPTURAL INTERPRETATION
DAS 12, 14–22, 35–41; SME 1–3; DV 12;
IBC 11–73, 241–42

THOMAS AQUINAS, SAINT
IBC 129

VATICAN I
See First Vatican Council

VATICAN II
See Second Vatican Council

VIGILANTIAE (LEO XIII)
DAS 5

VULGATE
DAS 1, 8, 14, 20–22; DV 22

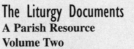 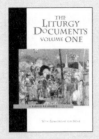

Rite of Christian Initiation of Adults

These books include all the rites for the catechumenate. Appendix I contains special "combined" rites used in celebrations involving both catechumens and candidates. Appendix II contains acclamations, hymns and songs for the rite. Appendix III supplies the statutes for use in the dioceses of the United States. Available in English and in Spanish.

English Ritual Edition

Designed for the presider's use at liturgy. Set in highly readable type. Easy to follow and easy to read in a public setting. Features two-color printing throughout and three ribbons. Hardcover.

English Study Edition

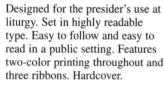

Use this paperback edition, with ample margins for notes, to prepare and plan the liturgies of the RCIA.

Spanish Ritual Edition

The complete text of the *Rite of Christian Initiation of Adults* translated into Spanish for use in the dioceses of the U.S. Hardcover. Appropriate for use during the liturgy.

Spanish Study Edition

Paperback edition intended for study and preparation.

Order of Christian Funerals

These resources have been designed to assist in the preparation for and celebration of the various rites of Christian funerals. The same handsome design by artist Steve Erspamer, sm, is used on the editions intended for use at the liturgy.

Order of Christian Funerals
Ritual edition

This complete hardcover edition is designed for use by the presider at funeral liturgies. Includes three ribbons and a 16-page cremation appendix.

Order of Christian Funerals
Study Edition

This paperback study edition is ideal for office use, for students and workshops, and for families who want to help in preparing the funeral liturgy. Includes a 16-page cremation appendix. Not intended for use during liturgy.

Wake Leader's
Ritual Edition

Contains the Vigil for the Deceased, Morning and Evening Prayer for the Dead, and prayers for the dead. Scripture readings are also included so this book can be used as a lectionary for all services. Two ribbons are provided. Includes a 16-page cremation appendix.

Rite of Committal
Presider's Edition

Includes the rites to be used at the place of final committal. One ribbon is provided. Includes a 16-page cremation appendix.

The Revised NAB Sunday Lectionary
Ritual Edition

These 10 x 14 volumes feature the readings for Sundays arranged in sense lines for ease of proclamation. Each cover is stamped in five beautiful, light reflecting foils. Inside, you'll find over 40 pieces of original art, a ribbon marker and a dedication page. Available for Year A, Year B and Year C or as a three-volume set.

Lectionary for Mass
Study Edition

This comprehensive paperback volume contains all of the readings for the Sundays of Year A, Year B and Year C and those for solemnities and feast days. All of the readings are in the RNAB translation for the United States. To help with the long-range planning of liturgy and music, you'll also find seven useful tables and charts. These tables include a list of the three readings for each Sunday in the three-year lectionary cycle, a list of the dates of Sundays through 2013, a list of the dates of principal feasts through 2025, and a list of all the readings and responsorial psalms in the order of the books in the Bible and where each may be found in the lectionary.

LITURGY TRAINING PUBLICATIONS
1800 North Hermitage Avenue
Chicago IL 60622-1101

Phone	1-800-933-1800
Fax	1-800-933-7094
E-Mail	orders@ltp.org
Website	www.ltp.org

The Book of the Gospels

Angel, ox, lion, eagle: four creatures that came to represent the four evangelists in the early church now grace the cover of LTP's *Book of the Gospels*. This traditional design connects today's church with the riches of our past.

This impressive book draws the assembly into the mystery and the wonder of the Word. The gleaming cover is visible to those near and far. It encases pages designed to prevent mistakes in proclamation. Excelling not only in function, the beauty of this book earns the reverence due an icon.

Over 30 pieces of art decorate the pages of this edition. The art acknowledges and honors the diversity in our American communities. It invites all Catholics, not just those of European descent, to see themselves in the gospel stories. What a just embodiment of the gospel for our times!

- Beautiful foil stamped cover with imagery based on the icons of the four evangelists: eagle, ox, angel and lion

- Rubrics set apart from texts to prevent mistakes in proclamation

- Over 30 pieces of full-color interior art by Laura James

- Acid-free paper

- Wide ribbon marker

- Gilded edges

11$\frac{1}{2}$ x 17$\frac{3}{8}$, 464 pages
1-56854-111-2

LAURA JAMES lives and works in Brooklyn. She paints biblical themes in the iconographic tradition of Ethiopian Christian art. Using bright color and intricate patterns, her work displays a unique style and vision.

PLEASE SUPPORT YOUR LOCAL BOOKSTORE OR CONTACT:

LITURGY TRAINING PUBLICATIONS
1800 North Hermitage Ave
Chicago IL 60622-1101

| Phone | 1-800-933-1800 | E-Mail | orders@ltp.org |
| Fax | 1-800-933-7094 | Website | www.ltp.org |

GET ACQUAINTED WITH SOMEONE YOU KNOW QUITE WELL...

Art Zannoni has the amazing gift of expressing deep theological insights in language all can understand. The scriptures invite us to discover and encounter a God who is beyond our limited vision, and Zannoni lights our path with this book. All who take the time to read and reflect on his insights will travel a journey worth taking.

– David Haas, director, The Emmaus Center for Prayer, Music and Ministry, Eagan, Minnesota

TELL ME YOUR NAME

Images of God in the Bible

Arthur E. Zannoni

Art Zannoni

Tell Me Your Name:
Images of God in the Bible

by Arthur E. Zannoni

All of us who take religion and faith as a serious part of our lives are constantly wrestling with the meaning of God. Our existence is derived from God and destined for God. And, in between, we long to know God. But how?

This important new book offers any reader the opportunity to contemplate, know and adore God more deeply. Each chapter looks at various names, images and metaphors for God—male and female, animate and inanimate—used in both testaments of the Bible, including images of Jesus and images used by Jesus.

Spend some time within these highly readable pages and discover a new level of intimacy, awe, wonder and humility in your own personal relationship with God.

7 x 10, 128 pages
1-56854-167-8